EXPEDITION TO BORNEO.

G. Hawkins, lith. Day & Haghe Lith^{rs} to the Queen.

H.M.S. DIDO at SARAWAK.

THE

EXPEDITION TO BORNEO

OF

H.M.S. DIDO

FOR

THE SUPPRESSION OF PIRACY:

WITH EXTRACTS FROM

THE JOURNAL OF JAMES BROOKE, ESQ.

OF SARĀWAK.

(NOW AGENT FOR THE BRITISH GOVERNMENT IN BORNEO.)

BY

CAPTAIN THE HON. HENRY KEPPEL, R.N.

IN TWO VOLUMES.

VOL. I.

Rediscovery Books

Reproduced by kind permission of the
Royal Geographical Society

Published by
Rediscovery Books Ltd
Unit 10, Ridgewood Industrial Park,
Uckfield, East Sussex,
TN22 5QE England
Tel: +44 (0) 1825 749494
Fax: +44 (0) 1825 765701

This edition © Rediscovery Books Ltd 2006

To find out more about Rediscovery Books
and its range of titles visit
www.rediscoverybooks.com

Published in association with
Royal Geographical Society
with IBG

Advancing geography
and geographical learning

The **Royal Geographical Society with IBG** was founded in 1830 to advance geographical science. Today it supports geographical research, promotes geography in schools and through outdoor learning, in society and to policy makers. Geography connects us to the world's people, places and environments.

The **Rediscovery Books** series allow us to see how previous geographers and travellers understood and recorded the world.

In reprinting in facsimile from the original, any imperfections are inevitably reproduced and the quality may fall short of modern type and cartographic standards.

TO

THE EARL OF ALBEMARLE.

———◆———

MY DEAR FATHER,

You could scarcely have anticipated, from my Profession, the dedication of a *Book* in testimony of my gratitude and affection; but, having had the good fortune to acquire the friendship of Mr. JAMES BROOKE, and to be entrusted by him with a narrative of his extraordinary career in that part of the world where the services of the ship I commanded were required, I am not without a hope that the accompanying pages may be found worthy of your approval, and not altogether uninteresting to my country.

I am, my dear Father,

Your affectionate Son,

HENRY KEPPEL.

Droxford, January 1846.

PREFACE.

THE visit of her Majesty's ship Dido to Borneo, and her services against the pirates, occupy comparatively so small a portion of these volumes, that some excuse may be necessary for their leading title.

It was only by undertaking to make the account of them part of the narrative, that I could prevail upon my friend Mr. Brooke to entrust me with his Journal for any public object; and when I looked at his novel and important position as a Ruler in Borneo, and was aware how much of European curiosity was attached to it, I felt it impossible not to consent to an arrangement which should enable me to trace the remarkable career through which he had reached that elevation. I hope, therefore, to be considered as having conquered my own disinclination to be the relater of events in which I was concerned, in order to overcome the scruples which he entertained against being the author of the autobiographical sketch, embracing so singular a portion of his life, which I have extracted from the rough notes confided to me.

That his diffidence in this respect was groundless will, I trust, be apparent from these pages, however indifferently I may have executed my unusual task, during a long homeward sea-voyage; and, from the growing interest which has arisen throughout the country for intelligence on the subject of Borneo and the adjacent Archipelago, I venture also to indulge the belief, that the general information will be deemed no unfit adjunct to the story of personal adventure.

H. K.

Droxford, January 1846.

CONTENTS OF VOLUME I.

CHAPTER I.

The Chinese War having terminated, Captain Keppel in H.M.S. Dido appointed to command of the Straits station. Meeting with Mr. Brooke. Sketch of his life. Mr. Brooke's outward voyage in the Royalist. Touch at Singapore. Arrival off the coast of Borneo. Land at the island of Talang Talang. Intercourse with the Bandar . . *Page* 1

CHAPTER II.

Progress: observations. Description of the coast of Borneo. Account, &c. of a Pangeran. Arrival at Sarāwak. Meetings with Rajah Muda Hassim, and conversations. The town. Interchange of visits and presents. Excursion to Dyak tribes. Resources and commercial products . . 22

CHAPTER III.

Second cruise: up the river Lundu. The Sibnowan Dyaks. Their town of Tungong. Their physical proportions, and words of their language. Their customs. Skull-trophies. Religious ceremonies and opinions. Their ornaments. Appearance of both sexes. Dress and morals. Missionary prospects of conversion, and elevation in the social scale. Government, laws, and punishments. Dances. Iron manufacturing. Chinese settlement. Excursion continued . 50

CHAPTER IV.

Renewed intercourse with the Rajah. Prospects of trade. Orang-outang, and other animals. The two sorts of mias. Description of the Rajah, his suite, and Panglimas, &c.

x CONTENTS OF VOLUME I.

The character of the natives. Leaves Saräwak. Songi Dyaks. Visits Seriff Sahib. Buyat tongue. Attack by pirates. Sails for Singapore . . . . *Page* 72

CHAPTER V.

Summary of information obtained during this visit to Borneo. Geographical and topographical observations. Produce. Various Dyak tribes. Natural history. Language. Origin of races. Sails from Singapore. Celebes. Face of the country. Waterfall 94

CHAPTER VI.

Dain Matara, the Bugis. Excursions in Celebes. Dispute with the Rajah's son-in-law. Baboon shot. Appearance of the country. Visits the Resident. Barometrical observations. The Bugis. Geography. Coral reefs. Visits the Rana of Lamatte. Population and products of the country . 114

CHAPTER VII.

Mr. Brooke's second visit to Saräwak. The civil war. Receives a present of a Dyak boy. Excursion to the seat of war. Notices of rivers, and settlements on their banks. Deaths and burials. Reasons for and against remaining at Saräwak. Dyak visitors. Council of war. Why side with the Rajah. Mode of constructing forts. State of enemy's and Rajah's forces. Conduct of the war . . . 137

CHAPTER VIII.

Appearance of the country. Progress of the rebel war. Character of the Sow and Singè Dyaks. Their belief in augury. Ruinous effects of protracted warfare. Cowardice and boasting of the Malays. Council of war. Refuse to attack the enemy's forts. Rebels propose to treat. The Malays oppose. Set out to attack the rebels, but frustrated by our allies. Assailed by the rebels. Put them to flight. Treat with them. They surrender. Intercede with the Rajah for their lives. Renewed treachery of the Malays . 159

CHAPTER IX.

Retrospect of Mr. Brooke's proceedings and prospects. Visit of a pirate fleet. Intercourse with the chief leaders, and other characteristic incidents. War-dances. Use of opium. Story of Si Tundo. Preparations for trading. Conditions of the cession of Sarāwak . . . . *Page* 189

CHAPTER X.

Obstacles in coming to a satisfactory conclusion with Muda Hassim. The law of force and reprisal considered. Capabilities of Sarāwak. Account of Sarebus and Sakarran pirates. Excursion up the river. Visit to the Singè Dyaks. Description of Mr. Brooke's house at Sarāwak. Circumstances relating to the wreck off Borneo Proper . . 214

CHAPTER XI.

Return of the Royalist from Borneo Proper, with intelligence of the sufferers from the wreck of the Sultana. Effect of the arrival of the Diana on the negotiations for their release. Outrage and oppression of Macota. Fate of the Sultana and her crew. Mr. Brooke made Rajah of Sarāwak. Liberation of rebel prisoners. State of Dyak tribes. Court of justice opened. Dyak burials, and respect for the dead. Malay cunning and treachery . . 240

CHAPTER XII.

Reflections on the new year. The plundered village, and other wrongs. Means for their suppression. The new government proceeds to act. The constitution. Preparation for an expedition against the Sea-Dyaks. Form of a treaty. Wreck of the Viscount Melbourne. Administration of justice. Difficulties and dangers. Dyak troubles. Views and arrangements of the Chinese. Judicial forms. Wrongs and sufferings of the Lundus 261

CHAPTER XIII.

Ascent of the left-hand river to the Stabad. Remarkable cave in the Tubbang. Diamond-works at Suntah. Return.

Infested by Dyak pirates. A meeting of prahus, and fight. Seriff Sahib's treatment of the Suntah Dyaks. Expedition against the Singè. Their invasion of the Sigos, and taking heads. The triumph over these trophies. Arms and modes of war. Hot and cold council-houses. Ceremonies on the installation of the Orang Kaya Steer Rajah. Meeting of various Dyak tribes. Hostile plans of Seriff Sahib, and their issue. Resolves to proceed to Borneo Proper . . . . *Page* 290

CHAPTER XIV.

Visit of Captain Elliott. Mr. Brooke sails for Borneo Proper. Arrival. Visited by leading men. Condition of the country. Reception by the Sultan. Objects in view. The different chiefs, and communications with them. The Sultan and his Pangerans. Objects of the visit accomplished. Return to Sarāwak. Ceremonies of the cession. Sails for Singapore 316

APPENDIX.

I. Natural History. Mr. Brooke's report on the Mias . i
II. Philology xii
III. Epistle of Laputongei, Rajah of Waju, and Consort, to Mr. James Brooke, and to the company of Merchants at Singapore xxvii

ILLUSTRATIONS TO VOLUME I.

H.M.S. Dido at Sarāwak	*to face the Title*
Jungle near Santobong	26
The Rajah Muda Hassim	29
Night-attack on the Panglima's prahu	90
Map of Malayan Archipelago	*at end of vol.*
,, Province of Sarāwak	*ditto*

ERRATA.

Page	line	for	read
30	9	Burni	Bruni
35	23	9°	59°
37	3	100	3000
119	6	Batang	Balong
121	3	idem	idem
123	15	idem	idem
125	1	claim	climb
161	12	cannonades	carronades
209	7	his	this
211	20	in the law	*i. e.* the written law
233	16	Sika	Situ
275	22	Laconia	Luconia
276	26	of	off
281	26	of a Chinaman	to a Chinaman
283	13	Montrado	those of Montrado
332	20	bought by	brought from

A

VISIT TO BORNEO.

CHAPTER I.

The Chinese War having terminated, Captain Keppel in H.M.S. Dido appointed to command of the Straits station. Meeting with Mr. Brooke. Sketch of his life. Mr. Brooke's outward voyage in the Royalist. Touch at Singapore. Arrival off the coast of Borneo. Land at the Island of Talang Talang. Intercourse with the Bandar.

At the conclusion of the Chinese war, the commander-in-chief, Vice-Admiral Sir William Parker, ordered the Dido to the Malacca Straits, a station in which was included the island of Borneo; our principal duties being the protection of trade, and suppression of piracy.

In the month of March 1843, while at Pinang, I received intimation from the governor of various daring acts of piracy having been committed near the Borneon coast on some native vessels trading to Singapore. I proceeded to that port; and, while undergoing a partial refit, made the acquaintance of Mr. Brooke, who accepted my invitation to return to Sarāwak in the Dido; and I could not have visited Borneo with a more agreeable or intelligent companion.

The objects of Mr. Brooke in leaving England, the reasons which induced him to settle at Sarāwak, and the circumstances which have led him to take so deep an interest in promoting the civilisation and improving the condition of the singular people whom he has adopted, form indeed a story very unlike the common course of events in modern times.

But before illustrating these circumstances from his own journals, it may be acceptable to say a few words respecting the individual himself, and of his extraordinary career. I am indebted to a mutual friend, acquainted with him from early years, for the following brief but interesting outline of his life; and have only to mention in the first instance, that Mr. Brooke is the lineal representative of Sir Robert Vyner, Baronet, and Lord Mayor of London in the reign of Charles II.; Sir Robert had but one child, a son, Sir George Vyner, who died childless, and his estate passed to his heir-at-law, Edith, the eldest sister of his father, whose lineal descendant is our friend. Sir Robert was renowned for his loyalty to his sovereign, to whom he devoted his wealth, and to whose memory he raised a monument.

" Mr. Brooke was the second, and is now the only surviving son of the late Thomas Brooke, Esq., of the civil service of the East India Company; was born on the 29th April, 1803; went out to India as a cadet, where he held advantageous situations, and distinguished himself by his gallantry in the Burmese war. He was shot through the body in an action with the Burmese, received the thanks of the government, and returned to England for the recovery of his prostrated strength. He resumed his station, but shortly afterwards relinquished the service, and in search of health and amusement left Calcutta for China in 1830. In this voyage, while going up the China seas, he saw for the first time the islands of the Asiatic Archipelago— islands of vast importance and unparalleled beauty —lying neglected and almost unknown. He inquired and read, and became convinced that Borneo and the Eastern Isles afforded an open field for enterprise and research. To carry to the Malay races, so long the terror of the European merchant-vessel, the blessings of civilisation, to suppress piracy and extirpate the slave-trade, became his humane and generous objects; and from that hour the energies of his powerful mind were devoted to this one pursuit. Often foiled—often disappointed, with a perseverance and enthusiasm which defied all obstacle, he was not until 1838 enabled to set sail from England on his darling project. The intervening years had been devoted to preparation and inquiry—a year spent in the Mediterranean had tested his vessel, the Royalist, and his crew—and so completely had he studied his subject and calculated on contingencies, that the least sanguine of his friends felt as he left the shore, hazardous and unusual as the enterprise appeared to be, that he had omitted nothing to insure a successful issue. 'I go,' said he, 'to awake the spirit of slumbering philanthropy with regard to these islands; to carry Sir Stamford Raffles' views in Java over the whole Archipelago. Fortune and life I give freely; and if I fail in the attempt, I shall not have lived wholly in vain.'

" In the admiration I feel for him, I may farther be permitted to add, that if any man ever possessed in himself the resources and means by which such noble designs were to be achieved, that man was James Brooke! Of the most enlarged views; truthful and generous; quick to acquire and appreciate; excelling in every manly sport and exercise; elegant and accomplished; ever accessible; and above all, prompt and determined to redress injury and relieve misfortune,—he was of all others the best qualified to impress the native mind with the highest opinion of English character. How he has succeeded, the influence he has acquired, and the benefits he has conferred, his own uncoloured narrative contained in the following pages best declares, and impresses on the world a lasting lesson of the good that attends individual enterprise, when well directed, of which every Englishman may feel justly proud."

Such is the sketch of Mr. Brooke by one well competent to judge of that to which he bears witness. In pursuance of the mission he has so eloquently and truly described, that gentleman left his native shores, in his yacht the Royalist schooner, of 142 tons, belonging to the Royal Yacht Squadron, with a crew of upwards of twenty men, in the year 1838. His general views were distinct and certain; but the details into which they shaped themselves have been so entirely guided by unforeseen occurrences, that it is necessary to look to his first visit to Borneo for their explanation; and in order to do so, I must refer to his private journal, which he kindly confided to me, after my having in vain tried to persuade him to publish it himself, as it contains much new and interesting intelligence.

EXTRACTS FROM MR. BROOKE'S JOURNAL.

" I had for some years turned my mind to the geography of the Indian Archipelago, and cherished an ardent desire to become better acquainted with a country combining the richest natural productions with an unrivalled degree of luxuriant beauty. Circumstances for a time prevented my entering on this field for enterprise and research; and when the barriers were removed, I had many preparations to make and some difficulties to overcome.

"In an expedition conducted by government, the line of discipline is so distinctly understood, and its infringement so strictly punished, that small hazard is incurred of any inconvenience arising from such a source. With an individual, however, there is no such assurance, for he cannot appeal to the articles of war; and the ordinary legal enactments for the protection of the mariner will not enable him to effect objects so far removed beyond the scope of the laws. I was fully aware that many would go, but that few might stay; for whilst a voyage of discovery *in prospectu* possesses great attractions for the imagination, the hardship, danger, and thousand other rude realities, soon dissipate the illusion, and leave the aspirant longing for that home he should never have quitted. In like manner, seamen can be procured in abundance, but cannot be kept from desertion whenever any matter goes wrong; and the total previous ignorance of their characters and dispositions renders this more likely, as the admission of one 'black sheep' goes far to taint the entire crew.

"These considerations fully convinced me that it was necessary to form *men* to my purpose, and by a line of steady and kind conduct, to raise up a personal regard for myself and attachment for the vessel, which could not be expected in ordinary cases. In pursuance of this object, I was nearly three years in preparing a crew to my mind, and gradually moulding them to consider the hardest fate or misfortune under my command as better than the ordinary service in a merchant-vessel. How far I have succeeded remains yet to be proved; but I cannot help hoping that I have raised the character of many, and have rendered all happy and contented since they have been with me; and certain am I that no men can do their duty more cheerfully or willingly than the crew of the Royalist.

"I may pass over in silence my motives for undertaking so long and arduous a voyage; and it will be sufficient to say, that I have been firmly convinced of its beneficial tendency in adding to knowledge, increasing trade, and spreading Christianity. The prospectus of the undertaking was published in the *Geographical Journal*, vol. viii. part iii. of 1838, when my preparations for sea were nearly complete. I had previously avoided making any public mention of my intentions, for praise before performance is disgusting; and I knew I should be exposed to prying curiosity, desirous of knowing what I did not know myself.

"On the 27th October, 1838, the Royalist left the river; and, after a succession of heavy gales, finally quitted the land on the 16th December. I may here state some farther particulars, to enable my readers to become better acquainted with her and her equipment. The Royalist, as already noticed, belonged to the Royal Yacht Squadron, which in foreign ports admits her to the same privileges as a man-of-war, and enables her to carry a white ensign. She sails fast, is conveniently fitted up, is armed with six six-pounders, a number of swivels, and small arms of all sorts, carries four boats, and provisions for four months. Her principal defect is being too sharp in the floor, which, in case of taking the ground, greatly increases the risk; but I comfort myself with the reflection, that a knowledge of this will lead to redoubled precaution to prevent such a disaster. She is withal a good sea-boat, and as well calculated for the service as could be desired.

"Most of her hands had been with me for three years or upwards, and the rest were highly recommended. They are, almost without exception, young, able-bodied, and active, fit in all respects for enduring hardship and privation, or the more dangerous reverse of self-indulgence, and willing to follow the fortunes of the Royalist and her commander through all the various shades of good or evil fortune which may betide. A fine, though slow, passage took us to Rio Janeiro, which presents features of natural beauty rarely equalled. The weather during our stay was hot in the extreme, and very wet, which marred, in some degree, the satisfaction I should otherwise have enjoyed in wandering about this picturesque country. I passed ten days, however, very agreeably, and departed with some regret from this brief visit to America and from my friends (if they will so allow me to call them) on board H.M.S. Calliope. I must not omit to mention that, during my stay, I visited a slaver, three of which (prizes to our men-of-war) lay in the harbour. It is a most loathsome and disgusting sight. Men, women, and children — the aged and the infant — crowded into a space as confined as the pens in Smithfield; not, however, to be released by death at the close of the day, but to linger, diseased and festering, for weeks or months, and then to be discharged into perpetual and hopeless slavery. I wish I could say that our measures tended toward the abolition of this detestable traffic; but from all that I could learn and observe, I am forced to confess that the exertions made to abolish slavery are of no avail in this country, and never will be till harsher means are resorted to.

" There are points of view in which this traffic wears a more cheering aspect; for any one comparing the puny Portuguese or the bastard Brazilian with the athletic negro, cannot but allow that the ordinary changes and chances of time will place this fine country in the hands of the latter race. The negro will be fit to cultivate the soil, and will thrive beneath the tropical sun of the Brazils. The enfeebled white man grows more enfeebled and more degenerate with each succeeding generation, and languishes in a clime which nature never designed him to inhabit. The time will come when the debased and suffering negroes shall possess this fertile land, and when some share of justice shall be awarded to their cheerful tempers and ardent minds.

" Quitting Rio on the 9th, we cruised for a day or two with H.M.S. Calliope and Grecian; and on the 11th, parting company, prosecuted our voyage for the Cape of Good Hope."

The next notice runs thus:—" The aspect of Tristan d'Acunha is bold even to grandeur. The peak, towering upwards of eight thousand feet above the sea, is inferior only to Teneriffe, and the precipitous cliffs overhanging the beach are a fitting base for such a mountain. I regretted not being able to examine this island on many accounts, but principally, perhaps, on account of the birds of the South Atlantic I had hoped to collect there, many of which are so often seen by voyagers, yet so little known and so vaguely described.

" On the 29th March, after being detained a fortnight [at the Cape of Good Hope] by such weather as no one could regret, we sailed again in a south-easter, and after a passage of six weeks reached Java Head.

" I had been suffering for some time under a severe indisposition, and I consequently hailed the termination of our voyage with double satisfaction, for I greatly required rest and quiet — two things impossible to be had on ship-board. From Java Head we glided slowly through Prince's Strait, and, coasting along the island, dropped our anchor in Anjer Roads. The scenery of this coast is extremely lovely, and comprises every feature which can heighten the picturesque: noble mountains, a lake-like sea, and deeply indented coast-line, rocks, islets, and, above all, a vegetation so luxuriant that the eye never wearies with gazing on its matchless tints. Anjer combines all these beauties, and possesses the incalculable advantage of being within a moderate ride of the refreshing coolness of the hills. We here procured water and provisions in abundance, being daily visited by crowds of canoes filled with necessaries or curiosities. Fowls, eggs, yams, cocoa-nuts, and sweet potatoes, were mixed with monkeys of various sorts, paroquets, squirrels, shells, and similar temptations on the stranger's purse or wardrobe. Great was the bartering for old clothes, handkerchiefs, and hats; and great the number of useless and noisy animals we received in exchange. Great, too, was the merriment aboard, and the excitement when the canoes first came. The transition from the monotony of a sea-life to the loquacious bustle of barter with a half-civilised people is so sudden, that the mind at once feels in a strange land, and the commonest productions proclaim the luxuriant climes of the tropics. Until this impression is made, we hardly know why we have been sailing onward for four months past, so quiet and unvarying is the daily tenor of a life aboard ship.

"*1st June, Singapore.*—On reaching Singapore I was most hospitably received by the kind inhabitants, and took up my abode with Mr. Scott. The quiet and repose of my present life, the gentle ride in the cool of the morning, and the evening-drive after an early dinner, are already restoring my shattered strength, and I trust soon to be enabled to prosecute my farther undertaking. In the mean time the Royalist is undergoing a refit after her passage, and, like her owner, is daily improving in good looks.

"I could say much of Singapore, for it is the pivot of the liberal system in the Archipelago, and owes its prosperity to the enlightened measures of Sir Stamford Raffles. The situation is happily chosen, the climate healthy, the commerce unshackled, and taxation light; and these advantages have attracted the vessels of all the neighbouring nations to bring their produce to this market in order to exchange it for the manufactures of England.

"The extent of the island is about 27 miles by 11 broad. The town of Singapore stands on the south side, facing the shores of Battam, and is intersected by a salt-water stream, which separates the native town from the pleasant residences of the European inhabitants; the latter stretch along the beach, and cover a space which extends to the foot of a slight eminence, on which stands the governor's house. Off the town lie the shipping of various countries, presenting a most picturesque and striking appearance. The man-of-war, the steamer, and the merchant-vessels of the civilised world, contrast with the huge, misshapen, and bedizened arks of China! The awkward prahus of the Bugis are surrounded by the light boats of the island. The semi-civilised Cochin Chinese, with their vessels of antiquated European construction, deserve attention from this important step towards improvement; and the rude prahus of some parts of Borneo claim it from their exhibiting the early dawn of maritime adventure.

"*27th July.*— After various causes of delay I sailed on this day from Singapore. When I contrast my state of health at my arrival with what it now is, I may well be thankful for the improvement. Every kindness and hospitality has been shewn me.

" On Saturday at noon we got under weigh with a light breeze, and stood down the Strait on our way to Borneo.

"*28th.* — In the morning we were well out in the China Sea, running six knots per hour, N. ¾ E. Lines of discoloured water were seen about us, and about 11 A.M. we entered a field some two miles long and 400 yards wide. The consistence of this dirty mass was that of pea-soup, which it likewise resembled in colour; and I doubt not the white water of the China Sea (vide *N. Magazine*) is referable to this appearance seen in the night, as may the report of rocks, &c. The Malays on board called it 'sara,' and declared it to come from the rivers. On examination it appeared, when magnified, somewhat like a grain of barley or corn. The particles were extremely minute, soft, and, rubbed between the fingers, emitted a strong smell like paint-oil; a potent odour arose whilst passing through the thick patch.

"It may not be superfluous to recount here the preparations I have made for this trip to Borneo, or my intentions when I get there. Borneo Proper, once the seat of piracy, which few vessels could approach with safety, is now under the sway of the Rajah Muda Hassim. The character given this rajah by many persons who know and have traded with him is so good, and he is spoken of as generous and humane, and greatly inclined to the English. These reasons have induced me to abandon my intention of proceeding direct to Malludu Bay, and during the season of the southwest monsoon to confine myself principally to the north-west coast. Muda Hassim being at present reported to be at Sarāwak, I propose, after taking a running sketch of the coast from Tanjong Api, to enter the river of that name, and proceed as far as the town.

"I believe I have availed myself of every means within my reach to render my visit agreeable to the rajah. I carry with me many presents which are reported to be to his liking—gaudy silks of

Surat, scarlet cloth, stamped velvet, gunpowder, &c., besides a large quantity of confectionery and sweets, such as preserved ginger, jams, dates, syrups, and, to wind up all, a huge box of China toys for his children! I have likewise taken coarse nankeen to the amount of 100*l.* value, as the best circulating medium in the country. Besides the above-mentioned preparations, I carry letters from the government of Singapore, to state, as far as can be done, the objects of my voyage, and to caution the rajah to take every care of my safety and that of my men. The Board of Commerce have at the same time entrusted me with a letter and present to him, to thank him for his humanity to a crew of an English vessel wrecked on his coast. The story, as I had it from the parties shipwrecked, is highly creditable to his humanity. The vessel, called the Napoleon, was wrecked on the bar of Sarāwak river in the northeast monsoon. The people were saved with difficulty, and remained in the jungle, where they were after a time discovered by some Malays. Muda Hassim, on receiving intelligence of this, sent down and brought them to his town, collected all that he could recover from the wreck, clothed them handsomely, and fed them well for several months, and, on an opportunity arriving, sent them back to Singapore free of expense.

" At the same time, however, that I have prepared to meet the natives as friends, I have not neglected to strengthen my crew, in case I should find them hostile. Eight stout men of the Orang Laut, or men of the sea (Malays), have been added to the force. They are an athletic race, cheerful and willing; and though not seamen in our sense of the term, yet well calculated for this expedition. They pull a good oar, and are invaluable in saving the Europeans the exposure consequent to wooding and watering. They possess, likewise, the knowledge of the jungle and its resources, and two of them have before been to Sarāwak and along the coast. Besides these, a young gentleman named Williamson accompanies me as interpreter; and I have fortunately met with a medical gentleman, Mr. Westermann, a Dane, who is surgeon for this voyage, Mr. Williams having left me at Singapore. With these arrangements I look without apprehension to the power of the Malays; but, without relaxing in measures of the strictest vigilance, I shall never sleep less soundly when it comes to my turn so to do.

"*August 1st.*—I am, then, at length, anchored off the coast of Borneo! not under very pleasant circumstances, for the night is pitchy dark, with thunder, lightning, rain, and squalls of wind.

"*2d.*—Squally bad night. This morning, the clouds clearing away, was delightful, and offered for our view the majestic scenery of Borneo. At nine got under way, and ran in on an east-by-south course $4\frac{1}{2}$ or 5 miles towards Tanjong Api.

Came to an anchor about 5 miles from the land, and despatched the boat to take sights ashore, in order to form a base-line for triangulation. The scenery may really be called majestic. The low and wooded coast about Tanjong Api is backed by a mountain called Gunong[1] Palo, some 2000 feet in height, which slopes down behind the point and terminates in a number of hummocks, shewing from a distance like islands.

" The coast, unknown, and represented to abound in shoals and reefs, is the harbour for pirates of every description. Here every man's hand is raised against his brother-man; and here sometimes the climate wars upon the excitable European, and lays many a white face and gallant heart low on the distant strand.

" 3d.—Beating between Points Api and Datu. The bay, as far as we have seen, is free from danger; the beach is lined by a feathery row of beautiful casuarinas, and behind is a tangled jungle, without fine timber; game is plentiful, from the traces we saw on the sand; hogs in great numbers, troops of monkeys, and the print of an animal with cleft hoofs, either a large deer, tapir, or cow. We saw no game save a tribe of monkeys, one of which, a female, I shot, and another quite young, which we managed to capture alive. The captive, though the young of the black monkey, is greyish,

---

[1] Gunong, a mountain, part of a chain.

with the exception of his extremities, and a stripe of black down his back and tail. Though very young, he has already taken food, and we have some hope of preserving his life.

"We witnessed at the same time an extraordinary and fatal leap made by one of these monkeys. Alarmed by our approach, he sprang from the summit of a high tree at the branch of one lower, and at some distance. He leaped short, and came clattering down some 60 or 70 feet amid the jungle. We were unable to penetrate to the spot on account of a deep swamp, to ascertain his fate.

"A rivulet flows into the sea not far from where we landed — the water is sweet, and of that clear brown colour so common in Ireland. This coast is evidently the haunt of native prahus, whether piratical or other. Prints of men's feet were numerous and fresh, and traces of huts, fires, and parts of boots, some of them ornamented after their rude fashion. A long pull of five miles closed the day.

"*Sunday, 4th.*—Performed divine service myself! manfully overcoming that horror which I have to the sound of my own voice before an audience. In the evening landed again more to the westward. Shore skirted by rocks; timber noble, and the forest clear of brushwood, enabling us to penetrate with ease as far as caution permitted. Traces of wild beasts numerous and recent, but none discovered. Fresh-water streams, coloured as yesterday, and the trail of an alligator from one of them to the sea. This dark forest, where the trees shoot up straight and tall, and are succeeded by generation after generation varying in stature, but struggling upward, strikes the imagination with pictures trite yet true. Here the hoary sage of an hundred years lies mouldering beneath your foot, and there the young sapling shoots beneath the parent shade, and grows in form and fashion like the parent stem. The towering few, with heads raised above the general mass, can scarce be seen through the foliage of those beneath; but here and there the touch of time has cast his withering hand upon their leafy brow, and decay has begun his work upon the gigantic and unbending trunk. How trite, and yet how true! It was thus I meditated in my walk. The foot of European, I said, has never touched where my foot now presses — seldom the native wanders here. Here I indeed behold nature fresh from the bosom of creation, unchanged by man, and stamped with the same impress she originally bore! Here I behold God's design when He formed this tropical land, and left its culture and improvement to the agency of man. The Creator's gift, as yet neglected by the creature; and yet the time may be confidently looked for when the axe shall level the forest, and the plough turn the ground.

"*6th.*— Made sail this morning, and stood in for an island called Talang Talang, anchoring about eight miles distant, and sending a boat to take correct observations for a base-line.

"Our party found Malays of Sarāwak on the island, who were civil to them, and offered to conduct us up to-morrow, if we wanted their assistance. The pirates, both Illanuns and Dyaks, have been gone from the bay but a few days — the former seaward, the latter up the rivers.

"*7th.*— Morning calm. In the afternoon got under way, and anchored again near the island of Talang Talang — the smaller one a conical hill bearing south. The Bandar[1] of the place came off in his canoe to make us welcome. He is a young man sent by Rajah Muda Hassim to collect turtles' eggs, which abound in this vicinity, especially on the larger island. The turtles are never molested, for fear of their deserting the spot; and their eggs, to the amount of five or six thousand, collected every morning and forwarded at intervals to Sarāwak as articles of food.

"Our visitor was extremely polite, and, in common with other Asiatics, possessed the most pleasing and easy manners. He assured us of a welcome from his rajah; and, in their usual phrase, expressed himself that the rajah's heart would dilate in his bosom at the sight of us. His dress consisted of trousers of green cloth, a dark green velvet jacket, and his sarong round his waist, and

[1] Pronounced short, for (properly) Bandhāra; a treasurer, chief steward.

thrown gracefully over two krisses, which he wore at his girdle. His attendants were poorly attired, and mostly unarmed — a proof of confidence in us, and a desire to assure us of his own friendly intentions. I treated him with sweetmeats and syrup, and of his own accord he took a glass of sherry, as did his chief attendant. On his departure he was presented with three yards of red cloth, and subsequently with a little tea and gunpowder.

CHAPTER II.

Progress: observations. Description of the coast of Borneo. Account, &c. of a Pangeran. Arrival at Sarāwak. Meetings with Rajah Muda Hassim, and conversations. The town. Interchange of visits and presents. Excursion to Dyak tribes. Resources and commercial products.

I RESUME Mr. Brooke's Journal, which requires no introductory remark.

"*Aug.* 8*th.*—A cloudy day, preventing us taking our wished-for observations. I made a boat-excursion round the two islands. The north one is somewhat the largest; the southern one, running north and south, consists of two hills joined by a low and narrow neck of land. The water between these islands deep, varying from seven to six fathoms; but between the smaller one and the main there are rocks and reefs; and though a passage may exist, it would not be advisable for a vessel to try the passage. These two small islands possess all the characteristic beauties of the clime. Formed of brown granite, with a speck of white sandy beach, and rising into hills covered with the noblest timber, wreathed with gigantic creepers. The cream-coloured pigeons flit from tree to tree, and an eagle or two soared aloft watching their motions. The frigate-birds are numerous, and several sorts of smaller birds in the bush difficult to get at. A small species of crocodile, or alligator, was likewise seen; but we were not fortunate enough to shoot one. The natives, when asked whether they were alligators, answered in the negative, calling them crocodiles. The tides appear to be as irregular as tides usually are in a deep bay. The rise and fall of the tide is about fifteen feet.

" 9*th*. — After breakfast this morning took our sights, and at twelve o'clock the latitude of the smaller Talang Talang and the ship for a base-line. We yesterday took the same base-line by sound, firing alternately three guns from the vessel and three from the shore.

" 10*th*. — A squall from the northward brought in a chopping sea in the morning. We were favoured with a visit from another native party, but the chief was in every respect inferior to our first acquaintance, Bandar Dowat.

" 11*th, Sunday*. — Got under weigh early, after a night of torrents of rain. The breeze being directly out of Lundu river, I stood as near it as I could, and then bore away for Santobong, in order to reach Sarāwak. From Gunong Gading the coast gradually declines, and forms two points. The first of these is Tanjong Bloungei, near which, on the right hand, runs a small river, of the same name. The next point is Tanjong Datu, which shews prominently from most parts of the bay. From Tanjong Datu the coast recedes into a bay, and again forms a low point, which I have christened Tanjong Lundu. The river Lundu disembogues itself into the bay just beyond the point of the same name; and the land on its far bank forms a bight of considerable depth. The Lundu is a barred river, with but little water; though, judging from the opening, it is by no means small. Our pilots inform me, at the same time, however, that within the bar there is a considerable depth of water.

"From the Sungei Lundu the land rises behind a wooded beach. The first hill, which may be said to form the larboard entrance of the river, is peaked, and called Sumpudin, and near it is a barred river of the same name. This range of high land runs some distance; and near its termination is the river Tamburgan. The low coast runs into another bight; and the first opening after the termination of the high land is the mouth of the river Seboo. Then comes another river; after which the land rises into hills, gradually larger, till they terminate in a round-topped hill, which forms the starboard entrance (going in) of the Sarāwak river.

"This river discharges itself at the east corner of the bay; and its locality is easily recognised by the highest peak of Santobong, which towers over its left bank, close to the entrance. A ship rounding Datu will readily perceive the high land of Santobong, shewing like a large island, with another smaller island at its northern extremity. Both these, however, are attached to the main: and the northernmost point, called Tanjong Sipang, is distinguished by two peaks, like horns, one small, the other larger. Steer from Datu a direct course towards this high land, and when within a mile and a half or two miles of the shore, haul in along the land, as there is a sand nearly dry at low water on the starboard hand, stretching from the shore to the Saddle island, or Pulo Satang. The leading mark to clear this sand is to bring the hollow formed between the round hill at the right entrance of the Sarāwak river and the next hill a-head, and as you approach the river's mouth, steer for a small island close to the shore, called Pulo Karra, or Monkey Island. These marks will conduct you over a shoal with $\frac{1}{4}$ three, the least water at high water; you will then deepen your water, and keep away for the low green point on the far side of the river, edging gradually in; and when you are some distance from the opposite low point on the port hand, cross the bar in three fathom (high water) nearly in the centre of the river. You must not, however, encroach on the larboard side. The bar is narrow, and just within is 7 and $7\frac{1}{2}$ fathom, where we are at present anchored. The scenery is noble. On our left hand is the peak of Santobong, clothed in verdure nearly to the top; at his foot a luxuriant vegetation, fringed with the casuarina, and terminating in a beach of white sand. The right bank of the river is low, covered with pale green mangroves, with the round hill above mentioned just behind it. Santobong peak is 2050 feet, or thereabouts, by a rough trigonometrical measurement.

"12th.—Lay at anchor; took angles and observations, and shot in the evening, without any success. There is a fine species of large pigeon of a grey colour I was desirous of getting, but they were too cunning. Plenty of wild hogs were seen, but as shy as though they had been fired at all their lives. When the flood made, despatched my gig for Sarāwak, in order to acquaint the rajah of my arrival.

"13th.—Got under weigh, and in the second reach met our gig returning, followed by a large canoe, with a Pangeran of note to welcome us. We gave him a salute of five guns; whilst he, on his part, assured us of his rajah's pleasure at our arrival, and his own desire to be of service. With the Pangeran Oula Deen (or Illudeen, anglicè Aladdin), came the rajah's chief writer, his shroff, a renegade Parsee, a war-captain, and some others, besides a score of followers. They made themselves much at home, ate and drank (the less scrupulous took wine), and conversed with ease

JUNGLE near SANTAOBONG.

London Chapman & Hall, 180 Strand, Jany 15th 1846.

and liveliness. No difference can be more marked than between the Hindoostani and the Malay. The former, though more self-possessed and polished, shews a constraint in manners and conversation, and you feel that his training has made him an artificial character. The Malay, on the contrary, concealing as well the feelings uppermost in his mind, is lively and intelligent, and his conversation is not confined to a dull routine of unmeaning compliments.

"*August* 13*th*.—The Pangeran spoke to me of some ship-captain who was notoriously cruel to his Lascars, and insolent in his language to the Malays. He was murdered by his crew; and the circumstance related to me, as though I was to approve the act! 'No Malay of Borneo (added the Pangeran) would injure a European, were he well treated, and in a manner suitable to his rank!' and I am sure such a declaration, in a limited sense, is consonant with all known principles of human nature, and the action of the passions and feelings.

" Our Pangeran was quite the gentleman, and a manly gentleman too. His dress was a black velvet jacket, trimmed with gold lace, and trousers of green cloth, with a red sarong and kris. He was the only one of the party armed whilst aboard. The rest were good quiet men, and one or two of them very intelligent. They took their leave of us to get back to the town at sunset; but the ebb making, returned and stayed until twelve at night, when the tide turned in their favour. We had some difficulty in providing beds. The Pangeran slept in my cabin, and the rest were distributed about on couches or carpets.

"*August* 14*th*. — Got under weigh with the flood; and, favoured by a light breeze, proceeded up the river nearly as far as the town. From the ignorance of the pilots, however, we grounded on a rock in the middle of the river in $1\frac{1}{2}$ fathom water, and it took us an hour to heave the vessel off by the stern. Had the tide been falling, we should have been in a critical situation, as the rock is dry at low water; but as it was we received no damage. Shortly after getting off, several boats with assistance came from the place, despatched in haste by the rajah. The intention was kind, though we needed not the aid. Being dark, we dropped anchor in $5\frac{1}{2}$ fathom, about $1\frac{1}{2}$ miles from the town.

"15*th*.—Anchored abreast of Sarāwak at seven, and saluted the rajah with twenty-one guns, which were returned with eighteen from his residence. The rajah's own brother, Pangeran Mahammed, then saluted the vessel with seven guns, which were returned. Having breakfasted, and previously intimated our intention, we pulled ashore to visit the great man. He received us in state, seated in his hall of audience, which outside is nothing but a large shed, erected on piles, but within decorated with taste. Chairs were placed on each

R. J. Hamerton, lith. Day & Haghe Lith[rs] to the Queen.

THE RAJAH MUDA HASSIM.

London Chapman & Hall, 180 Strand, Jan[y] 15th 1846.

side of the ruler, who occupied the head seat. Our party were placed on one hand; on the other sat his brother Mahammed, and Macota and some others of his principal chiefs; whilst immediately behind him his twelve younger brothers were seated.

"The dress of Muda Hassim was simple, but of rich material, and most of the principal men were well, and even superbly, dressed. His countenance is plain, but intelligent and highly pleasing, and his manners perfectly elegant and easy. His reception was kind, and, I am given to understand, highly flattering. We sat, however, trammelled with the formality of state, and our conversation did not extend beyond kind inquiries and professions of friendship. We were presented with tobacco rolled up in a leaf, each about a foot long, and tea was served by attendants on their knees. A band of music played wild and not unmusical airs during the interview, and the crowd of attendants who surrounded us were seated around in respectful silence. After a visit of half an hour, we rose and took our leave.

"Sarāwak is but an occasional residence of the Rajah Muda Hassim, and he is now detained here by a rebellion in the interior. On my inquiring whether *the war* proceeded favourably, he replied that there was *no war*, but merely *some child's play among his subjects*. From what I hear, however, from other quarters, it is more serious than he represents it; and hints have been thrown out that the rajah wishes me to stay here *as a demonstration* to intimidate the rebels. We shall see.

" The town consists of a collection of mud huts, erected on piles, and may contain about 1500 persons. The residences of the rajah and his fourteen brothers occupy the greater part, and their followers are the great majority of the population. When they depart for Borneo (or Būrni), the remainder must be a very small population, and apparently very poor. The river affords a few fish; but there is little sign of cultivation either of rice or other grain. Fowls and goats seem the only other means of subsistence of these people. The geological features of the country are easily described. Vast masses of granite rock are scattered along the coast; for instance, Gunong Poe, Gading, Santobong, &c. &c., which have evidently at some former period been detached islands. The spaces between these granite masses is now filled in with alluvial soil, intersected in every direction with rivers and streams, and on the low alluvial bank of the Sarāwak· river stands this little town. The distance from the sea is about twenty-five miles, through banks of mangrove, and the Nepa palm, until approaching the town, where some jungle-trees first appear. The breadth is about 100 yards, and the depth six fathoms at low water spring-tides in mid river opposite the rajah's residence. In some places below, the river is narrower and the depths considerable, varying from three to seven fathoms. The prominent points, however, are shallow, and the rocks below the town lay on the starboard hand coming up just as the first houses appear in sight. The larboard hand should then be kept close aboard. Some other rocks are likewise reported; and in ascending the stream, though it be generally clear, a vessel *with* or without a pilot should have a boat a-head sounding. In the evening I went ashore suddenly to pay a visit to the rajah, in order, if possible, to break through the bonds of formality. The great man soon made his appearance, and received us very well. We talked much of the state of his country and of ours; but he was very guarded when I spoke of the Dutch. "He had no dealings whatever (he said) with them, and never allowed their vessels to come here, and therefore could not say what they were like." We sat in easy and unreserved converse, out of hearing of the rest of the circle. He expressed great kindness to the English nation; and begged me to tell him *really* which was the most powerful nation, England or Holland, or, as he significantly expressed, which is the "cat and which the rat?" I assured him that England was the mouser, though in this country Holland had most territory. We took our leave after he had intimated his intention of visiting us to-morrow morning.

"16*th*.—We were ready to receive the rajah

after breakfast: but these affairs of state are not so easily managed. There came two diplomatists on board to know, in the first place, how many guns we intended to salute with, and, in the second, whether I would go ashore in my *gig*, in order to fetch the chief and his brother off. The latter request I might have refused, and in a diplomatic light it was inadmissible; but I readily conceded it, because, in the first place, it was less troublesome than a refusal; and in the next, I cared not to bandy paltry etiquettes with a semi-savage; and whatever pride might whisper, I could not, as an individual traveller, refuse an acknowledging of the supremacy of a native prince. I went accordingly. The great man came on board, and we treated him with every distinction and respect. Much barbaric state was maintained as he quitted his own residence. His sword of state, with a gold scabbard, his war-shield, jewel-hilted kris, and flowing *horse*-tails, were separately carried by the grand officers of state. Bursts of wild music announced his exit. His fourteen brothers and principal Pangerans surrounded him, and a number (formidable on the deck of a vessel) covered the rear. He stayed two hours and a half; ate and drank, and talked with great familiarity, till the oppressive heat of the crowded cabin caused me to wish them all to another place. However, he departed at last, under a salute of twenty-one guns, and the fatigues of the day were satisfactorily brought to a close. I afterwards sent the rajah the presents I had brought for him, consisting of a silk sarong, some yards of red cloth and velvet, a pocket-pistol, scissors and knives, with tea, biscuits, sweetmeats, China playthings, &c. &c. A person coming here should be provided with a few articles of small importance to satisfy the crowd of inferior chiefs. Soap, small parcels of tea, lucifers, writing-paper, a large stock of cigars, biscuits, and knives, are the best; for, without being great beggars, they seem greatly to value these trifles, even in the smallest quantity. The higher class inquired frequently for scents; and for the great men I know no present which would be more acceptable than a small pier-glass. All ranks seemed greatly pleased with those aboard; and some of the lower orders, quite ignorant of the reflection, laughing, moving, sitting, and rising, to observe the corresponding effect.

"18*th*. — In the morning I intimated my intention of paying a visit to the Pangeran Muda Mahammed; and being apprised of his readiness to see us, I went ashore to his house. He was not, however, in the room to receive us; nor, indeed, was I much surprised at this slight, for he is a sulky-looking, ill-favoured savage, with a debauched appearance, and wanting in the intelligence of his brother the rajah. I seated myself, however, and remained some time; but the delay exceeding what I considered the utmost limit of my forbearance, I expressed to the Pangeran Macota my regret that his compeer was not ready to receive me, adding that, as I was not accustomed to be kept waiting, I would return to my vessel. I spoke in the quietest tone imaginable, rose from my seat, and moved away; but the assembled Pangerans, rising likewise, assured me it was a mistake, that he was not yet dressed, and would greatly regret it himself. I repeated, that when I visited the rajah, he received me in the hall. Whilst this brief discussion passed, the culprit Muda Mahammed appeared, and apologised for his remissness, assuring me that the error was his attendants', who told him I was not coming for an hour. The excuse, of course, passed current, though false, as excuses generally are. I vindicated my independence, not until it was necessary; and I am well aware that any endeavour of a native to commit an indirect rudeness, if met with firmness and gentleness, always recoils on his own head. The routine of the visit resembled our last — tea, cigars, complimentary conversation, and departure. The Pangeran afterwards sent me a present of fowls and goats, and I was right glad to have it over. Muda Mahammed is the 'own' brother to Muda Hassim, and next in rank here. As yet I had not made any request to the rajah to allow me to visit various parts of his country; but thinking the time was arrived (the ceremonial of arrival being past) to do so, I sent Mr. Williamson, my interpreter, to express my wish to travel to some of the Malay towns and into the country of the Dyaks. The latter request, I fully expected, would be evaded, and was therefore the more pleased when an answer came giving a cheerful consent to my going amongst the Dyaks of Lundu, and visiting the towns of Sadung, Samarahan, &c. At the same time the rajah informed me, that if I went up the river, he could not be answerable for my safety, as the rebels were not far distant, and constantly on the watch. Sarebus, another large Dyak town, he advised me not to visit, as they were inimical to his government, and a skirmish had lately taken place between them and some of his subjects.

"18th, Sunday.—Performed service. In the evening walked ashore, but the jungle was wet after rain. Every day or night since arriving it has rained, sometimes in torrents, at others in showers, and the sky has been so obscured that no observations can be obtained. The thermometer never ranges above 81°, and sometimes stands at 9°.

"At 12 at night we were surprised by a boat sent from the rajah, to say he was taken ill, and wanted some physic. We despatched our surgeon, but it was found impossible to admit him into the sacred precincts of the seraglio, and he returned with the information that the rajah was asleep.

"21st.—Our fleet were in readiness before daylight, and by 5 o'clock we left Kuching,[1] and dropped down the river. The Pangeran Illudeen and the Panglima, both in prahus, accompanied us, and with our long-boat (the Skimalong) formed quite a gay procession. The prahu of the Pangeran pulled twelve paddles, mounted two brass swivels, and in all had a crew of about twenty men. The Panglima's boat likewise carried a gun, and had about ten men; whilst the Skimalong mounted an iron swivel, and carried six Englishmen and one of our Singapore Malays. With this equipment we might be pronounced far superior to any force of the rajah's enemies we were likely to meet.

"We passed from the Sarāwak river into the Morotaba. At the junction of the two streams the Morotaba is narrow; but at no great distance, where it meets the Quop, it becomes wider, and in some places more than half a mile across.

"The river Quop is a fine stream, fully, as far as I could see, as broad as the Morotaba or Sarāwak. Beyond the junction of the Quop and Morotaba the latter river divides into two branches — the left-hand one, running to the sea, retains the name of Morotaba, whilst the right is called Riam.

"The Riam is a fine stream; at its junction with the Morotaba it takes that name, as the Morotaba does that of Sarāwak where they join. Low mangrove or Nepa palm banks characterise

---

[1] The old name for the town of Sarāwak.

EXCURSION. 37

these streams; and occasionally slight eminences, with timber, are to be seen. The highest hill is about 100 feet high, called Matang, and is at the point of junction between the Morotaba and Riam.

" The next river on the starboard hand is the Tanjan, a small stream; and some distance from it, the Kulluong, or Parwheet river, more properly the continuation of the Riam. On the port hand is a smaller river, running N. 35° E. We pursued this stream, called Ugong Passer; and after a hard pull against a strong tide, emerged into the larger river of Samarahan. The tide was so strong against us that we brought up for a couple of hours till it slacked, and between 4 and 5 got under weigh again, with the expectation of shortly arriving at our place of destination. Hour after hour passed, however; the sun set; the glorious moon rose upon our progress as we toiled slowly but cheerfully onward. Silence was around, save when broken by the wild song of the Malay boatmen, responded to by the song of our tars to the tune of 'Bonnie laddie, Highland laddie.'

" It was such a situation as an excitable mind might envy. The reflection that we were proceeding up a Borneon river hitherto unknown, sailing where no European ever sailed before; the deep solitude, the brilliant night, the dark fringe of retired jungle, the lighter foliage of the river bank, with here and there a tree flashing and shining with fireflies, nature's tiny lamps glancing and flitting in countless numbers and incredible brilliancy! At eleven at night we reached Samarahan, having been eighteen hours in the boat, and fifteen at the oars, chiefly against tide. The men were tired, but cheerful. Indeed, I can give them no praise beyond their merits for conduct spirited, enduring, and yet so orderly as never to offend the native inhabitants, or infringe upon their prejudices. A glass of grog with our supper, and we all soon closed our eyes in comfortable sleep, such as fatigue alone can bring.

"22d.—The village of Samarahan consists of a few houses, built, as usual, upon posts, and standing close to the brink of the river. It contains from sixty to eighty inhabitants in all, and there is nothing in its site different from the rest of the country. Whilst here, a boat, with a Dyak family, came alongside, consisting of a father, his son, and two daughters. They belonged to Sibnowan tribe, and had a 'ladang,' or farm, on the Samarahan, towards the sea. The women were good-looking; one, indeed, handsome, plump, and intelligent. They were naked to the waist, and ornamented with several cinctures of brass and coloured rattans scraped very thin.

"About 10 we quitted Samarahan and proceeded up the river, stopping only to take a set of sights, and about seven in the evening reached Sibnow, having previously passed the villages of Rembas and Siniawan. Siniawan and Sibnow are not above half a mile from each other, and Rembas not far distant. They are all about the same size, consisting each of eight or ten houses, and containing sixty or eighty inhabitants. The river, during its course so far, is characterised by the same claymud bank, evidently an alluvial deposit, without one rock to be seen. The banks are low, and for the most part cleared a quarter of a mile or more on either side, but the jungle is rarely disturbed beyond that distance. Occasionally, however, the scene is varied by the rich foliage of this jungle, which here and there kisses the tide as it flows by, and in some spots on the cleared ground arise clumps of trees that would be the pride of any park in Europe. Monkeys in great numbers frisked among the branches; and though unable to shoot them, they amused us often by their grotesque attitudes and the tremendous leaps they made. On one occasion we saw as many as twenty throw themselves, one after the other, from the branch of a high tree into a thick bush full forty feet below, and not one missed his distance or hold! On our way to Sibnow the Pangeran had collected a number of men for a deer-hunt. The nets used for this purpose are formed of rattans strongly wove together, which, being stretched along the jungle, have nooses of the same material, at three feet apart, attached to this ridge-rope. Beaters and dogs then hunt from the opposite quarter, and the deer, in escaping them, is caught in this trap. Several hundred fathoms is stretched at once, each separate part of thirty or forty fathoms being joined on as required; and I was told that in this way many deer were taken.

"A heavy rain came on directly after we had brought up, and quickly dispelled all our preparations for supper, by putting out our fire, cooling our hot water, and soaking our half-broiled fowls. To a hungry man such an event is very disastrous; but nothing could exceed the kindness of our Malay friends. They took us to the best house in the village, prepared our supper, and provided us with comfortable mats and pillows to sleep on. Some of our party preferred a bad supper and wet bed to these accommodations; and to consummate their discomfort, they were kept awake a great part of the night by sandflies. Our lot in the house was more fortunate. We heard the rattling of the pitiless rain, and pitied those whose choice or distrust kept them in the boat. I obtained by this means an excellent opportunity of seeing a Malay *ménage* in its primitive simplicity. Women, children, and all their domestic arrangements, were exposed to view. Nothing appeared to be concealed, nor could anything exceed the simple kindhearted hospitality of the inhabitants. The women gazed upon us freely; and their children, with the shyness natural to their age, yet took a glance at the strangers. Never having seen a white man, their curiosity was naturally excited, but it was never offensive. Our supper consisted of an excellent curry and cold venison broiled on a stick, flavoured with a glass of sherry, and concluded by a cigar. We retired to a dry bed, laying our head on the pillow with as entire a feeling of security as though reposing in England.

"A description of this Malay dwelling, situated so far up this hitherto unknown river, may be interesting. Built, like other Malay houses, on posts, floored with split bamboo, and covered with the leaf of the Nepa palm, it presents the very *beau ideal* of fragility, but affords, at the same time, many advantages, and with a little improvement might be rendered admirably calculated for a new settler in any warm country. It is built at very small expense, is remarkably roomy, free from damp, and weather-proof. The interior of the house consists of four rooms; the centre one large and commodious, the front narrower, but thirty-six feet in length, a family sleeping-apartment on one side, and a kitchen at the back. These apartments are divided one from the other by partitions made of the Nepa; the floors were nicely spread with strong mats of Dyak manufacture, and on our arrival finer white mats were laid over these. The entrance of the house is approached by a steep ladder, which in case of attack is easily removed. The river Samarahan is admirably calculated for trade; and, indeed, the same may be said of the whole country, from the great facility it offers of inland communication. There is no impediment for small vessels of 200 or 300 tons navigating as far as Sibnow, the stream being deep and clear of danger. The tides in the river are strong, but not dangerously so; and sounding occasionally in every reach we never found less water than three fathoms. The distant mountains, called Bukar (and some other name), are inhabited by Dyaks, and offer many valuable articles of trade, and we may presume this true from the riches whence the Sarāwak river takes its rise. It is highly probable, indeed, that both these rivers, as well as the Quop and others, have their source in the same range, and will be found to afford the same mineral productions. Tin, the natives confidently assert, can be procured, and birds' nests in very considerable quantities. The latter article, I have heretofore understood, was found only in the vicinity of the sea, whence the material of which they are composed is gathered; but both here and at Sarāwak the best-informed and most intelligent Malays assure me it likewise is found in the interior, and brought by the Dyaks from the mountains. The alluvial soil is a rich clay loam. The principal production at present is rice, of which considerable quantities are grown on the banks of the river, which accounts for the clearing of so many miles of the jungle. The mode of cultivation is similar to what is pursued in Sumatra, and so well described by Marsden. A small spot is cleared of jungle, and when the soil is exhausted of its primeval richness, is deserted for another, which again in turn is neglected, and returns to its wild state. The rice produced is of excellent quality, and of a smaller grain than the Java rice we have with us. It is very white, and of excellent flavour; and I am inclined to think is the 'Padi ladang,' or rice grown on dry ground. (For rice, cultivation of, &c. &c., vide Marsden's *Sumatra*, p. 65.)

"Besides rice, rattans are found in great quantities, and likewise Malacca canes, but whether of good quality I am not able to say. On my expressing a wish to see one, a man was despatched into the jungle, and returned with one in a few minutes. Bees-wax is another article to be procured here *at present* to the amount of thirty or forty peculs per year from Sibnow, Malacca canes a small ship-load, rattans in abundance, and any quantity of the Garu wood.[1] When we consider the antimony of Sarāwak, besides the other things previously mentioned (to say nothing of gold and diamonds), we cannot doubt of the richness of the country; but allowance must be made for the exaggeration of native statements.

"It must likewise be borne in mind, that these articles are collected in small quantities in a country thinly populated; and for the purposes of trade it would be necessary to have a resident European

---

[1] Aloes wood, *Lignum aloes*.

on the spot to gather the produce of the country ready for exportation. I have no doubt that permission might be obtained for an English merchant to reside in the country, and that during the lifetime of the Rajah Muda Hassim he would be secure from outrage. The produce of the country might likewise be obtained (at first) at a low rate in exchange for European goods suited to native tastes. In addition to the articles I have already mentioned, I must here add pins, needles and thread, both gold and white, showy cheap velvets, yellow, green, and red cloth, Surat silks, cottons, coloured beads (for the Dyaks), nankeens in small quantities, gold-lace of various qualities, gunpowder, muskets, pistols, flints, &c. &c. The head man of Sibnow (Orang Kaya), when I asked him why he did not collect the produce of the country, replied, that the inhabitants were few, and unless an English merchant was settled at Kuching to buy the things, it was no use collecting them. The uncertainty of sale, as well as the very small prices to be obtained from trading Malays, prevents these people using the advantages of their country, and as yet they seemed to consider it impossible that vessels would come for them. That they will one day or other be convinced to the contrary I am sure; that it will be soon I sincerely hope; for I can see no reason, with a population and rulers so pacific, why a trade highly advantageous to Singapore should not be opened. I considered our reception as an additional proof how much better the natives are disposed where they have had no intercourse with Europeans; how perfectly willing they are to extend a friendly hospitality when never previously injured or aggravated; and as the first white men who ever visited their country, we can bear the most cordial testimony to their unaffected kindness.

"It is true that we were under the protection of the rajah and accompanied by a Pangeran, and could have insisted on obtaining what was readily granted. But in case the natives had shewn any aversion or antipathy towards us, it would easily have been observed.

"23d.—Heavy rain all the morning. Our salt provisions being exhausted, we procured a goat, which was cooked to last during our upward passage.

"At 12, the flood making, we quitted Sibnow, and passing through the same description of country, reached the village of Guntong, consisting of eight houses, and about sixty or seventy inhabitants. The scattered population on the banks of the river amounts, however, to an equal, or probably greater number than in the villages. Beyond Guntong the country becomes wild, but beautiful, and the river gradually narrows until not above twenty-five yards wide. The depth, however, was three fathoms at high water, where we brought up for the night, about five hours' pull from Guntong.

The course of the river is so tortuous, that in one place two reaches are only divided by a neck of land five yards across!

"We were now fairly in the bush, and beyond the range of our Pangeran's knowledge; and I was not therefore surprised (though disappointed) when he intimated the necessity of returning. 'There was nothing to see; the river was narrow, rapid, and obstructed by trees; the Dyaks hostile; the rajah's enemies in ambush.'

"I had nothing to answer, save my desire to proceed; but I felt, at the same time, bound in honour to return; for to abuse the indulgence of a native prince on our first excursion would have been a poor way to obtain his future permission to visit other places.

"I did every thing man could do to shake the Pangeran's resolution; and I believe I should have been successful, had his stock of tobacco and sirih[1] not been expended. My last resource was resorting to the means found efficient with most men to induce them to alter their opinion. I was content to gain a consent to our proceeding some miles farther up the stream in the morning, and then returning with the ebb. Nothing during this contention could be more polite than the Pangeran's manner, for he not only expressed but looked his

---

[1] The Malay name for the betel, the aromatic leaves of which are chewed along with the pinang or areca nut, a little pure lime, and various spices.

regret, and urged on me his responsibility to the rajah. The plea was unanswerable, though I could not help suspecting the want of tobacco and betel as the leading motive.

"24th.— We proceeded, as previously agreed, up the river some ten or twelve miles farther, during which distance it narrows to an inconsiderable but deep stream. In many places it was not above eighteen feet wide, with trees overhanging the water. The depth was $2\frac{1}{2}$ fathoms high water, but being the rainy season it would not be deeper than necessary for boats all the year round. In the early morning the jungle presented a charming scene. Long vistas of noble trees with a diversity of richest foliage were before us — in some places overarching the water and forming a verdant canopy above our heads. Birds were numerous, and woke the woods with their notes, but rarely approached within shot. Pigeons in numbers and of several varieties were seen, but very shy and wild.

"We pushed on ahead of our attendant Pangeran, and pulled up long after the ebb had made. He had a long chase, and exhausted his lungs in shouting to us to return; and at last, from pity and according to promise, I did so. Poor fellow, he was very glad, fired his swivel-gun, and then brought up for breakfast. I believe a few hours' progress would have brought us to the vicinity of the hills and into the country of the Dyaks; and although disappointed at not being allowed to proceed thither, I nevertheless comfort myself that we have penetrated a hundred miles up a Borneon river hitherto unknown — a river likewise (as far as we have yet examined it) admirably calculated for the purposes of navigation and trade, and which may at some future period become of importance not only to the trade of our settlement of Singapore, but even to the commercial interests of Great Britain. The general character of the Samarahan river is similar to other streams flowing through alluvial soils; the stream is deep, with muddy banks and bottom, and apparently free from danger or obstruction. Of course these remarks are not meant to prevent the necessity of caution in any vessel proceeding up, as our survey was necessarily very brief; and, like other rivers, one bank will usually be found deep, the other shallow, which must be attended to.

"It now remains for us to proceed up the river from its mouth to its junction with the Ugong Passer; and should it prove to have sufficient water for vessels on the bar, nothing more will be desired.

"Returning, it took us five hours with a fair tide to Sibnow; the next ebb we reached Samarahan in three hours, where we stopped for the night. A heavy rain set in after we brought to, and continued till morning.

"25th.—The morning was cold and raw, but cleared up as the sun rose. At 7 we started, and at a quarter past 10 reached the mouth of the

Ugong Passer, and thence into the Riam. Thus it took us 11¼ hours, with a strong ebb tide, to pull the distance. We had ascended the river from the junction of the Ugong Passer. Mr. Murray's plan of the river will shew the distance as taken of each reach, together with its bearing. The ebb tide lasted us some distance up the Riam; but the flood making, we entered a small creek, called Tarusongong, scarce wide enough for the boat to get through, and entirely overarched with the Nepa palm. The general direction of the creek was N.W., and we emerged from it into the Boyur river; and pulling through several reaches, got into the Quop,[1] and thence, after a while, into the Morotaba; from the Morotaba into the Sarā-wak river, reaching the schooner at sunset, all well and happy. Thus ended our first cruise into the interior of Borneo."

[1] The banks of the Boyur and Quop are Nepa palm.

CHAPTER III.

Second cruise: up the river Lundu. The Sibnowan Dyaks. Their town of Tungong. Their physical proportions, and words of their language. Their customs. Skull-trophies. Religious ceremonies and opinions. Their ornaments. Appearance of both sexes. Dress and morals. Missionary prospects of conversion, and elevation in the social scale. Government, laws, and punishments. Dances. Iron manufacturing. Chinese settlement. Excursion continued.

"*Aug.* 30*th.*—Our flotilla, similar to the last time, quitted Sarāwak with the ebb tide, and reached Santobong, at the mouth of the river, soon after the flood had made. We waited for the turn of the tide; and in wandering along the sand, I had a shot at a wild hog, but unluckily missed. I likewise saw a deer, very like a red deer, and nearly as large. The hog I fired at was a dirty white, with a black head, very unlike in this particular to any wild hogs I have hitherto seen either in India or Europe; but several young pigs likewise seen were black.

" With the flood we weighed anchor, intending to bring up at the mouth of the Seboo river; but the Skimalong outsailing the prahus, foolishly parted company, causing me much uneasiness, and keeping the prahus under weigh all night. I was at this time aboard the Pangeran's boat, where I usually slept. About 10 on the 31st we reached Lobrek Bay, and rejoined our boat.

" With the flood tide we proceeded up Lundu river, which has Gunong Gading on the right hand. The course of the river is very tortuous, but it appears every where of more than sufficient depth. The Dyak village of Tungong is situated about eighteen miles from the mouth, and takes its name from a small stream which joins the Lundu just below on the left hand. It was dark when we arrived, and we ran against a boom formed of large trees run across the river as a defence against adverse Dyak tribes. We could see nothing of the town, save that it appeared longer than any we had yet visited.

" *September 1st.*—The river Lundu is of considerable breadth, about half a mile at the mouth, and 150 or 200 yards off Tungong. Tungong stands on the left hand (going up) close to the margin of the stream, and is enclosed by a slight stockade. Within this defence there is *one* enormous house for the whole population, and three or four small huts. The exterior of the defence between it and the river is occupied by sheds for prahus, and at each extremity are one or two houses belonging to Malay residents.

" The common habitation, as rude as it is enormous, measures 594 feet in length, and the front room, or *street*, is the entire length of the building, and 21 feet broad. The back part is divided by mat-partitions into the private apartments of the various families, and of these there are forty-five separate doors leading from the public apartment. The widowers and young unmarried men occupy the public room, as only those with wives are entitled to the advantage of separate rooms. This edifice is raised twelve feet from the ground, and the means of ascent is by the trunk of a tree with notches cut in it — a most difficult, steep, and awkward ladder. In front is a terrace fifty feet broad, running partially along the front of the building, formed, like the floors, of split bamboo. This platform, as well as the front room, besides the regular inhabitants, is the resort of pigs, dogs, birds, monkeys, and fowls, and presents a glorious scene of confusion and bustle. Here the ordinary occupations of domestic labour are carried on — paddi ground, mats made, &c. &c. There were 200 men, women, and children counted in the room and in front whilst we were there in the middle of the day; and allowing for those abroad and those in their own rooms, the whole community cannot be reckoned at less than 400 souls. Overhead, about seven feet high, is a second crazy story, on which is stowed their stores of food and their implements of labour and war. Along the large room are hung many cots, four feet long, formed of the hollowed trunk of trees cut in half, which answer the purpose of seats by day and beds by night. The Sibnowan Dyaks are a wild-looking but apparently quiet and inoffensive race. The apartment of their chief, by name Sejugah, is situated nearly in the centre of the building, and is larger than any other. In front of it nice mats were spread on the occasion of our visit, whilst over our heads dangled about thirty ghastly skulls, according to the custom of these people. The chief was a man of middle age, with a mild and pleasing countenance and gentle manners. He had around him several sons and relations, and one or two of the leading men of his tribe; but the rest seemed by no means to be restrained by his presence, or to shew him any particular marks of respect — certainly not the slightest of the servile obsequiousness observed by the Malays before their prince. Their dress consists of a single strip of cloth round the loins, with the ends hanging down before and behind, and a light turban, composed of the bark of trees, round the head, so arranged that the front is stuck up somewhat resembling a short plume of feathers.

"Their figures are almost universally well-made, and shewing great activity without great muscular development, but their stature is diminutive, as will be shewn by the following measurements, taken at random amongst them, and confirmed by general observation :—

"Sejugah, the chief, height, 5 ft. 1¾ in. Head round, 1 ft. 9 in. Anterior portion, from ear to ear, 1 foot; posterior, 9 in.; across the top, 1¼ ft.

"Kalong, the chief's eldest son, height, 5 ft. 2¼ in. Anterior portion of head, 1 ft.; posterior, 8¾ in.; across the top, 1 ft., wanting a few lines.

	Height.
Man from the crowd	5 ft. 1¾ in.
Another	5 1½
Another	5 4
Another	4 10
Another	5 3
Another	5 4

"The following is a specimen of their names, and some few words of their dialect, the only ones I could get not Malayan. The fact, indeed, appears to be that, from constant intercourse, their Dyak language is fast fading away; and whilst retaining their separate religion and customs, they have substituted the soft and fluent Malay for their own harsher jargon. The names are Jugah, or Sejugah, Kalong, Bunshie, Kontong, Lang, Rantie.

"The vocabulary:—

hairs, *bōk* (similar to the Lundu Dyaks).
thigh, *pāh*.
woman, *indo*.
father, *api*.
sea, *tasiek*.
slave, *ulon*.
spear, *sancho*.

black, *chelum*.
good, *badass*.
bad, *jaïe*.
quick, *pantass*.
slow, *bagadïe*.
that, *kneah* (nasal, like *kgneah*).
this, *to*.

to go, *bajali*.	to give, *bri*.
there, *kein*.	give all, *bri samonia* (M).
come, *jali*.	to bring, *bīi*.
here, *keto*.	bring that, *bīi kneah*.
come here, *jali keto*.	bring here, *bīi keto*.

"The corruptions of the Malay are, *langan* for *tangon*, arm; *ai* for *ayer*, water; *menua* for *benua*, country; *komah* for *rumah*, house; *besi* for *besar*, great.

" Like the rest of the Dyaks, the Sibnowans *adorn* their houses with the heads of their enemies; but with them this custom exists in a modified form; and I am led to hope, that the statements already made public of their reckless search after human beings, *merely* for the purpose of obtaining their heads, will be found to be exaggerated, if not untrue; and that the custom elsewhere, as here and at Lundu, will be found to be *more accordant* with our knowledge of other wild tribes, and to be regarded merely as a triumphant token of valour in the fight or ambush; similar, indeed, to the scalps of the North American Indian.

" Some thirty skulls were hanging from the roof of the apartment; and I was informed that they had many more in their possession; all, however, the heads of enemies, chiefly of the tribe of Sarebus. On inquiring, I was told, that it is indispensably necessary a young man should procure a skull before he gets married. On my urging them that the custom would be more honoured in the breach than in the observance, they replied, that it was established from time immemorial, and could not be dispensed with. Subsequently, however, Sejugah allowed that heads were very difficult to obtain now, and a young man might sometimes get married by giving presents to his ladye-love's parents. At all times they denied warmly ever obtaining any heads but those of their enemies; adding, they were bad people, and deserved to die.

"I asked a young unmarried man whether he would be obliged to get a head before he could obtain a wife. He replied, 'Yes.'—'When would he get one?' 'Soon.'—'Where would he go to get one?' 'To the Sarebus river.' I mention these particulars in detail, as I think, had their practice extended to taking the head of any defenceless traveller, or any Malay surprised in his dwelling or boat, I should have wormed the secret out of them.

"The men of this tribe marry but one wife, and that not until they have attained the age of seventeen or eighteen. Their wedding ceremony is curious; and, as related, is performed by the bride and bridegroom being brought in procession along the large room, where a brace of fowls is placed over the bridegroom's neck, which he whirls seven times round his head. The fowls are then killed, and their blood sprinkled on the forehead of the pair, which done, they are cooked, and eaten by the new married couple *alone*, whilst the rest feast and drink during the whole night.

"Their dead are put in a coffin, and buried; but Sejugah informed me that the different tribes vary in this particular; and it would appear they differ from their near neighbours the Dyaks of Lundu.

"Like these neighbours likewise the Sibnowans seem to have little or no idea of a God. They offer prayers to Biedum, the great Dyak chief of former days. Priests and ceremonies they have none; the thickest mist of darkness is over them; but how much easier is it to dispel darkness with light, than to overcome the false blaze with the rays of truth!

"The manners of the men of this tribe are somewhat reserved, but frank; whilst the women appeared more cheerful, and more inclined to laugh and joke at our peculiarities. Although the first Europeans they had ever seen, we were by no means annoyed by their curiosity; and their honesty is to be praised; for, though opportunities were not wanting, they never on any occasion attempted to pilfer any thing. Their colour resembles the Malay, and is fully as dark; and the cast of their countenance does not favour the notion that they are sprung from a distinct origin. They never intermarry with the Malays so as to intermingle the two people, and the chastity of their women gives no presumption of its otherwise occurring. Their stature, as I have before remarked, is diminutive, their eyes are small and quick, their noses usually flattened, and their figures clean and well formed, but not athletic. Both sexes generally wear the hair long and turned up, but the elder men often cut it short. As is natural, they are fond of the water, and constantly bathe; and their canoes are numerous. I counted fifty, besides ten or twelve small prahus, which they often build for sale to the Malays at a very moderate price indeed. The men wear a number of fine cane rings, neatly worked (which we at first mistook for hair), below the knee, or on the arm, and sometimes a brass ring or two; but they have no other ornaments. The ears of a few were pierced, but I saw nothing worn in them except a roll of thin palm-leaf, to prevent the hole closing. The women are decidedly good-looking, and far fairer than the men; their figures are well shaped, and remarkable for their *embonpoint*. The expression of their countenance is very good-humoured, and their condition seems a happy one. Their dress consists of a coarse stuff, very scanty (manufactured by the Sakarran Dyaks), reaching from the waist to the knee; around the waist they have rings of rattan, either black or red, and the loins are hung round with a number of brass ornaments made by their husbands. Above the waist they are entirely naked, nor do they wear any covering or ornament on the head. They have a few bracelets of brass, but neither ear-rings or nose-rings; and some, more lucky than the rest, wear a necklace of beads. They prefer the smallest Venetian beads to the larger and more gaudy ones of England. The labour of the house, and all the drudgery, falls upon the females. They grind the rice, carry burdens, fetch water, fish, and work in the fields; but though on a par with other savages in this respect, they have many advantages. They are not immured, and eat in company with the males; and, in most points, hold the same position towards their husbands and children as the European women. The children are entirely naked, and the only peculiarity I observed is filing their teeth to a sharp point like those of a shark. The men marry but one wife, as I have before observed. Concubinage is unknown; and cases of seduction or adultery very seldom arise. Even the Malays speak highly of the chastity of the Dyak women; yet they are by no means shy under the gaze of strangers, and used to bathe before us in a state of nudity.

"That these Dyaks are in a low condition there is no doubt, but comparatively theirs is an innocent state, and I consider them capable of being easily raised in the scale of society. The absence of all prejudice regarding diet, the simplicity of their characters, the purity of their morals, and their present ignorance of all forms of worship and all idea of future responsibility, render them open to conviction of truth and religious impression. Yet, when I say this, I mean, of course, only when their minds shall have been raised by education; for without previous culture, I reckon the labours of the missionary as useless as endeavouring to read off a blank paper. I doubt not but the Sibnowan Dyaks would readily receive missionary families amongst them, provided the consent of the Rajah Muda Hassim was previously obtained. That the rajah would consent, I much doubt; but if any person chose to reside at Tungong for the charitable purpose of leading the tribe gradually, by means of education, to the threshold of Christianity, it would be worth the asking, and I would exert what influence I possess with him on the occasion. I feel sure a missionary would be safe amongst them as long as he strictly confined himself to the gentle precepts and practice of his faith; he would live abundantly and cheaply, and be exposed to no danger except from the incursion of hostile tribes, which must always be looked for by a sojourner amid a Dyak community.

"I must add, that this day, when so many of my friends are destroying partridges, I have had my gun in my hand, to procure a few specimens.

"2d.—To continue my account of the Sibnowan Dyaks. I made particular inquiry about the superstition stated to exist regarding birds, and the omens said to be drawn from their flight; but I could trace no vestige of such a belief, nor did they seem at all acquainted with its existence.

The government of the Sibnowans may be called patriarchal. The authority of the chief appears limited within very narrow bounds; he is the leader in war, and the dispenser of the laws; but possesses no power of arbitrary punishment, and no authority for despotic rule. The distinction between Sejugah and the lowest of his tribe is not great, and rather a difference of riches than of power. A few ornamented spears presented by the Malays seem his only insignia of office; and these were never displayed in our presence save in the dance. The chiefship would appear to be elective, and not hereditary; but I could not distinctly understand whether the appointment rested with the rajah or the tribe. The former claims it, but the latter did not speak as though it were a matter of necessity or certainty. On asking Kalong, the eldest son of Sejugah (a young man of twenty years of age, active, clever, and intelligent), whether he would succeed his father, he replied, he feared he was not *rich* enough; but two or three of the tribe, who were present, asserted that he would be made chief. The Rajah Muda Hassim told me, that the only hold he had on the Dyaks was through the chief and his family, who were attached to him, but that the tribe at large cared nothing for the Malays. I can easily believe this, as any ill-treatment or cruelty directed against a Dyak community would soon drive them beyond the power and the territory of the prince. It is the best safeguard of the Dyaks, and the Malays are well aware that a Dyak alliance must be maintained by good treatment. They are called subjects and slaves, but they are subjects at pleasure, more independent and better used than any Malay under his native prince.

"The laws of this Dyak tribe are administered by the chief and the two principal men. They have no fixed code, or any standard of punishment, each case of crime being judged according to its enormity. In the event of murder in their own tribe, the murderer suffers death by decapitation, *provided he be in fault.* Theft is punished by fine; and adultery (stated as a heinous offence) by severe beating and heavy mulct. Other crimes are, in like manner, punished by fine and beating,—one or both, according to their various shades of evil. The latter varies greatly in degree, sometimes being inflicted on the head or arm, with a severity which stops short only of death. The arm is often broken under this infliction; so, according to their representation, it is a risk to be dreaded and avoided.

"Slavery holds amongst them; and, like the Malay, a debtor is reduced to this state until his debt be discharged. Children are likewise bought, and must be considered as slaves.

"In the evening I requested Sejugah to collect his tribe, and to shew me their dances and musical instruments. They readily consented;

and about nine at night we went to witness the exhibition. The musical instruments were the tomtom or drum, and the Malayan gong, which were beat either slow or fast, according to the measure of the dance. The dances are highly interesting, more especially from their close resemblance, if not identity, with those of the South Sea Islanders. Two swords were placed on the mat, and two men commenced slowly from the opposite extremities, turning the body, extending the arms and lifting the legs, in grotesque but not ungraceful attitudes. Approaching thus leisurely round and round about, they at length seize the swords, the music plays a brisker measure, and the dancers pass and repass each other, now cutting, now crossing swords, retiring and advancing, one kneeling as though to defend himself from the assaults of his adversary; at times stealthily waiting for an advantage, and quickly availing himself of it. The measure throughout was admirably kept, and the frequent turns were simultaneously made by both dancers, accompanied by the same eccentric gestures. The effect of all this far surpasses the impression to be made by a meagre description. The room partially lighted by damar torches — the clang of the noisy instruments — the crowd of wild spectators — their screams of encouragement to the performers — the flowing air and rapid evolutions of the dancers, formed a scene I wish could have been reduced to painting by such a master as Rembrandt or Caravaggio. The next dance was performed by a single person with a spear, turning like the last; now advancing, retiring, poising, brandishing, or pretending to hurl his weapon. Subsequently we had an exhibition with the sword and shield, very similar to the others, and only differing in the use of the weapons; and the performance was closed by a long and animated dance like the first, by two of the best performers.

"The dance with the spear is called Talambong; that with the sword, Mancha. The resemblance of these dances to those of the South Seas is, as I have observed, a remarkable and interesting fact, and one of many others which may, in course of time, elucidate the probable theory, that the two people are sprung from a common source. The Malays of Sarāwak, and other places in the neighbourhood of the Dyak tribes, dance these dances, but they are unknown to Borneo Proper, and the other Malay islands; and although the names may be given by the Malays, I think there is no doubt that the dances themselves belong to the Dyaks: a correcter judgment can be formed by a better acquaintance with other Dyak tribes.

"The household utensils in use here are few and simple. The mode of grinding padi clear of the husk is through the trunk of a tree cut into two parts, the upper portion being hollow, the lower solid; small notches are cut where the two pieces fit, and handles attached to the upper part, which being filled with padi and kept turning round, the husk is detached and escapes by the notches.

"The Dyaks, as is well known, are famous for the manufacture of iron. The forge here is of the simplest construction, and formed by two hollow trees, each about seven feet high, placed upright, side by side, in the ground; from the lower extremity of these, two pipes of bamboo are led through a clay-bank three inches thick, into a charcoal-fire; a man is perched at the top of the trees, and pumps with two pistons (the suckers of which are made of cocks' feathers), which being raised and depressed alternately, blow a regular stream of air into the fire. Drawings were taken of these, and other utensils and instruments. The canoes are not peculiar, but the largest prahus (some forty feet long, with a good beam) are constructed in the first place exactly like a small canoe: a single tree is hollowed out, which forms the keel and kelson, and on this foundation the rest of the prahu is built with planks, and her few timbers fastened with rattans. A prahu of fifty feet long, fitted for service, with oars, mast, attops, &c. was ordered by the Panglima Rajah, whilst we were with him, which completed was to cost thirty reals, or sixty Java rupees, or 6*l.* English. During the course of the day we ascended the river to visit the settlement of Chinese, lately established here. It is situated about 2½ miles up the river, on the same side as Tungong, and consists of thirty men (real Chinese), and five women of the mixed breed of Sambas. Nothing can be more flourishing than this infant settlement; and I could hardly credit their statement, that it had only been formed between four and five months. The soil they represented as most excellent, and none are better judges; many acres were cleared and under cultivation; rice, sirih, sweet potatoes (convolvulus), Indian corn, &c. &c. were growing abundantly; and they were able to supply us with seven pecul, or 933 lbs., of sweet potatoes, without sensibly diminishing their crop. They shewed me samples of birds-nests, bees-wax, garu wood (lignum aloes), and ebony, collected in the vicinity, chiefly from Gunong Gading. Several peculs of birds-nests and bees-wax, and the wood in large quantity, could *now* be brought to market; and no doubt, when demand stimulates industry, the quantities would greatly increase. The Dyaks, they told me, collected rattans, and likewise canes, which are plentiful. The mixed breed of the Chinese with the Malay or Dyak are a good-looking and industrious race, partaking much more of the Chinese character than that of the natives of this country. This mainly arises from education and early formed habits, which are altogether Chinese; and in religion and customs they likewise follow, in a great measure, the paternal stock. The race are worthy of attention, as the future possessors of Borneo. The numbers of this people cannot be stated, but it must amount to many thousand persons : 3000 were said to be on their way to the Borneon territory.

"The head man of this settlement, a Chinese of Quantung, or Canton, but long resident in the vicinity of Sambas, gave me some valuable information respecting the Sarāwak mountains. He had, with a considerable party of his countrymen, been employed there at the gold-mines, and he spoke of them as abundant, and of the ore as good. Tin they had not found, but thought it existed. Antimony-ore was to be had in any quantities, and diamonds were likewise discovered. I mention these facts as coming from an intelligent Chinese, well able from experience to judge of the precious metals, and the probability of their being found.

"3d.— Night as usual set in with torrents of rain, which lasted until the morning: the days, however, are fine, though cloudy. Got sights in the afternoon; and leaving our Dyak friends, we dropped down to the mouth of the river, where we slept.

"4th.— At 2 A.M. got under weigh for the Samatan river, which we reached at 8 A.M. I had been given to understand that the Lundu and Sibnowan Dyaks were to be found on this river; but on arriving, I was informed we must proceed to Seru, where we should see plenty of Dyaks.

I accordingly started immediately after breakfast, and reached Seru after midday. Here we found a small Malay fishing-village, with two or three stray Dyaks of the Sibnowan tribe; and on inquiring, we were told by them that their country was far away. Being convinced that the Pangeran had dragged me all this distance to answer some purpose of his own, I re-embarked on the instant, and set off on my return to Lundu, indignant enough. However, I had the poor satisfaction of dragging them after me, and making them repent their trick, which I believe was nothing else than to visit the island of Talang Talang for turtles' eggs. We were pretty well knocked up by the time we reached Samatan, having been pulling thirteen hours, the greater part of the time under a burning sun.

"The Samatan river, like the others, is enclosed in a bay choked with sand: the boat-passage is on the right-hand side, going in near Point Samatan. The sands are mostly dry at low water, and stretch out a considerable distance. There is a fishing-station here, though not so large as at Seru, and the fish at both places are very plentiful, and are salted for exportation to Sambas, and along their own coast. Seru is a shallow creek; the village may consist of 50 or 60 inhabitants, and the sands stretch a long way out. We thus lost two days, through the cunning of our Malay attendant; and the only advantage gained is being enabled to fill up the details of our survey of this bay.

"*5th.*—The day consumed returning along the coast to the Lundu, and we did not reach Tungong till late.

"*6th.*—Remained at Tungong. Every impediment was thrown in my way, to prevent my reaching the Lundu Dyaks—the distance was great, the tribe small and unsettled, the little probability of finding them, &c. I would, however, have gone; but another cause had arisen of a more serious nature. My feet, from the heat of the sun, mosquito-bites, and cuts (for I foolishly went without shoes that unlucky day to Seru), had become so painful and inflamed that I felt great doubt whether, if I walked in pain to Lundu, I could come back again. With the best grace I could, I yielded the point; with a vow, however, never to have the same Pangeran again. I did *manage* to be civil to him, from policy alone. He was superfluously kind and obliging.

"*7th.*—Left Tungong on our return to the vessel, and brought-to for the night at Tanjong Siri. In the evening I walked along the fine sandy beach as far as the entrance of the Sumpudin river. We saw many wild hogs; and on one occasion I was able to get within twenty yards of some ten of them together amongst some large drift-wood. Just as I was crawling over a tree and balancing, I found myself confronted by these animals; but they were out of sight almost before I could cock my gun and fire.. They were of a large size, and most of them we saw during the evening either dirty white, or white and black. At night, after we had retired to our quarters in the Pangeran's boat, she filled with water, and was near going down. The first intimation we had of it was the water wetting our mats on which we were sleeping. She was beached and baled out, and a hand kept baling all night, as they had laden her so deep that she leaked considerably.

"8th.—In the morning we got our anchor at daylight, and breakfasted on the island of Sumpudin. There are deer, hogs, and pigeons on Sumpudin island; but what was more interesting to me was, the discovery of the wild nutmeg-tree in full flower, and growing to the height of twenty or thirty feet. The nutmegs lay in plenty under the trees, and are of considerable size, though elongated in shape, and tasteless, as usual in the wild sorts. Whilst the East India Company were sending Captain Forest from their settlement of Balambangan as far as New Guinea in search of this plant, how little they dreamed of its flourishing so near them on the island of Borneo! The soil on which they grow is a yellowish clay mixed with vegetable mould. I brought some of the fruit away with me. After breakfast, a breeze springing up, we sailed to the mouth of the Sarāwak river, waited for the tide, and pushed on for the vessel, getting aboard about half-past 3 in the morning. Our Malay attendants were left far far behind, and there is little chance of their being here to-morrow, for their boats sail wretchedly."

CHAPTER IV.

Renewed intercourse with the Rajah. Prospects of trade. Ourang-outang, and other animals. The two sorts of mias. Description of the Rajah, his suite, and Panglimas, &c. The character of the natives. Leaves Sarāwak. Songi Dyaks. Visits Seriff Sahib. Buyàt tongue. Attack by pirates. Sails for Singapore.

HAVING returned to Sarāwak, Mr. Brooke renewed his intercourse with the Rajah; and his Journal proceeds:

"*Sept. 9th.*—Visited the rajah; civil and polite —I ought indeed to say, friendly and kind. Der Macota was on board, speaking on the trade, and very anxious for me to arrange the subject with the rajah. I could only say, that if the rajah wished I would do so, as I believed it would be greatly for the benefit of their country and Singapore.

"10*th.*—Laid up with my bad legs, and hardly able to crawl. Muda Hassim presented us with another bullock, which we salted. At Lundu we bought eight pigs, which arrived to-day in charge of Kalong, the young Dyak. He is a fine fellow.

I gave him a gun, powder-flask, powder, &c. He was truly delighted. Our Pangerans arrived at the same time.

"11th.—Very bad; got a novel, and read all day. Went ashore to see Muda Hassim in the evening. He gave us a private audience; and we finished our discussion respecting the trade, and I think successfully.

" I began by saying, that I, as a private gentleman, unconnected with commerce, could have no personal interest in what I was about to speak; that the rajah must clearly understand that I was in no way connected with the government of Singapore, and no way authorised to act for them; that he must, therefore, look upon it merely as my private opinion, and act afterwards as his wisdom thought fit. I represented to him that the kingdom of Borneo was the last Malay state possessing any power, and that this might be in a great measure attributed to the little intercourse they had had with European powers. I thought it highly advisable to call into play the resources of his country, by opening a trade with individual European merchants. Sarāwak, I stated, was a rich place, and the territory around produced many valuable articles for a commercial intercourse — bees-wax, birds-nests, rattans, besides large quantities of antimony-ore and sago, which might be considered the staple produce of the country. In return for these, the mer--

chants of Singapore could send goods from Europe or China which his people required, such as gunpowder, muskets, cloths, &c.; and that both parties would thus be benefited by their commercial interchange of commodities. I conceived that Singapore was well fitted for trade with this place. The Rajah must not suppose I was desirous of excluding other nations from trading here, or that I wished he should trade with the English alone; on the contrary, I thought that the Americans, the French, or any other nation, should be admitted on the same terms as the English.

"Of course, I was not allowed to proceed without much questioning and discussion; many of the views were urged and re-urged, to remove their false notions. That Mr. Bonham had the supreme command of the trade of Singapore was the prominent one; and when he died, or was removed, would not the next governor alter all kind intentions and acts? 'What friend should they have at Singapore then?'

"Again, they thought that a few ships might come at first; but then they would deceive them, and not come again. It was very difficult to explain, that if they procured cargoes at an advantageous rate, they would come here for their own advantage; if not, of course it would not be worth their while to come at all. The entire discussion proceeded with the utmost goodwill and politeness.

"That the political ascendancy of the English

is paramount here is apparent. They might, if they pleased, by means of an offensive and defensive alliance between the two powers, gain the entire trade of the north-west coast of Borneo, from Tanjong Datu to Malludu Bay.

" I obtained subsequently from Macota the following list of imports and exports, which I here commit to paper, for the information of those whom it may concern.

"*From Singapore.*—Iron ; salt, Siam ; nankeen ; Madras, Europe, and China, cotton cloth, coarse and fine ; Bugis and Pulicat sarongs ; gold and other threads, of sorts and colours ; brass wire, of sizes ; iron pans from Siam, called qualis ; chintzes, of colours and sorts ; coarse red broadcloth, and other sorts of different colours ; China crockery ; gunpowder ; muskets ; flints ; handkerchiefs (Pulicat and European) ; gambir ; dates ; Java tobacco ; soft sugar ; sugar-candy ; biscuit ; baharri ; common decanters ; glasses, &c. &c. ; China silk, of colours ; ginghams ; white cottons ; nails ; besides other little things, such as Venetian beads ; ginger ; curry-powder ; onions ; ghee ; &c. &c.

" The returns from Sarāwak are now : antimony-ore, sago, timber (lackah, garu), rattans, Malacca canes, bees-wax, birds-nests, rice, &c. Other articles, such as gold, tin, &c. &c., Macota said, would be procured after the war, but at present he need say nothing of them. The articles above mentioned might subsequently be greatly increased by demand; and, in short, as every person of experience knows, that in a wild country a trade must be fostered at first.

"To the foregoing list I must add, the pipe-clay, the vegetable tallow, which might be useful in commerce, being of fine quality; and the ore, found in abundance round here, of which I can make nothing, but which I believe to be copper.

"12*th*.—I received from the Rajah a present of an ourang-outang, young, and like others I have seen, but better clothed, with fine long hair of a bright chestnut-colour. The same melancholy which characterises her race is apparent in Betsy's face; and though but just caught, she is quite quiet unless teased.

"From the man who brought Betsy I procured a *Lemur tardigradus*, called by the Malays *Cucan*, not *Poucan* as written in Cuvier — Marsden has the name right in his dictionary—and at the same time the mutilated hand of an ourang-outang of *enormous* size. This hand far exceeds in length, breadth, and power, the hand of any man in the ship; and though smoked and shrunk, the circumference of the fingers is half as big again as an ordinary human finger. The natives of Borneo call the ourang-outang the *Mĭas*, of which they say there are two distinct sorts; one called the *Mĭas rombi* (similar to the specimen aboard and the two in the Zoological Gardens), and the *Mĭas pappan*, a creature far larger, and more difficult to procure. To the latter kind the hand belongs. The mïas pappan is represented to be as tall or taller than a man, and possessing vast strength: the face is fuller and larger than that of the mïas rombï, and the hair reddish, but sometimes approaching to black. The mïas rombï never exceeds four or four and a half feet; his face, unlike the pappan, is long, and his hair redder. I must own myself inclined to this opinion from various reasons:—1st. The natives appear so well agreed on the point, and so well acquainted with the distinction and the different names, that it is impossible to suppose it a fabrication for our peculiar use. Of the many whom I asked respecting them, at different times and in different places, most of them of their own accord mentioned the difference between the mïas pappan and the mïas rombï. The animal when brought aboard was stated to be the mïas rombï, or small sort. In short, the natives, whether right or wrong, make the distinction. 2d. The immense size of the hand in my possession, the height of the animal killed on the coast of Sumatra, and the skull in the Paris Museum, can scarcely be referred to an animal such as we know at home; though by specious analogical reasoning, the great disparity of the skulls has been pronounced the result merely of age.

" However, facts are wanting, and these facts

I doubt not I can soon procure, if not actual proof; and whichever way it goes, in favour of Buffon's Pongo or not, I shall be contented, so that I bring truth to light.

"19*th*.—From the 12th to the 19th of September we lay, anxious to be off, but delayed by some trifling occurrence or other, particularly for the letters which I was to receive for the merchants of Singapore. Our intercourse the whole time was most friendly and frequent; almost daily I was ashore, and the rajah often visited the vessel. How tedious and *ennuyant* to me can only be known by those who know me well, and how repugnant these trammels of society and ceremony are to nature. Nevertheless, I suffered this martyrdom with exemplary outward patience, though the spirit flagged, and the thoughts wandered, and the head often grew confused, with sitting and talking trifling nonsense, through a poor interpreter.

" I here bid adieu to these kind friends, fully impressed with their kindness, and the goodness of their dispositions. To me they are far different from any thing I was at all prepared to meet, and devoid of the vices with which their countrymen are usually stigmatised by modern writers. I expected to find an indolent and somewhat insolent people, devoted to sensual enjoyments, addicted to smoking opium, and eternally cock-fighting or gambling: let me speak it to the honour of the Borneons, that they neither cock-fight nor smoke opium; and in the military train of their rajah they find at Kuching few conveniences and fewer luxuries. Like all the followers of Islam, they sanction polygamy; and the number of their women, and, probably, the ease and cheerfulness of the seraglio, contrasted with the ceremonial of the exterior, induces them to pass a number of their hours amid their women, and excites habits of effeminacy and indolence. I should pronounce them indolent and unwarlike; but kind and unreserved to foreigners, particularly to Englishmen. They are volatile, generally speaking very ignorant, but by no means deficient in acuteness of understanding; and, indeed, their chief defects may be traced entirely to their total want of education, and the nature of their government. The lower orders of people are poor and wretched, and the freemen are certainly poorer and more wretched than the slaves. They are not greatly addicted to theft, and yet, unlike the scrupulous honesty of the Sibnowans, they pilfered some trifling articles occasionally when left in their way. The retainers of the court shewed much the same mean intriguing spirit which is too often found in courts, and always in Eastern ones; and the rajah himself seldom requested any favour from me direct, but employed some intermediate person to sound me— get whatever was required for himself if possible, if not for the rajah. I took the hint, and always expressed my wishes through the interpreter when not present myself. In this way we were enabled to grant or refuse without the chance of insult or offence. The suite of the rajah consists principally of slaves, either purchased or debtors: they are well treated, and rise to offices of some note. The Panglima Rajah was a slave-debtor, though we did not know it for some time after our arrival. I never saw either cruelty or undue harshness exercised by the great men during my stay, and in general their manners were affable and kind to those about them. The Rajah Muda Hassim is a remarkably short man, and slightly built; about 45 years of age; active and intelligent, but apparently little inclined to business. His disposition I formed the highest estimate of, not only from his kindness to myself, but from the testimony of many witnesses, all of whom spoke of him with affection, and gave him the character of a mild and gentle master. Muda Hassim's own brother, Muda Mahammed, is a reserved and sulky man, but they spoke well of him, and the rajah said he was a good man, but given to fits of sulkiness.

" Der Macota, unlike other Malays, neither smokes tobacco or chews sirih. He sought our society, and was the first person who spoke to me on the subject of the trade. His education has been more attended to than others of his own rank. He both reads and writes his own language, and is well acquainted with the government, laws, and customs of Borneo. From him I derived much information on the subject of the Dyaks and the geography of the interior; and if I have failed to put it down, it is because I have not departed from my general rule of never giving any native statements unless they go far to verify my own actual observations. I parted from the Rajah with regret, some six or seven miles down the river. Never was such a blazing as when we left Sarāwak; twenty-one guns I fired to the Rajah, and he fired forty-two to me —at least we counted twenty-four, and they went on firing afterwards, as long as ever we were in sight. The last words the Rajah Muda Hassim said, as I took my leave, were—' Tuan Brooke, do not forget me.'

" Amongst the curiosities in my possession are spears, swords, and shields, from various tribes; a coat of mail, made to the northward of Borneo, and worn by the pirates; specimens of Sakarran Dyak manufacture of cloth, and Sarebus ditto; ornaments and implements of the Sibnowans; and, last not least, a gold-handled kris, presented me by the Rajah, which formerly belonged to his father, and which he constantly wore himself. I likewise presented him with a small English dagger with a mother-of-pearl handle; and my favour was so high with him, that he used always to wear my gift, and I, to return the compliment, wore his.

" The climate of Sarāwak is good, and seldom hot: the last eight or ten days were oppressive, but previous to that we could sleep with a blanket, and seldom found it too warm in the day. Rain at this season falls in great quantities; and from imprudence, our crew suffered on their first arrival from colds and rheumatism; but getting more careful, we had latterly no sick-list.

"Farewell to Sarāwak! I hope to see it again; and have obtained a promise from the Rajah that he will go with me to Borneo, and shew me every part of the country by the way.

" I may here state the result of some inquiries I have made respecting the government of Borneo. The form of government may be considered aristocratic rather than oligarchical: it is ruled by the Sultan, but his power is kept in check by four great officers of government. These are, the Rajah Muda Hassim, the Bandar, in whose hands is the government of the country; Pangeran Mumin, the Degadon, the treasurer, or as Mr. Hunt says, comptroller of the household of the Sultan; Pangeran Tizudeen, Tumangong, or commander-in-chief; and Pangeran Kurmaindar, the Pen-dāmei, or mediator and interceder. This officer is the means of communication or mediation between the Sultan and his Pangerans; and in cases of condemnation, he sues for the pardon or mercy of his sovereign. Mr. Hunt, in his short but excellent paper on Borneo, mentions some other officers of state: I will not follow him; but in the names, as well as duties of these officers, his account agrees with my information. Farther than this, I have not yet learned, therefore state not; for I am not *manufacturing* a book, but gaining information. I may add, however, that these offices are elective, and not hereditary; as far as I yet know, I am inclined to believe the election rests with the chief Pangerans of the state; not only those in office, but others. When I reach Borneo I can detail this information.

"*23d.* — Quitted the Royalist at the entrance of the Morotaba, and accompanied by Pangerans Subtu and Illudeen, set sail for the river Sadung.

" The town called Songi is of considerable size, and the entire population along the river may certainly be reckoned at from 2000 to 3000 persons, independent of Dyaks. The country has a flourishing aspect, but the soil is represented as bad, being soft and muddy. There is a good deal of trade from this river, and it annually sends several large prahus to Singapore: two were lying off the town when we arrived, and two others had sailed for that place twenty days before. The produce of the country is bees-wax, birds-nests, rice, &c. &c., but they seem to be procured in less abundance than in the other contiguous rivers. There is nothing peculiar about the Malay population, except that it struck me, generally speaking, that they appeared better off than the people of Sarāwak, or others I have visited hereabouts. We ascended the river by night, anchored a short distance from the Songi, in a tide-way like a sluice, and entered the smaller river shortly after daylight. Having sent the Pangerans ahead to advise Seriff Sahib of our arrival, we pulled slowly up to the campong of the Datu Jembrong, where we brought up to breakfast. Datu Jembrong is a native of Mindanao, an Illanun and a pirate; he is slightly advanced in years, but stout and resolute-looking, and of a most polite demeanour—as oily-tongued a cut-throat as a gentlemen would wish to associate with. He spoke of his former life without hesitation, and confessed himself rather apprehensive of going to Singapore. He was remarkably civil, and sent us a breakfast of some fruit, salt fish, stale turtles' eggs, and coffee sweetened with syrup; but spite of all this, his blood-thirsty education and habits prejudiced me against him. Breakfast finished, we went forward to visit Seriff Sahib, who received us in an open hall; promised to get us as many animals as he could now; regretted our short stay, and assured me he would collect more by the time I returned. Amongst these is to be a mïas pappan, living or dead. I at the same time offered ten dollars for the skeleton belonging to the hand already in my possession, and a less sum for the parts. Being the first European Seriff Sahib had ever met, he was rather puzzled to know what we were like; but we had every reason to be satisfied with his kindness and the civility of his people: the inhabitants, though crowding to see us, are by no means intrusive, and their curiosity is too natural to be harshly repressed. I need hardly remark here how very erroneously the position of the Sadung river is laid down in the charts, it being placed in the bay, to the westward of Santobang, and nearly in the position of the Samatan river.

" 25*th*. — The last night was passed off Datu Jembrong's house, and I left him with a firm impression that he is still a pirate, or at any rate connected with them. He resides generally at Tawarron, to the northward of Borneo Proper, where his wives and children now are, and he has come here to superintend the building of a prahu. The people about him speak of his pursuits without disguise, and many informed us the prahu near his house is intended for a piratical vessel. Nothing could exceed the polite kindness of our rascally host, and I spent the rainy evening in his house with some satisfaction, acquiring information of the coast to the northward, which he is well able to give.

" In the morning we dropped down with the last of the ebb to the mouth of the Songi, and took the young flood to proceed up the Sadung. Beyond the point of junction with the Songi the Sadung retains an average breadth of from three quarters of a mile to a mile. The banks continue to be partially cleared, and here and there are a few Dyaks residing in single families or small communities on their ladangs or farms. The Campong Dyak, which terminated our progress up the stream, consists of three moderately long houses inhabited by Sibnowans. The manners, customs, and language of the Sibnowans of the Sadung are the same as those of their Lundu brethren; but they are a wilder people, and appear poor. Like other Dyaks, they had a collection of heads hanging at the entrance of their chief's private apartments. Some of these heads were fresh, and, with the utmost *sang-froid*, they told us they were women. They declared, however, they never took any heads but those of their enemies, and these women (unhappy creatures) had belonged to a distant tribe. The fresh heads were ornamented with fowl's feathers, and suspended rather conspicuously in separate rattan frames of open work. They professed themselves willing to go with me up the river to the mountains; and on the way, they informed me, were some large Malay towns, besides some more campongs of their own countrymen. Farther up they enumerated some twenty tribes of Dyaks, whose names I thought it useless to preserve. Late in the evening we set off on our return, and anchored once again off Datu Jembrong's house.

"26*th*.—Again visited Seriff Sahib. His name and descent are Arabic; his father, an Arab, having married a daughter of the Borneo rajah. The Malays evidently honour this descent, and con-

sider his birth very high. His power, they say,
equals his family, as he is, in some measure, independent; and were he to instigate the Sadung
country to take arms against Borneo, it is very
probable he would overthrow the government, and
make himself Sultan of Borneo. In person, this
noble partakes much of his father's race both in
height and features, being tall and large, with a
fine nose and contour of face. His manners are
reserved, but kind; and he looks as if too indolent
to care much about acquiring power, too fat for an
active traitor, though a dangerous man to oppress.
We were the first Europeans he had ever seen;
but, on our second visit, he lost much of his previous reserve, and was curious in examining our
arms and accoutrements. We, as usual, *exchanged*
presents; mine consisting of some nankeen, red
cloth, knife, scissors, and handkerchief; whilst
he gave me the shield of a great Kayan warrior,
a Bukar spear, a goat, fowls, and our dinner and
breakfast daily. He promised me the arms of
all the Dyak tribes, and plenty of animals, particularly my much-desired mïas pappan; and I,
in return, agreed to bring him two small tables,
six chairs, and a gun. Subsequent to our interview he sent me a tattooed Dyak, the first I had
seen. The lines, correctly and even elegantly laid
in, of a blue colour, extended from the throat to his
feet. I gained but little information; yet the
history of the poor man is curious, and similar to

that of many other unfortunates. He represented a chief amongst his own people in the country of Buyat, five days' journey up the Cotringen river (*vulgo* Coti river). Going in his canoe from the latter place to Banjamassim, he was captured by Illanun pirates, with whom he was in bondage for some time, but ultimately sold as a slave to a resident of Sadung. It was now five years since he became first captive, but having lately got money enough to buy his liberty, he is again a freeman; and having married, and turned to the religion of Islam, desires no longer to revisit his native country. The language of the tribe of Buyat he represents as entirely Malay. I made him a small present for the trouble I had given him, and he departed well content.

"About 3 o'clock in the afternoon we had a heavy thunder-storm, with lightning as vivid as the tropics produce. Torrents of rain descended, and continued a great part of the night; but, sheltered by our kajangs or mats, we managed to keep tolerably dry. Indeed, the voyager on this coast must be prepared for exposure to heavy rains, and considerable detention from thick and cloudy weather. The latter obstruction, so little noticed or even agreeable to those making a passage, is a cause of much vexation in surveying the coast, as for days together no observations are to be had.

"*27th*.—About 7 A.M. we quitted Songi, and dropped down as far as Tanjong Balaban, a low point forming the larboard entrance into the Sadung river, and bounding the bay, which lies between it and Tanjong Sipang. Coming to this point gave us a good offing for our return, and enabled me to take a round of angles to finish the survey as far as this point and Pulo Burong, which lies off it. We crossed over the sand flats with a light breeze, and reached the Royalist at 4 P.M. In the evening the Datu Jembrong, who had preceded us from Sadung, spent the evening aboard. He expressed his willingness to accompany me next season : whether I shall take him is another question ; but, could he be trusted, his services might be highly useful.

"Our Pangerans arrived early this morning from Sadung; and to-morrow was fixed for our departure, when an unforeseen occurrence caused a farther detention. The day passed quietly : in the evening I was ashore, and took leave of the Pangerans Subtu and Illudeen, who returned to Sarāwak, leaving the Panglima Rajah to pilot us out. The first part of the night was dark; and the Panglima in his prahu, with twelve men, lay close to the shore, and under the dark shadow of the hill. About nine, the attention of the watch on deck was attracted by some bustle ashore, and it soon swelled to the wildest cries ; the only word we could distinguish, however, being 'Dyak ! Dyak !' All hands were instantly on deck. I gave the order to charge and fire a gun with a blank cartridge, and, in the mean time, lit a blue light. The gig was lowered, a few muskets and cutlasses thrown into her, and I started in the hope of rescuing our poor Malay friends. The vessel, in the mean time, was prepared for defence; guns loaded, boarding-nettings ready for running up, and the people at quarters; for we were ignorant of the number, the strength, or even the description of the assailants. I met the Panglima's boat pulling towards the vessel, and returned with her, considering it useless and rash to pursue the foe. The story is soon told. A fire had been lit on the shore, and, after the people had eaten, they anchored their boat, and, according to their custom, went to sleep. The fire had probably attracted the roving Sarebus Dyaks, who stole upon them, took them by surprise, and would inevitably have cut them off but for our presence. They attacked the prahu fiercely with their spears; five out of twelve jumped into the water, and swam ashore; and the Panglima Rajah was wounded severely. When our blue light was lit they desisted; and, directly the gun fired, paddled away fast. We never saw them. The poor Panglima walked aboard with a spear fixed in his breast, the barb being buried, and a second rusty spear-wound close to the first; the head of the weapon was cut out, his wounds dressed, and he was put to bed. Another man had a wound from a wooden-headed spear; and most had been struck more or

G. Hawkins, lith.

Day & Haghe Lith^{rs} to the Queen.

NIGHT ATTACK on the PANGLIMA'S PRAHU.

London Chapman & Hall, 180 Strand, Jany 15th 1846.

less by these rude and, luckily, innocuous weapons. A dozen or two of Dyak spears were left in the Malay boat, which I got. Some were well shaped, with iron heads; but the mass simply pieces of hard wood sharp-pointed, which they hurl in great numbers. Fire-arms the Dyaks had none, and whilst attacking made no noise whatever; whilst the Malays, on the contrary, shouted lustily, some perhaps from bravery, most from terror. The force that attacked them was differently stated; some said the boat contained eighty or a hundred men, others rated the number as low as fifty; and, allowing for exaggeration, perhaps there might have been thirty-five—not fewer, from the number of spears thrown. Being fully prepared, we set our watch, and retired as usual to our beds; the stealthy and daring attack, right under the guns of the schooner, having given me a lesson to keep the guns charged in future. The plan was well devised, for we could not fire without the chance of hitting our friends as well as foes, and the deep shadow of the hill entirely prevented our seeing the assailants.

"*29th.*—I considered it necessary to despatch a boat to Sarāwak to acquaint the Rajah with the circumstance of the attack made on his boat. The wound of the Panglima was so severe, that in common humanity I was obliged to wait until all danger for him was past. He was soon well, and, like natives in general, his wound promises favourably;

on a European constitution a similar wound would be imminently dangerous.

"30th.— Took the long boat, and sounded along the edge of the sand; soundings very regular. In the evening Mr. Williamson returned in the gig, and a host of Pangerans; the Pangeran Macota at the head. He urged me much to go and see Muda Hassim. The Rajah, he said, desired it so much, and would think it so kind, that I consented to go up to-morrow. I am very desirous to fix their good feelings towards us; and I was prompted by curiosity to see the Rajah's *ménage* as his guest.

"*October* 1*st.*—We had a heavy pull against tide, and arrived at Sarāwak about 4 P.M. We had eaten nothing since breakfast at 8; and we had to sit and talk, and drink tea and smoke, till 8 in the evening; then dinner was announced, and we retired to the private apartments — my poor men came willingly too! The table was laid *à la 'Anglais*, a good curry and rice, grilled fowls, and a bottle of wine. We did justice to our cheer; and the Rajah, throwing away all reserve, bustled about with the proud and pleasing consciousness of having given us an English dinner in proper style; now drawing the wine; changing our plates; pressing us to eat; saying, you are at home. Dinner over, we sat, and drank, and smoked, and talked cheerfully, till, tired and weary, we expressed a wish to retire, and were shewn to a private room. A crimson silk mattress, embroidered with gold, was my couch; it was covered with white gold-embroidered mats and pillows. Our men fared equally well, and enjoyed their wine, a luxury to us: our stock of wine and spirits having been expended this some time.

"*2d.*— Once more bade adieu to our kind friends; reached the vessel at 4 P.M., and got under weigh directly. At dusk anchored in the passage between the sands.

"*3d.*—Five A.M. under weigh. Clear of the sands about mid-day, and shaped our course for Singapore.

"*4th.*—Strong breeze from w.s.w. Beating from leeward of Datu to Pulo Murrundum, in a nasty chop of a head sea."

CHAPTER V.

Summary of information obtained during this visit to Borneo. Geographical and topographical observations. Produce. Various Dyak tribes. Natural history. Language. Origin of races. Sail from Singapore. Celebes. Face of the country. Waterfall.

MR. BROOKE's journal continues his observations on the people and country he had just left; and I need hardly say, communicates much of novelty and interest in his own plain and simple manner.

"*Oct. 5th.*—Just laying our course. I may here briefly recapitulate the information acquired during the last two months and a half. Beginning from Tanjong Api, we have delineated the coast as far as Tanjong Balaban; fixing the principal points by chronometer and observation, and filling in the details by personal inspection. The distance, on a line drawn along the headlands, may be from 120 to 130 miles, the entire coast being previously quite unknown.

" Within this space are many fine rivers, and some navigable for vessels of considerable burden,

and well calculated for the extension of commerce;
such as Sarāwak, Morotaba, and Sadung. The
others, equally fine streams, are barred, but offer
admirable means for an easy inland communication;
these are, the Quop, Boyur, Riam, Samarahan,
Lundu, Samatan, &c. In our excursions into the
interior of the island, most of these streams have
been ascended to a distance of 25 or 30 miles, and
some farther. We traced the Samarahan river for
70 or 80 miles from its mouth, and passed through
portions of the intermediate streams of the Riam,
Quop, and Boyur. The Morotaba, which is but
another mouth of the Sarāwak, we passed through
several times, from the sea to its junction with that
river. The Lundu and Sadung rivers were likewise ascended to the distance of near 30 miles; and
plans of all these rivers have been taken as accurately as circumstances would permit, by observations of the latitude and longitude, and various
points, and an eye-sketch of the distance of each
reach, and the compass-bearing. The entrances
into the Sarāwak and Morotaba were carefully examined, and the former accurately laid down. The
productions of the country attracted our attention,
and the articles best fitted for commerce have been
already enumerated. Amongst these are, firstly,
minerals: say gold, tin, probably copper, antimony-ore, and fine white clay for pipes. Secondly, vegetables: woods of the finest descriptions, for ship-building, and other purposes; besides aloes wood

(*lignum aloes*), and arang or ebony wood, canes, and rattans. To these may be added, in the vegetable productions, sago, compon, rice, &c. &c.

"The wild nutmeg was found growing on the islands of Sadung and Sumpudin in abundance and perfection, proving that by cultivation it might be brought into the market as cheap, and probably as good, as those produced in the Moluccas. We have various specimens of ores and stones, which, on being tested, may prove valuable commodities. Amongst these is decomposed granite rock (I believe), containing minute particles of what we conceive to be gold, and an ore believed to be copper. Besides the articles above enumerated, are birds-nests and bees-wax in considerable quantities, and others not worth detailing here. We have been able, during our residence amongst the Borneons, to continue on the most friendly terms with them, and to open a field of research for our subsequent inquiries in the proper season. My attention has been anxiously directed to acquiring a knowledge of the Dyak tribes; and for this purpose I passed ten days amongst them at Lundu. I have made such vocabularies of the language of the Sibnowans and Lundus as my means allowed, and a farther addition of their various dialects will offer, I conceive, matter of high importance to those interested in tracing the emigration of nations. I may here briefly notice, that the nation of Kayans, included under the common denomination of Dyak, are a tattooed race, who use the sumpitan, or blow-pipe; whilst the other Dyak tribes (which are very numerous) are not tattooed, and never use the blow-pipe.

" The arms and instruments of many tribes are in my possession; and amongst the Sibnowans I had the opportunity of becoming acquainted with their habits, customs, and modes of living.

" The appellation of the Dyak tribes near the coast is usually the same as the rivers from which they originally came. The Dyaks of Sibnow come from the river of that name, just beyond Balaban Point; though large communities are dispersed on the Lundu and the Sadung. The same may be said of the Sarebus tribe (the most predacious and wild on the coast), which has powerful branches of the original stock on the Sakarran river. Beyond Point Balaban is a bay — between that point and Point Samaludum; the first river is the Sibnow; the next the Balonlupon, which branches into the rivers of Sakarran and Linga; passing Tungong and Samaludum, you come to the two islands of Talison; and between it and the next Point, or Banting Marron, lies the Sarebus river. Between Banting Marron and Tanjong Siri, is the Kalcka river, a high mountain called Maban, and then Rejong, the chief river of the Kayans. I may here likewise correct some of the statements and names usually current in England. The Idaan, represented as a Dyak tribe, are a hill-people, and probably not Dyaks; and the name Marat is applied by the natives of Borneo to the various wild tribes, Dyaks and others, without any specific meaning.

"In natural history the expedition has done as much as was in their power, by forming collections of birds, animals, and reptiles; but these collections are as small as our means. Specimens of woods and seeds have been preserved; but the season was not the proper one for flowers, as very few indeed were seen. The specimen of the hand of the mĭas pappan and the head of an adult mĭas rombĭ will, I believe, go far to establish the existence of an animal similar to the Pongo of the Count Buffon. I have little doubt that I shall be able in the ensuing season to establish the fact, or set it at rest for ever; though I confess myself greatly inclined to think that the former will be the case. I here leave the coast, with an excellent prospect for the coming year; and I would not now have quitted it so soon, but for the want of provisions; added to which, the change of the monsoon, bringing squally and dark weather, greatly interferes with our farther progress in surveying.

"*Nov. 22d*, 1839.—The Malayan language has been compared to the *lingua franca* of Europe. They are both indeed used by various nations in their commercial transactions; but beyond this, nothing can be more unjust or absurd than the comparison. The *lingua franca* is a jargon compounded at random, devoid of grammar or elegance; the Malayan, on the contrary, is musical, simple in its construction, and well calculated for the expression of poetry. It boasts many dialects, like the Italian, of superior softness; and, like the Italian, it is derived from many sources, refining all to the most liquid sounds by the addition of a final vowel. I fully concur with Mr. Marsden in his opinion, that the Malayan tongue, though derived from the Sanscrit, the Arabic, the Hindoostani, &c. &c., is based on the language which he calls the Polynesian; a language which may be considered original (as far as we know), and which embraces so vast an extent of geographical surface. The proof of this rests mainly on the fact, that the simple wants of man, as well as the most striking features of nature, are expressed in the Polynesian; whilst the secondary class of ideas is derived from the Sanscrit, or other language, and usually grafted in a felicitous manner on the original stem. By an original language, I must be understood, however, to mean only a language which cannot be derived from any other language. I seek not to trace the language of Noah, or to raise a theory which shall derive the finished and grammatical Sanscrit, the pure and elegant Greek, from some barbarous stock, whether Celtic or Teutonic. Such inquiries are fitted for those with leisure and patience to undertake a hopeless task, and learning enough to achieve better things. When we look for the origin of languages, we are lost; for those existing afford us no help. They present some affinities, as might be expected; but their discrepancies are irreconcilable; and amidst many equally good claims, who shall be able to demonstrate the only one which is right? All languages agreeing even in primary ideas, it would be difficult to determine the original; but when this primary class of ideas is expressed by sounds entirely and totally different, the task becomes utterly hopeless, and the labour as vain as that of Sisyphus. Indeed, it would be very difficult to shew how languages, derived from one stock, could possibly differ so far in the simplest expression of their ideas and wants as not to be traceable: and indeed, until this is done (which I conceive impossible), I am content to rest in the belief that there are more original languages *than one*—a conclusion agreeable to common sense, and consonant with the early history of the Hebrews.

"To trace the original identity of distant races, and their early migrations, through the affinity of language, is indeed a limited task, compared with the other; but one both feasible and useful. To further this labour, the smallest additional information is valuable; and the dialects of the rude people inhabiting the interior of the islands of Borneo and Celebes would be highly important. Previous, however, to instituting such a comparison as in my power, I propose taking a brief glance at the different races whose languages may be included under the common name of Polynesian.

"In the first place, the Malayan. Issuing from the interior of Sumatra, there is reason to think, as well as facts to prove, that originally the dialect of Menangkābau resembled the other dialects of its birthplace. The gradual extension of a warlike race gave a polish to the language; additional wants, increasing luxury, extended knowledge, and contact with the merchants of many Eastern nations,—all combined to produce the Malayan in its present form. But, during the progress of this change, the radical Polynesian root remained; and we find, consequently, that the words necessary to mankind in their earliest stage bear a striking and convincing resemblance to the dialects of Rejong and Lampung, in Sumatra. Subsequent improvements were largely adopted from the Sanscrit and the Arabic; but the fact of the primary ideas being expressed in the Polynesian, must preclude the conclusion of either of these being the source whence the Malayan is derived—its improvement and extension being alone referable to them. Marsden positively states his inability to trace the Polynesian to any other Eastern language; and, at the same time, he has demonstrated, in what he considers a convincing manner, the identity of this language from Madagascar and the islands of the Pacific to the Philippines and Sumatra.

"It may here be incidentally remarked, that whilst so many authors are endeavouring to prove that the Asiatic archipelago was peopled from the

Western continent, they overlook the fact of the radical difference of language. Unless the roots of the language can be traced either to India, Cambodia, or other parts, it must follow, as a matter of course, that the islands were peopled at a time previous to the introduction of the language now spoken on the continent; else, how are we to account for the simple dialects of a rude people being radically distinct from the language of the mother country? If the Dyaks of Borneo and the Arafuras of Celebes and New Guinea speak a dialect of the Polynesian, it will go far to prove an original people as well as an original language — that is, as original as the Celtic, the Teutonic, the South American; original, because not derived from any known source.

"These brief remarks on the Malayan will, I believe, apply to the language of the island of Java, which, equally improved and enlarged by the addition of Sanscrit and Arabic words, and differently modified, retains nevertheless its radical Polynesian root and its distinct written character, as do likewise the islands of Bally and Lombock. The districts of Rejong, Lampung, &c. in Sumatra, retain the original language in a much higher degree, possess distinctive written characters, and have little intermixture of Sanscrit or Arabic. Celebes, or Bugis-land, with a distinct language and character, will probably be found to follow the same rule; and the Philippines, including Mindanao, according to

Marsden, possess the same language, though altered and modified into the Tagala tongue.

"Madagascar, so far removed, exhibits in its language a dialect of Tagala, or, strictly speaking, of Polynesian; and the South Sea islands present striking and almost convincing proofs of the same origin.

"The inquiry ought to be pushed to the languages of the Mexicans and Peruvians of South America; and, as far as our knowledge permits, their identity established or disproved: for the language of this bygone people would go far towards tracing the course of emigration; it being evident that a strong argument would be raised in favour of the migration proceeding from east to west, if the language is common to South America and Sumatra, and not traceable to any country of the continent of India.

"It remains, however, to inquire into the language of the interior tribes of Borneo, Celebes, and New Guinea; and, on such inquiry, should they be found to possess the same radical roots as the rest, I believe the conclusion must ultimately be arrived at of the existence of a Polynesian language common to this vast geographical extent, and distinct from the languages of Asia. In tracing this identity we can only, of course, find it in few instances in the cultivated languages of Java and Malayan. Discrepancies, of course, must be great from the intermixture, from early recorded times, of all languages in the archipelago; but nevertheless, if the radical affinities be striking, they will be conclusive in establishing the original identity of all the races before mentioned. For, without this original identity, how can we account for these affinities of language? It may, indeed, be urged, that this language has gradually crept into the dialects of Java and Menangkābau. But, in the first place, the affinities will be found in the radical roots of the language—in the expression of the primary and necessary ideas, which seldom alter in any people; in the next, the high degree of improbability in supposing a rude dialect to transplant a substantial portion of a more polished one; and, thirdly, the collateral evidence of the similarity of conformation of the entire race from Polynesia to the archipelago —distinct alike from the Caucasian and the Mongolian.

"In tracing the identity of this language, we may reckon that of the Dyaks of Borneo, &c., as the lowest step of the ladder; the Pacific islands next; and so, through the dialects of Sumatra and the Tagala, up to the Malayan and Javanese. For this purpose a comparative view of all must be attained; and Eastern scholars should point out, when possible, the words taken from Sanscrit and other languages. For my own part, these remarks are made as a sketch to be enlarged on, and to assist in obtaining the vocabularies of the Dyaks and Arafuras.

"*Dec. 6th.*—In looking over Marsden's admirable introduction to his Malayan grammar, I find I have taken many of his views in the foregoing remarks; but I consider that his opinions may be pushed to conclusions more extended than he has ventured upon. Having described the 'exterior circumstances' of the Malayan language, he proceeds to point out those more original languages from whence we may presume it to be derived.

"'The words of which it consists may be divided into three classes; and that two of these are Hindoo and Arabic has been generally admitted. The doubts that have arisen respect only the third, or that original and essential part which, to the Malayan, stands in the same relation as the Saxon to the English, and which I have asserted to be one of the numerous dialects of the widely-extended language found to prevail, with strong features of similarity, throughout the archipelago on the hither side of New Guinea, and, with a less marked resemblance, amongst the islands of the Pacific Ocean..... To shew the general identity, or radical connexion, of its dialects, and, at the same time, their individual differences, I beg leave to refer the reader[1] to the tables annexed to a paper on the subject which I presented, so long ago as the year 1780, to the Society of Antiquaries, and is printed in vol. vi. of the *Archæologia;* also a

---

[1] Also vol. iv. of the *Bengal Asiatic Researches.*

table of comparative numerals in the appendix to vol. iii. of Captain Cook's last voyage; and likewise to the chart of ten numerals, in two hundred languages, by the Rev. R. Patrick, recently published in Valpy's *Classical, Biblical, and Oriental Journal.*'

" Again, Marsden states :

" ' But whatever pretensions any particular spot may have to precedence in this respect, the so wide dissemination of a language common to all bespeaks a high degree of antiquity, and gives a claim to originality, as far as we can venture to apply that term, which signifies no more than the state beyond which we have not the means, either historically or by fair inference, of tracing the origin. In this restricted sense it is that we are justified in considering the main portion of the Malayan as original, or indigenous, *its affinity to any continental tongue not having yet been shewn;* and least of all can we suppose it connected with the monosyllabic, or Indo-Chinese, with which it has been classed.'

" When we find an original language bearing no traces of being derived from any continental tongue, we must conclude the people likewise to be original, in the restricted sense, or, with their language, to have emigrated from some source hitherto unknown. The Sanscrit and Arabic additions to the original stock are well marked, though the period of the introduction of the former is hidden in darkness. It may be inferred, however, that it came with the Hindoo religion, the remains of which are yet in existence. It is evident that the question resolves itself into two distinct branches: first, the original language, its extent, the coincidence of its dialects, its source, &c.; secondly, its discrepancies, whence arising, &c.; together with the inquiry into the probable time and mode of the introduction of the Sanscrit. With the latter of these inquiries I have nothing to do; on the former subject I may collect some valuable information by adding the dialects of the savage tribes in the interior of Borneo and Celebes.

"The alphabets of the island of Java, of the Tagala, and the Bugis of Celebes, are given by Corneille, Le Brun, Thevenot, and Forrest."

Of Mr. Brooke's sojourn at Singapore it is unnecessary to speak; and I accordingly resume with his ensuing voyage from that port, and again for the Indian archipelago; but for reasons which need not be entered into at length, contenting myself with only that portion of his excursion to Celebes and among the Bugis which particularly bears upon his Borneon sequel.

"*Dec. 7th.*—Off Great Solombo. Never was there a more tedious passage than ours has been from Singapore. Sailing from that place on the 20th November, we have encountered a succession of calms and light winds—creeping some days a few miles, and often lying becalmed for forty-eight hours without a breath to fill the sails. Passing through the straits of Khio and Borea, and watering at the islands of Nooka, we stood thence for Pulo Babian, or Lubeck, lay a night becalmed close to the Arrogants Shoal, of which, however, we saw nothing, owing probably to the smoothness of the water. The depths are greater than laid down on Horsburgh's chart, varying from thirty-six to thirty-eight fathoms. A calm now keeps us off the greater Solombo, which it is my intention to visit when in my power.

"8th.—Drifted past Solombo in the calm, and, reluctant to return, I continued on my voyage with a light breeze from the eastward. This island is well laid down: from the sea, we made its longitude 113° 31'; Horsburgh gives it 113° 28', which, considering that both observations were made afloat, is a near enough approximation. The land is low, with a single hill, shewing round from the westward, flat or wedge-shaped from the eastward. The smaller Solombo is low: both wooded.

"10th.—In sight of Laurots islands.

"11th.—In the evening stood within four miles of the southern island of Laurots. These islands are high and steep, covered with wood, and uninhabited. The easternmost island seems, by bearings, badly laid down, being not far enough to the southward and eastward. The southern island is called by the Bugis, Mata Siri; the eastern, Kadapangan; the northern one, Kalambow. A few rocks and islets lay off them; water deep, and apparently clear of all danger.

"15th.—Turatte Bay. After experiencing continued calms and light winds, and falling short of water, we at length reached this bay, and anchored in 7½ fathom. The first impression of Celebes is highly favourable. The mountains present a bold outline, and rise in confused masses, until crowned by what is commonly called *Bonthian Hill.* The sides of the mountains slope gradually to the sea, and present an inviting and diversified aspect of wood and cleared land. I despatched a boat for water to a small village; and the crew were well received by the natives, after they became assured that they were not pirates.

"The outline of this bay, in Nories' chart, is not badly laid down; but, on either side, there is great room for improvement and survey. Turatte Bay may be fairly so called, as the district (or *negri*) generally bears that name. The larboard point of Turatte Bay (approaching) is called Malăsaro, which comes next to Tanjong Layken in the charts. The starboard point is Tanjong Uju Loke, and from Uju Loke the land runs low to the point of Galumpang, the entrance of a river marked in the charts. From Uju Loke (named Bolo Bolo in Nories' chart), the coast-line runs for twelve or fifteen miles to Bulo Bulo, which space is entirely omitted. Bulo Bulo forms the entrance of Bonthian Bay.

"16th.—Bonthian Bay. Called Banthi by the natives: is in lat. 5° 37' s.; long. 119° 33' E.

"The bay is pretty well laid down by Dalrymple. The small Dutch fort or entrenchment stands rather on the eastern bight of the bay, and is composed of a few huts, surrounded by a ditch and green bank. Two guns at each corner compose its strength, and the garrison consists of about thirty Dutchmen and a few Javanese soldiers. We were cordially and hospitably received by the officers, and, after a great deal of trouble and many excuses, here procured horses to carry us to the waterfall. Bonthian hill is immediately over this place, a flat space of rice-ground, some miles in extent, only intervening. The hill (so called) may with more propriety be designated as a range of mountains, which here attain their utmost height and sink down gradually almost across the peninsula. The view is most attractive: the green and refreshing rice-grounds on the front ground, and behind, the slopes of the mountain and its various peaks, verdant grass, wooded chasms, and all the inequalities which mark a mountain-region. I was very anxious to mount to the summit, but so many difficulties are thrown in the way, that I almost despair—horses and guides are not to be procured. The Dutch say the natives are lazy: the natives say they dare not go without authority—either way we are the losers; but the officers certainly exert themselves in our favour. Coming into this bay, there is some difficulty in distinguishing the fort, but, coming from the westward, its position may readily be known by steering for two lumps on the s.e. declivity of the mountain.

"18th.—Got ashore by seven o'clock to start for the waterfall; till nine we were detained by want of horses, but after much trouble the animals were procured, and off we started. Our party consisted of three doctors (him of the fortification, a German gentleman, Treacher, and Theylingen) and myself, with native guides. The road lay for a short way along the beach, then struck into the thicket, and we commenced a gradual ascent. The scenery was most striking and lovely; glades and glens, grassy knolls and slopes, with scattered trees, and the voice of a hidden river which reached our ears from a deep valley on our left hand. Proceeding thus for some distance, we at length plunged into the wood, and descending a short space, found ourselves by the side of the stream below the waterfall. Here, breakfast being finished, we all stripped to our trousers, entered the water, and advanced along the bed of the river to the fall. The banks on either hand, steep and woody, prevented any other mode of approach, and the stream rushing down and falling over huge rocks, rendered the only available one anything but easy. At times we were up to the arms, then crawling out and stealing with care over wet and slippery stones, now taking advantage of a few yards of dry ground, and ever and anon swimming a pool to shorten an unpleasant climb. In this manner we advanced about half a mile, when the fall became visible; thick trees and hanging creepers intervened; between and through the foliage we first saw the water glancing and shining in its descent. The effect was perfect. After some little farther and more difficult progress, we stood beneath the fall of about 150 feet sheer descent. The wind whirled in eddies, and carried the sleet over us, chilling our bodies, but unable to damp our admiration. The basin of the fall is part of a circle, with the outlet forming a funnel; perpendicular on all sides, bare cliffs form the upper portion of the vale, and above and below is all the luxuriant vegetation of the East; trees, arched and interlaced, and throwing down long fantastic roots, and creepers, shade the scene, and form one of the richest sylvan prospects I have ever beheld. The water, foaming and flashing, and then escaping amid huge grey stones on its troubled course—clear and transparent, expanding into tranquil pools, with the flickering sunshine through the dense foliage—all combine to form a scene such as Tasso has described.[1]

"Inferior in body of water to many falls in Switzerland, it is superior to any in sylvan beauty; its deep seclusion, its undisturbed solitude, and the difficulty of access, combine to heighten its charms

[1] Canto 15, stanza lv. lvi.

to the imagination. Our descent was like our upward progress. Having again dressed ourselves, we rested for a time, and then started for Bonthian—wearing away the rest of the day shooting amid the hills. Theylingen and myself procured many specimens, and returned laden with our spoil, and charmed with our day's excursion. The waterfall is called Sapo, from the neighbouring green peak of that name. The height of our resting-place, (not the highest point of the day's ascent) was 750·5 feet, by Newman's two barometers; yet this is the bottom of the mountain on its western slope. The officers dined with us; they are very polite and kind: and we retired early to rest, all the better for our excursion.

"19th.—At 6 A.M. went with the Dutch officers shooting, and reached the same stream which forms the waterfall. The scenery delightful; water cool, and pleasant for bathing, a luxury I enjoyed in high perfection. Aboard again to a late breakfast.

CHAPTER VI.

Dain Matara, the Bugis. Excursions in Celebes. Dispute with the Rajah's son-in-law. Baboon shot. Appearance of the country. Visits the Resident. Barometrical observations. The Bugis. Geography. Coral reefs. Visits the Rana of Lamatte. Population and products of the country.

"I MAY here indulge in a brief episode, to introduce my Bugis companion, Dain Matara,— which properly I should have done long since— a man well born, and, for his country, affluent and educated: he offered, at Singapore, to accompany me on this expedition, refusing all pay or remuneration, and stating that the good name to be acquired, and the pleasure of seeing different places, would recompense him. At first, I must own, this disinterestedness rendered me suspicious; but conceiving that the greatest utility might accrue from his assistance, I agreed to take him with his servant. Our long passage seemed to make us well acquainted, and, I believe, raised a mutual confidence. Dain, cheerful, good-tempered, and intelligent, gained daily on my esteem; and, by the time we reached Bonthian, I was rejoiced that he accompanied me.

"On this day we succeeded in procuring horses and guides for the *hill*, as it is called.

"*20th.*—By 8 A.M. our preparations were complete, and we mounted our horses; a motley group we formed, composed of Treacher, Theylingen, and myself, two seamen (Spence and Balls), Dain Matara, a son-in-law of the Bonthian Rajah, and six footmen. Provisions for four days was on one of the horses, and a goodly stock of fowling-pieces, besides my mountain barometer. The plain was soon cleared; and three hours' ride by a good horse-path brought us to the village of Senua, consisting of a dozen houses. We found the inhabitants hospitable, and took refuge from a heavy squall of wind and rain in the best house the place afforded. During the rain the thermometer sunk to 76°, but rose directly afterwards. At half-past one the rain cleared away, but we were detained until three by the Bugis getting their dinner. During this time I strayed along the sparkling stream which runs by the village, and after enjoying a bathe, called to horse, in order to proceed. Great was my surprise, however, to be told by the Rajah's son-in-law that he supposed we were going back. A discussion arose,—he declaring there was no road for the horses, and that we could not go farther; whilst I insisted, if he would not advance, I should continue my journey on foot. After much time had been lost, our guide set off slowly and reluctantly, and we proceeded for two or three miles, when, finding our head turned to the southward, and the road descending, I again called a halt, and was once more told it was not possible to mount farther. A scheme had been formed to lead us round about, and take us gradually down, until too late to mount again. A long parley ensued; both parties seemed resolute; and it finished by our unloading the baggage-horse, and making a small parcel of necessaries to carry on foot. Our guide, however, never intended matters to go so far, and we finished at last by taking half the horses, and allowing him (the Rajah's son-in-law) to descend with the rest. This being done, we had to retrace our road nearly to Senua; and a little before sunset our party crossed an awkward stream, and struck into the path up the mountains.

"A short walk brought us to Lengan Lengang about dusk, where we put up for the night. For the first time, this day I saw the cockatoo in his wild state; I was within easy shot of two of them, but the stream lay between us, and I felt some compunction at shooting these favourite birds.

"Lourikeets were in great plenty, and many varieties of pigeons and doves, besides other birds. Near Lengan Lengang we encountered a community of dusky baboons, many of them very large and powerful: after a hard scramble I got within shot of them; on my firing the first barrel, the young ones and females made off, but the leaders of the band disdained to retreat, and, with threatening gestures and grimaces, covered the retreat of their party. The consequence was, I sacrificed one of these heroes, of a large size: he fell from the branch on which he was seated into a deep valley, and his fall completed the rout of the rest. Spence, in the mean time, having arrived, I despatched him to secure the prize; but at the bottom of the valley the baboons again shewed themselves, and manifested every inclination to fall on him; another barrel put them to flight, and between us we dragged the fallen hero to the horses.

" The village of Lengan Lengang consists of about a dozen houses, is situated in a nook of the hills, and surrounded by cocoanut-trees. We were accommodated in the principal house, and treated with every hospitality. The people of the hills are poor, though their land is fertile, and produces abundance of rice and Indian corn. Theft is said to be common, especially of horses, and the care of the horses belonging to travellers devolves on the villagers; for, in case a horse is stolen, a fine is imposed on the population in general. To prevent this misfortune, our hosts kept playing, as long as we could bear it, on an instrument like a clarionet; but at 12 o'clock, after trying in vain to sleep, we were obliged to stop the noise and risk the horses.

" This instrument is about three feet long, with five or six holes, and a flat mouthpiece on the cane-tube; the sound is musical when gently breathed into, but in their usual mode of playing, it emits frightful shrieks. During the night the thermometer sunk to 69°, and we were glad of our blankets.

"21st.—Rose between five and six. Took some barometrical observations, and at half-past six continued our upward way. As far as Lengan Lengang the country presents beautiful woodland and mountain scenery, with luxuriant vegetation, thickly wooded valleys, and sparkling streams. The flats and valleys are occupied by rice-grounds, and the pasturage is of the very finest description for all sorts of cattle; the grass short and rich. Lengan Lengang is the last point where the cocoanut or other palms is seen, but there it grows remarkably well, and attains a great height. Above this point the wood, generally speaking, becomes smaller, and the vegetation more coarse, the hills being covered with a coarse high grass, and ferns, similar to those in England. Three hours' slow travelling brought us to the village of Lokar, situated at the foot of the peak of that name. I mounted, whilst breakfast was preparing, nearly to the top, and up to the belt of thick wood which surrounds the last 100 or 150 feet. Observations were repeated here, shewing a great fall of the mercury, and afterwards taken at the village. Lokar consists of a few scattered huts, situated amid gardens of fruit and vegetables: the mango, the guava, the jack, and the plantain, with cabbages and Indian corn, compose their stock; the latter constitutes their principal food, and is granaried for use in large quantities, not only in the house, but on frame-works of bamboo without, on which it is thickly hung in rows, with the heads downward, to protect it from the weather. The highest summit, called Lumpu Batang, was visible when we first arrived, some miles in advance: at breakfast-time the clouds entirely covered it, and rolled down upon Lokar in heavy rain, driving us into a miserable hut for shelter.

"During the rain the thermometer fell to 70°. At 3 P.M. started for some huts we saw at the foot of Lumpu Balong, having first sent our horses back to Lengan Lengang, being assured their farther progress was impracticable. When, however, our guide from Lokar understood our object of reaching Lumpu Batang, he objected to advance, on the plea that the village in advance was inhabited by people from Turatte. We managed to coax him on, and, after two and a half hours' walk, reached Parontalas. The country, ascending gradually, becomes more and more wild; the wood stunted, and the streams, finding their way through masses of rock, leave strong traces of their occasional violence. Parontalas stands on the edge of the forest which skirts Lumpu Balong, from which it has not long been retrieved. It consists of a few scattered huts, far apart. Potatoes, tobacco, and coffee are grown here, the former in great abundance. Like the rest of the people, their food consists of Indian corn; and, as in the other villages, they breed horses. Our host of Parontalas was very polite, and gave us some fowls and the accommodation of his house; the latter, indeed, was needful, for we were all badly provided with covering, and the mountain-air was chilly and cold. To our request for guides to ascend the mountain, he replied that it was necessary to consult the head man of the district, who lived some little distance off. In the interim we made ourselves very happy, determined to ascend with or without a guide or guides. We lay down at nine, in order to be ready for the morning's work, the thermometer standing at 59° in the house.

"22d.—At five, when we rose, the thermometer stood at 56° in the air. The head man had arrived, and willingly gave us guides, warning us only of the difficulty of the ascent. Nothing could exceed the kindness and attention of this simple old man. He remembered the time the English had the country, and spoke of their respect for our nation, and their regret that we had left the country. At 6 A.M. we started, and, after walking about a mile, plunged into the belt of forest which environs Lumpu Balong. From six till half-past two, we were alternately ascending and descending, scrambling over rocks or fallen timber, or cutting a path through the most tangled thicket that ever tore the wayfarer. To add to our difficulty, during the latter half of the ascent, we could procure no water, which caused us considerable suffering. At length, however, we stood at the summit of Lumpu Batang, and looked, on either side, over a vast sea of fleecy clouds which rolled beneath. The top is a narrow ridge, covered with stunted trees and luxuriant moss; and a second peak to the westward, of rather less elevation, is separated from it by a declivity. I climbed to the top of a tree to look along the mountain, and make certain that we were at the highest point; and having convinced myself of this, I proceeded with the barometric observations, which were concluded by 3 P.M.; for it was highly necessary to get down before night overtook us in the dreary and inhospitable forest. Our thirst, too, was tormenting, and increased by hearing the fall of a torrent deep in the valley to the northward.

"As far as I could observe, the northern face of the mountain was perpendicular; and the ascent on that side would have been attended with greater difficulty than from the point we chose. Our way down was easier, and the descent was made as expeditiously as the nature of the ground would allow. Having fairly worn our shoes off our feet, we were pierced by brambles and thorns in a cruel manner. Our guide, in going down, discovered a tree with a bee-hive in it containing great store of honey. The Bugis instantly attacked the tree; on seeing which, my first impression was, that it would be prudent to retreat to a distance; but their composure induced me to remain; and, to my surprise, when the tree was laid open, the honey was taken out in large quantities, and the bees brushed off the comb without offering to sting. Though flying round about us, and on the hands of all the people, they were quite innocent of harm; and I conclude, therefore, they were different from the common honey-bee. The honey was excellent, and refreshed us for a few minutes; but ultimately only added to our thirst. At length, about five, we reached a stream of water, and quenched our thirst with draughts of the coolest and most limpid mountain-stream. The Bugis, though, like ourselves, they had been without any water from nine o'clock in the morning till five in the evening, refused to drink, alleging that it was highly injurious after eating honey! Glad were we, just at dark, to get clear of the forest; and a short walk farther brought us to our temporary dwelling. We were much knocked up, and very much torn with the thorns. A brief dinner, and a delicious cigar, and we lay down to sleep—not even incommoded by the cold, which kept us awake the last night.

"23d.—Having, through mistake, forgotten to bring up any money, I had no means of repaying the obligations received from these simple hill-people except *by promises*. My old friend ordered the guide of yesterday to accompany us to the plains, to receive his own payment, and to bring some things, for others, up there. At ten we hobbled forth, very foot-sore, and lacking proper covering for our feet. The prospect of four or five hours' walk to Lengan Lengang was very unpleasant; and in proportion to our expected pain was our gratification on meeting *all* our horses within three miles of Parontalas—*all* the horses, which all the men swore could not, by any possibility, ascend, were there; and though without saddles and bridles, or the Bugis, we were too glad to mount. We went down by another road. Four hours brought us to Lengan Lengang, where we rested for two hours, and, remounting, reached Bonthian at about seven o'clock in the evening. Thus concluded this interesting excursion into a hill-region, where we attained the summit of Lumpu Balong, never before reached by European. The Dutch officers informed me that three successive Residents of Bonthian had attempted it and failed.

"Before I conclude, I may take a brief survey of the country. The hills are generally rounded or flat at top, and not offering any rugged or broken peaks. The scenery about Senua and Lengan Lengang is the perfection of woodland, with the picturesque characteristics of a mountain-region; the climate admirably suited, thence to the summit, for Europeans, and capable of producing most European and tropical plants to perfection. Coffee-plantations, on these hills, might be undertaken with certainty of success; and there is much in the character of the natives which would facilitate the operation. To the westward of Lakar, and somewhat lower, is a fine extensive plain, which we just skirted coming down: it was cultivated in every part, apparently with rice. The vegetable productions of the hills I have briefly mentioned; but I may add, that the wild raspberry was found, and that wild guavas grow in the greatest abundance, as well as oranges and grapes.

"The animal kingdom, of course, we had no time to examine; but the babi rupa is said to be found in the higher regions; and in the forest, towards the summit of Lumpu Balong, we saw the dung of wild cattle, which I am told are a species of urus. The birds we saw were, paroquets of two sorts, viz. the lourikeet, and a small green paroquet; a large green pigeon, specimens of which we got; the cream-coloured pigeon of Borneo; besides many others.

"The geological formation of the region I must leave to others. I brought down some specimens of the rocks and loose stones, which are, I believe, pummice; if so, I presume the formation volcanic, similar to Java.

"24th.—Called on the Resident, and saw the Rajah.

"25th.—Christmas, with his jolly nose and icy hands: here it is hot enough! Were I to live in this country, I should retire for the season up in the mountains. Dined with the Resident of Bonthian; by no means surprised that he and his congeners had failed in their attempt to claim the mountain: the Resident is a native! In the evening, celebrated the day with all sorts of sports.

"26th.— Mid-day quitted Bonthian, and ran to Boele Comba or Compa.

"27th.—I have little to say of Boele Comba. It is situated in the bight of the bay, eastward of Bonthian. There appears to be much confusion in Horsburgh's Directory about the latitude and longitude, and the hill called after the place. This hill is the last of the mountain-range, somewhat detached, covered with wood, of moderate elevation, and peaked. From our anchorage, two miles from the fort, it bore N.N.W. The fort is similar to the one at Bonthian; the country pretty, and nearly level. The Bonthian mountains (*i.e.* Lumpu Balong and the range) shew steep and well in the background. Game abounds, by report. Europeans are subject to complaints of the eyes, and occasionally to fever. Any vessel running in should be very careful, for the charts are defective, and Boele Comba reef is said to project farther to the westward of the fort than laid down.

"I here subjoin a list of our barometric observations, the upper barometer reduced to the rate of the lower and standard one:

Senua, 20th December, 1839.

	Bar.	A.	D.	
1.	30·054	86	87	} 3ʰ 15ᵐ P.M.
2.	28·385	79	80	

BAROMETRICAL OBSERVATIONS.

Lengan Lengang, 21st December.

	Bar.	A.	D.	
1.	30·119	79	78·5	6ʰ 30ᵐ A.M.
2.	27·988	70	69·5	6ʰ 0ᵐ ,,

Lokar Peak, 21st December, 100 feet below summit.

	Bar.	A.	D.	
1.	30·095	90	90	} 10ʰ 30ᵐ A.M.
2.	25·975	79	79	

Hill on the way to Lumpu Balong, 22d December.

	Bar.	A.	D.	
1.	30·144	90	90	Mean between 8ʰ and noon.
2.	23·612	66	65·5	10ʰ 40ᵐ A.M.

Lumpu Balong Peak, 22d December.

	Bar.	A.	D.	
1.	30·146	89·5	90·5	2ʰ 0ᵐ P.M.
2.	22·718	64	63·5	2ʰ 30ᵐ ,,

"28th.—Leaving Boele Comba after breakfast, we shaped our course for Point Berak.

"With the richest country, the natives of these places are poor, and they bear no good-will to their rulers. It is likewise certain that few active measures are resorted to for forwarding the development of the native character and local resources. The Resident is a Macassar-born native, and this fact alone speaks volumes for the mode and manner of government. The people of the country I found a kind and simple race; and though they are accused of pride and laziness by their masters, I could not, circumstances taken into consideration, discover any trace of the latter vice, and the former I can readily forgive them. That the Bugis are not an indolent race is well proved by their whole conduct, wherever circumstances offer any inducement to exertion. Even here, the cleared country and the neat cultivation prove them far otherwise; and traces are visible everywhere on the mountains, of their having been more highly cultivated than at present. Coffee-plantations once flourished, and being destroyed during a war, years ago, have never been renewed. Enclosures and partition-walls in decay are very frequent, marking the former boundary of cultivation. That they are independent enough to be proud, I honour them for! The officers allowed they were courageous; and one designated them as '*fier comme un Espagnol;*' and, on the whole, no doubt exists in my mind that they are people easily to be roused to exertion, either agricultural or commercial; that sullen and repulsive manners towards their masters, rather indicating a dislike to their sway, and the idleness complained of, only give a proof that the profits of labour are lower than they ought to be.

" Nothing so strongly marks the degradation of a race or nation as a cheerful acquiescence to a foreign rule. The more virtuous, the more civilised, the more educated a people, the more turbulent, indolent, and sullen, when reduced to a state of subjection; the fewer qualities will they have to please their masters, when foreign rule is oppressive, or looks solely to the advantage of the country of the conquerors, and not of the conquered. There is no race will willingly submit: the bayonet and the sword, the gallows and the whip, imprisonment and confiscation, must be constantly at work to keep them under.

"Leaving Boele Comba, as I before said, we shaped our course for Tanjong Berak, passing between that point and the north island. The passage is excellent, clear of all danger, as far as we could see, with deep water. The rocks reported to exist by Horsburgh, and put down on Nories' chart, have no existence. The Bugis prahus always use this channel, and know them not; and the captain of a Dutch cruiser informed me that he had often run through the passage at night, and that it was clear of all danger or obstruction.

"My own observation went to verify the fact, for every part of the passage appears deep and clear, and we passed over the spots where these rocks are marked. Approaching Tanjong Berak, there is a sandy beach, where a vessel may get anchorage in case the wind dies away. The tides in the channel are strong; here, and along the south coast, the ebb runs from the eastward, the flood from the west. Having cleared the channel, we hauled into the Bay of Boni, which, although running in a north and south direction, has some headlands extending to the eastward. There are two places marked on the chart, viz. Berak and Tiero; but these, instead of being towns or villages, are names of districts; the first, reaching from Tanjong Berak, about 15 miles, till it joins Tiero; Tiero, extending from the northern confine of Berak to Tanjong Labu, 15 miles in all. To the northward and eastward is a high island called Balunrueh. From Tanjong Berak the water along the coast is very deep; no soundings with 50 fathom. Towards evening we went into Tiero Bay, a pretty secluded spot. The southern part of the bay is foul, having a reef above water at low water. The northern headland has a spit running from it, with about 14 fathom water, half a mile (or little more) off. Within the bay there is no bottom with 50 fathom till near its northern extremity, where the water shoals suddenly. Running in, in a squall, we got into $3\frac{1}{4}$ fathom, where we anchored. This country belongs to the Dutch as far as Point Labu.

"*29th.*—Calm all day. Sounded the bay: the southern point has a steep coral-reef nearly a quarter of a mile off. The southern part of the bay is enclosed by a reef, part of which seems to me artificial, for the purpose of catching fish, and is shallow: outside the reef the water is deep close to. The western shore is lined by a reef close to it, and the water is deep. The centre part of the bay is very deep; and within 100 yards of where we lay we got no bottom at 17 fathoms. The next cast was 6, and the next 3 fathoms — hard clay bottom. A small river discharges itself, in the northern part, inside the anchorage: there is a considerable depth within, but the bar is shallow. The scenery on the river is beautiful; wild at first, and gradually becoming undulating and cultivated. Birds are plenty: cockatoos abound, of which I shot two. There is some geological interest: the hills round the bay are of slight elevation; and 80 or 100 feet from the sea-level are large masses of coral-rock, upheaved by some convulsion.

"29th.—Passed at Tïero—calm.

"30th.—Under weigh. Brought up in 23 fathoms, amid the coral-shoals.

"31st.—Visited the island of Balunrueh for sights.

"Tanjong Labu is bluff and bold, and of moderate elevation. The land from thence trends away westward, forming a long bay, which, for distinction, may be called Labu Bay, at the N.W. part of which is the town of Songï, the principal place about here. Between Labu and Songï are the following countries: Kupi Kajang, Pakah, Buah, Kalaku, Baringan, and Magnarabunbang; each with a separate petty rajah. The country is moderately well cleared; about an average height, near the shore, of 300 feet; with few habitations about, but no towns or villages. The mountain-range throws a spur downward to the sea, in the vicinity of Songï and the fine peaks of Lumpu Balong; and Wawa Karang, with the *confusion* of mountains, form a magnificent background to the prospect. From Magnarabunbang the land runs away to the eastward towards Tanjong Salaketa, which must be described on a future occasion. In the offing are several islands and numerous reefs. The principal island is Balunrueh, 400 or 500 feet high; bold, steep, and covered with trees, except at its northern extremity, where it is low, with a sandy point. Off this north point runs a coral-reef: direction 354^0, and extent about two miles. At the s.w. angle of the island there is likewise a reef stretching half a mile; and the shores all round, for a short distance, are lined with coral, outside of which the water is apparently very deep. We could get no soundings with a hand lead, half a mile to the westward.

"Off Balunrueh, to the s.e., is the islet of Liang Liang; next to Liang Liang, Tanbunoh, which is larger; then Cadingareh Batantampeh (the largest) Cotingduan Lariahriah, and two islands to the northward called Canallo. Balunrueh and Batantampeh have both indifferent fresh water; the former near the low point at the north end. From the s.w. end of Liang Liang a reef runs out. The bearing, from the small hill, over the watering place of Balunrueh, was $77°$. The reef extends to $104°$, and stretches to the southward besides: near Liang Liang it is narrow. Its limits I could not define.

"Between Liang Liang and Tanbunoh a narrow reef, and spits from most of the islands. Two patches lay off Balunrueh about 2 miles and a half: the first, bearing 319°, is narrow, and about half a mile long; the other smaller, and bearing 287°. Part of the day we passed on Balunrueh was very hot; but we got satisfactory sights, and sailed round the island, returning to the vessel about six in the evening.

"I must now return to Labu, to give some account of the channel between the reefs; as, from the appearance of the charts, it would seem impossible to navigate the western side of the bay. Having passed Tanjong Labu at a distance of 3½ or 4 miles, get the flat-topped hill called Bulu Tanna ahead. Close to the Bulu Tanna, in the foreground, is another smaller hill, with two remarkable tufts on the top: this hill, just open to the eastward of Bulu Tanna, is the leading mark for Songĭ, which stands to the westward. This mark will lead clear, or very nearly so, of all the reefs; but as there is uncertainty in the distance from Tanjong Labu, it may be necessary to diverge from the straight course in order to avoid some of the patches. In the daytime the coral is seen with the greatest ease; and a vessel with a look-out aloft, and a breeze, may proceed with safety. The first reef is on the starboard hand; part was dry, and shoal-water about. This first patch is in the proximity of the great reef called Melompereh, which runs to the eastward. Besides these, the channel is occasionally lined by patches on either hand; but is no where narrower than a mile and a half, and is any thing but difficult navigation; so far, in clear weather.

"*Jan. 4th,* 1840.—Arrived off Songĭ on the 1st, and despatched a boat to the old rajah, or rana, of Lamatte. Our answer was, that not having been to Boni, she feared receiving us, as she felt inclined; but if we would come to her house, she should be glad to see us. On the following day, accordingly, we paid our visit at her residence, which is situated about four miles up the river Tanca.

"The old lady is about sixty-five years of age, and (as she herself informed us) very poor. Her house, indeed, bears every mark of great poverty; having a leaky roof, and not sufficient matting to cover the bamboo floors. She was kind, and seemed pleased to see us; said I should henceforward be her son, and that nothing but her fear of the Boni rajah prevented her receiving me in the best way in her power; but pointing to the roof and to the floor, she repeated, 'I have nothing.' I presented her with such articles as I thought would be acceptable to her; and, in return, she gave me a sarong.

"The population of the country is considerable. The last district I mentioned was Magnarabunbang.

The town of that name, on the sea-side, consists of forty-five houses, besides a roving population of Badjows. Along the coast to the eastward, and close to Magnarabunbang, is the river of Songĭ. Proceeding up this shallow river, the first village is Tacolompeh, situated on the right bank, and consisting of twenty houses; nearly opposite the village of Pangassa, of thirteen houses; and farther up, about four miles from the river's mouth, stands Songĭ, consisting of 164 houses on the right bank, and 60 on the left. These places are all on the low ground, and surrounded with cocoanut-trees.

"Joining the district of Magnarabunbang, on the coast, is Lamatte, the rajanate of our old friend. The river, like the Songĭ, is shallow, and running through very low ground. On the left bank is Luppa, consisting of twenty-five houses; then, on the right, Ulo, twenty-two houses; and above Ulo comes Ulluĕ, of twelve houses. Nearly opposite Ulluĕ is Balammepa, with thirty houses, superior to the others, and inhabited by merchants who have made money in trading voyages. This village sends yearly two prahus to Singapore. Just above Ulluĕ stand seven houses; and above Balammepa is Tanca, the residence of the rajah of Lamatte, consisting of ten houses. The streams, as I have said, are shallow, and the ground low, neatly cultivated with Indian corn, and abounding in cocoa-nut-trees. Behind Magnarabunbang there is a narrow strip of low ground, which becomes wider as it advances to the eastward, with here and there moderate elevations.

" The chief product of the country is coffee, which is grown in great quantities on the hills, but brought down as it ripens, when it is collected by the Bugis merchants for their yearly shipments. The yearly produce is stated to be 2000 coyans or 80,000 peculs. The price is from fifteen to sixteen Java rupees the pecul; to which must be added the trouble and expense of storing and clearing from the inner skin. Tortoise-shell is brought in by the Badjows; and mother-of-pearl shells in any quantity there is demand for. Taking the number of houses in this small space, above described, the total will be 308 houses, which, reckoned at the low estimate of eight persons for each house, will give 2464 inhabitants: this, however, is far below the proper estimate, as there are villages scattered between the rivers, and numbers of detached houses; in all, therefore, safely computed at 5000 persons. The villages, with the exception of Balammepa, have an aspect of poverty, and the country is ravaged by that frightful scourge the small-pox, and likewise some cases of cholera, from the account given of the complaint. Near the hill of Bulu Tanna there is a hot spring, and likewise, by the report of the natives, some slight remains of an old building. I regretted much not seeing these; but the natives, with much politeness, begged me not to go previous to my visit to Boni, as they would be answerable for allowing strangers to see the country without orders from the chief rajah. All I see and hear convinces me that the Rajah of Boni has great power over the entire country. On a friendly communication with him, therefore, depends our chance of seeing something of the interior.

"The inhabitants here are polite, but shy and reserved: and the death of the Rana of Songï, and the absence of the Rajah Mooda, her reported successor, have been against us.

"*5th.* Sailing from Songï about 4 P.M., we directed our course for Tanjong Salanketo. The breeze was stiff, which caused us to use considerable precaution in sailing amongst the shoals. Assisted by a native Nacodah, by name Dain Pativi, we were enabled to keep the tortuous channel, of which otherwise we should have been ignorant. A little farther than the Tanca river is a shoal stretching from the shore, to avoid which we kept Canallo on our lee bow: this being cleared, we gradually luffed up, ran between two shoals, and passed several others."

CHAPTER VII.

Mr. Brooke's second visit to Sarāwak. The civil war. Receives a present of a Dyak boy. Excursion to the seat of war. Notices of rivers, and settlements on their banks. Deaths and burials. Reasons for and against remaining at Sarāwak. Dyak visitors. Council of war. Why side with the Rajah. Mode of constructing forts. State of enemy's and Rajah's forces. Conduct of the war.

MR. BROOKE continued his cruise for some time, and made very interesting collections of natural history, besides acquiring much insight into the native history, language, and customs, of which it is to be hoped he will at a future day permit the publication. He then returned to Singapore, where he was detained for several months by ill health; but availed himself of the opportunity to recopper and refit the Royalist, and set every thing else in order for his next visit to Sarāwak, the remarkable results of which are related in the following pages. Still sick and languid though he was, the very air of Borneo, and the prospect of activity, seemed to restore him to life, after the listless rest at Singapore, with " nothing to observe;" and only cheered by the kindest attentions and hospitalities of the inhabitants of that interesting and important settlement.

On the second visit of Mr. Brooke to Sarāwak, about the end of August 1840, he found the inhabitants in nearly the same state as at first, although there was much talk of reinforcements, and decisive measures for bringing the war to a close. The two parties lay within thirty miles of each other, the rebels holding the upper part of the river, and communication with the interior. The sultan, however, had sent down the Orang Kaya de Gadong to take more active measures, and his arrival stimulated Muda Hassim to something like exertion. This appears, by Mr. Brooke's journal, to have occurred on the 4th September, 1840; and I shall give various extracts from it, as it will not only help to form some opinion of the character of my friend, whose ideas were written down at the time the impressions were made, but also supply a distinct picture of the progress of this novel and amusing civil warfare, and demonstrate the unwarlike character of the Sarāwak Borneons.

"An army of mixed Malays and Dyaks was raised to attack the Dyak tribes in rebellion, and this service was successfully performed; the rebel Dyaks were defeated, and most of them have since come over to the rajah. Their forces, being weakened by desertion, were reported not to amount to more than 400 or 500 men, in four or five forts situated on the river; and it now remained to drive them from their last stronghold of resistance. It was confidently asserted by the Rajah and Macota, that, were it not for the underhand assistance of the Sultan of Sambas, who had constantly supplied them with food and ammunition, the insurgents would long since have been dispersed.

"At the period in question they were said to be in great distress for want of provisions; and as a force was collecting to attack them from various quarters, it was greatly to be hoped that the war was verging to a termination. During my week's stay I have frequently visited Muda Hassim, and he has likewise been on board: our good understanding knows no interruption; and these savage, treacherous, bloodthirsty Borneons are our good friends, with whom we chat and laugh every evening in familiar converse. I find no cause to alter my last year's opinion, that they have few active vices; but indolence is the root of their evils.

"*Sept. 7th.*—Last night I received a strange and embarrassing present, in the shape of a young Dyak boy of five years old—a miserable little prisoner, made during this war, from the tribe of Brong. The gift causes me vexation, because I know not what to do with the poor innocent; and yet I shrink from the responsibility of adopting him. My first wish is to return him to his parents and his tribe; and if I find I cannot do this, I believe it will be better to carry him with me than leave him to become the slave of a slave: for, should I send him back, such will probably be his fate. I wish the present had been a calf instead of a child.

"*9th.* — Situ, my Dyak boy, seems content and happy; and judging by his ways, and his fondness for tobacco, he must be older than I at first supposed. In pursuance of my desire to restore him to his parents, I made every inquiry as to their probable fate; but have learned nothing that leaves me any hope that I shall be able to do so. The Brong tribe took part with the rebels, and were attacked by the Rajah's people; and many were killed and the rest scattered. Pino, the Brong, knows not whether Situ's parents are alive or dead; nor, if the former, whither they have fled. Supposing my endeavours to restore the child fail, I have resolved to keep him with me, for many reasons. The first is, that his future prospects will be better, and his fate as a freeman at Singapore happier, than as a slave in Borneo; the second, that he can be made a Christian. I can easily provide for him in some respectable household, or take him to England, as may hereafter be most advantageous for him; and at the former place he can always be made a comfortable servant with good training. Yet with all this, I cannot disguise from myself that there is responsibility — a heavy moral responsibility — attached to this course, that might be avoided: but then, *should*

it be avoided? Looking to the boy's interests—
temporal, perhaps eternal—I think it ought not;
and so, provided always I cannot replace him where
humanity and nature dictate, I will take the responsibility, and serve this wretched and destitute
child as far as lies in my power. He is cast on my
compassion; I solemnly accept the charge; and I
trust his future life may bear good fruit, and cause
me to rejoice at my present decision.

" *Oct. 2d.*—Lying at Sarāwak, losing valuable
time, but pending the war difficult to get away;
for whenever the subject is mentioned, Muda
Hassim begs me not to desert him just as it is
coming to a close, and daily holds out prospects of
the arrival of various Dyak tribes. The Rajah
urged upon me that he was deceived and betrayed
by the intrigues of Pangerans, who aimed at alien-
ating his country; and that if I left him, he should
probably have to remain here for the rest of his
life, being resolved to die rather than yield to the
unjust influence which others were seeking to acquire over him; and he appealed to me that after
our friendly communication I could not, as an
English gentleman, desert him under such circumstances. I felt that honourably I could not do so;
and though reluctantly enough, I resolved to give
him the aid he asked;—small indeed, but of consequence in such a petty warfare.

" *3d.*—I started to join Macota at Leda Tanah.
At 4h. 30m. P.M. a pouring rain delayed us some

time; and darkness setting in, rendered our pull a long and very disagreeable one. We did not reach Leda Tanah until 11, when we found *the army* in their boats, and a small fort they had built on the bank of the river. I moved into Macota's large boat, and slept there; whilst he, as commander-in-chief, went backwards and forwards from one post to another during the night.

"4th.—At Leda Tanah the river divided into two branches; one part running past Siniawan, the other to the left — likewise to another point of the mountain-range. Above Siniawan is Sarambo, a high detached mountain, perhaps 3000 feet in height, with a notch in the centre. Off Leda Tanah is a sand and pebble bank formed by the junction of the two streams, and the country around is well cleared for this part; whilst the graves on the right bank bear witness to the population of former days. It is represented to have been a flourishing place, and the neighbourhood well inhabited, until the breaking out of this unhappy war. The situation is delightful, and advantageously chosen at the confluence of the two streams.

"5th.—Ascended that to the left for a short distance. On the left hand, just above Leda Tanah, is the small creek of Sarāwak, the original settlement, and from which the larger river now takes its name. I intended to have returned today; but as the weather threatened another deluge, I stopped till the following morning. It was a curious sight to see the whole army bathe, with the commander-in-chief at their head, and his Pangerans. The fare of these people is any thing but luxurious, for they get nothing but rice and salt; and they were thankful in proportion for the small supplies of tea, sugar, and biscuit I was able to spare them.

"6th.— Quitted Leda Tanah, and reached the Royalist in five hours, one of which we were delayed by the way. The river is remarkably pretty; banks cleared of jungle, with fine trees, and a view of the mountains. Many parts are exceedingly shallow; but the natives state there is a channel for a moderate-sized vessel as far as Leda Tanah."

On Mr. Brooke's return on board the Royalist, he found his steward Rankin, who had been lingering some time, still alive; and a seaman named Daniel, whom he had left with a slight fever, suddenly expired at ten at night in a fainting fit. He writes in his journal : "It is difficult to allege the immediate cause of his death, which probably arose from some organic complaint of the heart or the brain, quite independent of fever. Five minutes before his decease the man's pulse was high and full. The steward will follow in a few days; and death, which has never before entered on board, will thus strike two blows. To me it is a satisfaction that neither is in any way attributable to climate.

"7th.—Muda Hassim rendered me every assistance. A grave was prepared, and wood for a coffin; so that by two o'clock we proceeded to inter the dead. His last resting-place was situated on a gently rising ground behind the Chinamen's houses. The ensign was placed over his simple bier, and he was carried by his shipmates to the grave. All who could be spared attended, and I performed the service—that impressive and beautiful service of the Church of England.

"8th.—Having the melancholy duty of yesterday over was a relief, only alloyed by the sad prospect of a near recurrence. I now turned my mind seriously to departure, having well weighed the pros and cons of the subject.

"In the first place, the greatest advantage would result from my accompanying the Rajah along the coast to Borneo; and if I could hope a reasonable time would leave him free to go there, I would wait spite of the season: for it is evident that by myself I should have to form fresh connexions amongst the chiefs, and without that I reckon it next to impossible to penetrate even a moderate distance from the coast in a strange place. The next reason is, that it has been intimated to me that a rival faction, headed by Pangeran Usop, exists in Borneo Proper, and that that Pangeran, from my known friendship to Muda Hassim, might endeavour to injure me, *i. e.* kill me. At any rate, during Muda Hassim's absence, I should be obstructed in all my proceedings, and could not do more than sketch the bare coast-line. These are strong and cogent reasons for remaining *for a time*, if the ultimate object be attainable; and to these may be added my own feelings — my reluctance to quit the Rajah in the midst of difficulty and distress, and his *very very sad* face whenever I mention the topic.

" On the other hand must be weighed the approach of the adverse monsoon, the loss of time, and the failure of provisions, which, though but luxuries to gentlemen which they can readily dispense with, are nevertheless necessaries to seamen, without which they get discontented, perhaps mutinous. There are good reasons on both sides.

" *9th.*—I sent Williamson to intimate my approaching departure; and when I went in the evening the little man had such a sorrowful countenance that my heart smote me. When I told him I would remain if there were the slightest chance of a close to the war, his countenance cleared, and he gaily repeated that my fortune and his would bring this struggle to an end, though others forsook him. I then consented to await the issue a few days longer, and to revisit Leda Tanah to ascertain if the news was true. It ran to the effect that the rebels, under the Pantingi and Tumangong, are fortified at the foot of the mountain of Sarambo, on which hill are three Dyak tribes below that of Sarambo; over them Bombak; and on the summit the Paninjow. The Bombak and Paninjow have already, in part, joined Macota, and the Sarambo are to come in as to-day. These three last Dyak tribes deserting the rebels will leave them surrounded in their forts, which are commanded by the rest of the hill; and every thing promises well, if the opportunity be vigorously used. The Sow and the Singè are in part at Leda Tanah, and more Dyaks daily joining. I must push the rajah on to action, for help from without is not likely to come. Yet I wish still more to accommodate matters; and if he would spare the leaders' lives, I believe they would lay down their arms on my guarantee. But though he does not say that he will kill them, he will listen to no terms of compromise; and when I reflect that an European monarch, in the same circumstances, would act in the same way—that the laws of my own country would condemn the men for the same offence—I cannot urge the subject into a personal matter.

"16*th*.—Rankin's (my steward's) death having been some time inevitable, it was a relief when the event occurred. He was cut off in the flower of manhood, from the effects of hard drinking, which even his fine constitution could not resist. I buried him near the other man, and had a neat inscription, and the name of the individual, his ship and age, placed over each.

" Days passed on, but not quite unrelieved by events. And now I may positively state, that the war will be over in a few days, or not over at all.

The first of these events was the desertion of the Dyaks, and the arrival of their chiefs with Macota. Next arrived 200 Chinese from Sambas, under a very intelligent Capitan. Rajah Ali came next, bringing some ourang-outangs' heads; then Datu Naraja; and lastly Pangeran Jedut from Sarebus, with the information that the Dyaks of that name, in consequence of a war with Linga, would not come here. Thus they not only refused to come themselves, but obliged the Linga people to stay at home to defend their country. To quiet this coast the Sarebus should receive a severe lesson.

"17th.—I had a large party of Dyaks on board in the evening, viz. the Singè, Sow, Bombak, and Paninjow, in all about fifteen men, with two old chiefs. They ate and drank, and asked for every thing, but stole nothing. One man wore a necklace of beads set with human teeth, taken of course in war, which I got from him for two yards of red cloth. Another was ornamented with a necklace of bears' teeth; and several had such a profusion of small white beads about their necks as to resemble the voluminous foldings of the old-fashioned cravat. As far as I could observe, they all seemed in earnest about attacking Siniawan; and their allegiance to the Rajah was as warm now (in words) as it had been heretofore defective in action.

"18th.—Proceeded in the long-boat to Leda Tanah, which we reached in three and a half hours' pulling, and just in time to witness the start of 150

Malays and 100 Dyaks of Lundu for the mountain of Sarambo, at the foot of which Siniawan and the enemies' forts are situated.

"19th.—Did every thing in my power to urge Macota to advance and divert the attention of the rebels from the party going up the mountain, but in vain : Malay-like, he would wait.

"20th.—I have before remarked that two rivers formed a junction at Leda Tanah ; and this day I ascended the left-hand stream, or, as they call it, the Songi besar (*i. e.* great Songi). The scenery is picturesque; the banks adorned with a light and variegated foliage of fruit-trees ; and every where bearing traces of former clearing and cultivation. In the background is the range of mountains, amongst which Stat is conspicuous from his noble and irregular shape. On our return, the white flag (a Hadji's turban) was descried on the mountain, being the pre-arranged signal that all was well. No news, however, came from the party; and in spite of the white banner, Macota took fright at the idea that the rebels had surrounded them.

"21st.—Detachments of Dyaks are coming in. Ten of the tribe of Sutor were despatched as scouts ; and in a few hours returned with the welcome intelligence that the detachment was safe on the top of the mountain, and that the three tribes of Paninjow, Bombak, and Sarambo, had finally decided on joining the Rajah, and surrendering their fortified houses. Soon after this news the chiefs of the tribes arrived with about 100 men, and were, of course, well received; for if chargeable with deserting their cause, it is done with the utmost simplicity, and perfect confidence in their new associates. From their looks it was apparent they had suffered greatly from want of food; and they frankly confessed that starvation was their principal motive for coming over. I did all in my power to fix their new faith by presents of provisions, &c. &c.: and I think they are trustworthy; for there is a straightforwardness about the Dyak character far different from the double-faced dealings of the Malay. Their stipulations were, forgiveness for the past, and an assurance that none of the Dyaks from the sea (*i. e.* Sarebus and Sakarran) should be employed; for they were, they said, hateful to their eyes. These terms being readily conceded—the first from interest, the second from necessity—they became open and communicative on the best means of attacking the forts. A grand council of war was held, at which were present Macota, Subtu, Abong Mia, and Datu Naraja, two Chinese leaders, and myself—certainly a most incongruous mixture, and one rarely to be met with. After much discussion, a move close to the enemy was determined on for to-morrow, and on the following day to take up a position near their defences. To judge by the sample of the council, I should form very unfavourable expectations of the conduct in action. Macota is lively and active; but whether from indisposition or want of authority, undecided. The Capitan China is lazy and silent; Subtu indolent and self-indulgent; Abong Mia and Datu Naraja stupid. However, the event must settle the question; and, in the mean time, it was resolved that the small stockade at this place was to be picked up, and removed to our new position, and there erected for the protection of the fleet. I may here state my motives for being a spectator of, or participator (as may turn out), in this scene. In the first place, I must confess that curiosity strongly prompted me; since to witness the Malays, Chinese, and Dyaks in warfare was so new, that the novelty alone might plead an excuse for this desire. But it was not the only motive; for my presence is a stimulus to our own party, and will probably depress the other in proportion. I look upon the cause of the Rajah as most just and righteous: and the speedy close of the war would be rendering a service to humanity, especially if brought about by treaty. At any rate much might be done to ameliorate the condition of the rebels in case of their defeat; for though I cannot, perhaps ought not, to save the lives of the three leaders, yet all the others, I believe, will be forgiven on a slight intercession. At our arrival, too, I had stated that if they wished me to remain, no barbarities must be committed; and especially that the women and children must not be fired upon. To counterbalance these motives was the danger, whatever it might amount to, and which did not weigh heavily on my mind. So much for reasons, which, after all, are poor and weak when we determine on doing any thing, be it right or be it wrong. *If* evil befall, I trust the penalty may be on me rather than on my followers.

"*22d.*—At daylight the fleet was astir, and in an hour the defences were cut down, the timber, bamboos, &c., formed into rafts ready for transportation, and the stockade, by breakfast-time, had as completely vanished as though it had been bodily lifted away by some genius of the Wonderful Lamp. Every thing was ready for a start, and we waited lazily for the flood-tide; but when it did make, the usual procrastination ensued, and there was no move till it was near done. Then, indeed, we proceeded up about two-thirds of the way, and brought up with two good hours' daylight, in spite of my remonstrances. No place could be better calculated than where we rested for an attack upon boats: high banks covered with grass and trees offered a safe shelter for musketry, against which no return could be made. The night, however, passed away quietly.

"*24th.*—Dawn found us on the advance to our proper position. A thick fog concealed us, and in half an hour the people were on shore busy re-erecting our fort, less than a mile from two forts of the enemy, but concealed from them by a point of the river. No opposition was offered to us; and in a few hours a neat defence was completed from the *débris* of the former. The ground was cleared of jungle; piles driven in a square, about fifteen yards to each face, and the earth from the centre, scooped out and intermixed with layers of reeds, was heaped up about five feet high inside the piles. At the four corners were small watch-towers, and along the parapet of earth a narrow walk connecting them. In the centre space was a house crowded by the Chinese garrison, a few of whose harmless gingalls were stuck up at the angles to intimidate rather than to wound. Whilst they laboured at the body of the defence, the Dyaks surrounded it by an outer work, made of slight sticks run into the ground with cross binding of split bamboo, and bristling with a *chevaux de frise* (if it may be so styled) of sharpened bamboos about breast-high. The fastenings of the entire work were of rattan, which is found in plenty. It was commenced at 7 A.M. and finished about 3 P.M., shewing how the fellows can get through business when they choose. This stockade, varying in strength according to circumstances, is the usual defence of the Sambas Chinese. The Malays erect a simple and quicker constructed protection by a few double uprights, filled in between with timber laid lengthways and supported by the uprights. Directly they are under cover, they begin to form the ranjows or sudas, which are formidable to naked feet, and stick them about their position.

Above our station was a hill which entirely commanded both it and the river; to the top of which I mounted, and obtained an excellent view of the country around, including the enemies' forts and the town of Siniawan. A company of military might finish the war in a few hours, as these defences are most paltry, the strongest being the fort of Balidah, against which our *formidable* assault was to be levelled. It was situated at the water's edge, on a slight eminence on the right bank of the river; and a large house with a thatched roof and a look-out house on the summit; a few swivels and a gun or two were in it, and around it a breastwork of wood—judging from a distance, about six or seven feet high. The other defences were more insignificant even than this; and the enemies' artillery amounted, by account, to three six-pounders and numerous swivels; from 350 to 500 men, about half of whom were armed with muskets, whilst the rest carried swords and spears. They were scattered in many forts, and had a town to defend, all of which increased their weakness. Their principal arm, however, consisted in the ranjows, which were stated to be stuck in every direction. These ranjows are made of bamboo, pointed fine and stuck in the ground; and there are besides, holes about three feet deep, filled with these spikes, and afterwards lightly covered, which are called patobong. Another obstacle consists of a spring formed by bending back a stiff cane with a sharp bamboo attached to it, which, fastened by a slight twine, flies forcibly against any object passing through the bush and brushing against it: they resemble the mole-traps of England. The Borneons have a great dread of these various snares; and the way they deal with them is by sending out parties of Dyaks during the night to clear the paths from such dangers.

"Though I have stated the insignificant nature of the enemies' lines, it must not be supposed I imagined them at all inferior to our own resources. Our grand army consisted of 200 Chinese, excellent workmen, but of whose qualities as soldiers I can say nothing. They were, however, a stout muscular set of men, though wretchedly armed, having no guns and scarcely any muskets; but swords, spears, and shields, together with forty long thin iron tubes with the bore of a musket and carrying a slug. These primitive weapons were each managed by two men, one being the carrier of the ordnance, the other the gunner; for whilst one holds the tube over his shoulder, the other takes aim, turns away his head, applies his match, and is pleased with the sound. Their mode of loading is as curious as the piece and its mode of discharge. Powder is poured in, the end knocked on the ground, and the slug with another knock sent on the powder, without either ramming or cartridge. Indeed, it is difficult to imagine any weapon more rude, awkward, or inefficient.

"Of Malays we had 250, of whom 150 were on the Sarambo mountain, occupied in defending the Dyak houses. Of the hundred remaining with the grand army, about half were armed with muskets. A few brass guns composed our artillery; and in the boats were a good many swivels. The Dyaks amounted to about 200, of various tribes, viz. Sibnowans, Paninjows, Bombak, Sarambo, Kampit, Tabah, Sanpro, Suntah; but these were merely pioneers, and would not face the report of fire-arms. The Borneons, in fighting, wear a quilted jacket or spencer, which reaches over the hips, and from its size has a most unservicelike appearance; the bare legs and arms sticking out from under this puffed-out coat, like the sticks which support the garments of a scarecrow. Such was our incongruous and most inefficient army; yet with 300 men who would fight, nothing would have been easier than to take the detached defences of the enemy, none of which could contain above thirty or forty men. But our allies seemed to have little idea of fighting except behind a wall; and my proposal to attack the adversary was immediately treated as an extreme of rashness amounting to insanity. At a council of war it was consequently decided that advances should be made from the hill behind our fort to Balidah by a chain of posts, the distance being a short mile, in which space they would probably erect four or five forts; and then would come a bombardment, noisy but harmless.

"During the day we were not left quiet. The beating of gongs, shouts, and an occasional shot, gave life to the scene. With my glass I could espy our forces at the top of the hill, pleased no doubt to see us coming to their support. At night loud shouts and firing from the rebels caused us to prepare for an attack; but it proved to be nothing but lights moving about the hill-side, with what intent we were ignorant. The jungle on the left bank having been cleared, we did not much expect any skirmishers; but some spies were heard near our boats. With this exception the night passed away unbroken on our part, though the rebels kept up an incessant beating of gongs,· and from time to time fired a few stray shots, whether against an enemy or not was doubtful.

"*25th.*—The grand army was lazy, and did not take the field when they possessed themselves of two eminences, and commenced forts on each. About 11 A.M. we got intelligence that the enemy was collecting on the right bank, as they had been heard by our scouts shouting one to another to gather together in order to attack the stockades in the course of building. Even with a knowledge of their usual want of caution, I could not believe this, but walked nevertheless to one of the forts, and had scarcely reached it when a universal rebel shout, and a simultaneous beating of the silver-tongued gongs, announced, as I thought, a general action. But though the shouts continued loud and furious from both sides, and a gun or two was discharged in air to refresh their courage, the enemy did not attack, and a heavy shower damped the ardour of the approaching armies and reduced all to inaction. Like the heroes of old, however, the adverse parties spoke to each other: 'We are coming, we are coming,' exclaimed the rebels; 'lay aside your muskets and fight us with swords.' 'Come on,' was the reply; 'we are building a stockade, and want to fight you.' And so the heroes ceased to talk, but forgot to fight, except that the rebels opened a fire from Balidah from swivels, all of which went over the tops of the trees. Peace, or rather rest, being restored, our party succeeded in entrenching themselves, and thus gained a field which had been obstinately assaulted by big words and loud cries. The distance of one fort from Balidah was about 800 yards, and manned with sixty Malays; whilst a party of Chinese garrisoned the other. Evening fell upon this innocent warfare. The Borneons, in this manner, contend with vociferous shouts; and, preceding each shout, the leader of the party offers up a prayer aloud to the Almighty, the chorus (or properly response) being the acclamation of the soldiery. We, on our side, kept up a firing and hallooing till midnight, to disguise the advance of a party who were to seize and build a stockade within a shorter distance of Balidah. When they reached the spot, however, the night being dark, the troops sleepy, and the leaders of different opinions, they returned without effecting any thing.

CHAPTER VIII.

Appearance of the country. Progress of the rebel war. Character of the Sow and Singè Dyaks. Their belief in augury. Ruinous effects of protracted warfare. Cowardice and boasting of the Malays. Council of war. Refuse to attack the enemy's forts. Rebels propose to treat. The Malays oppose. Set out to attack the rebels, but frustrated by our allies. Assailed by the rebels. Put them to flight. Treat with them. They surrender. Intercede with the Rajah for their lives. Renewed treachery of the Malays.

"26th. — I must here pause in my account of this extraordinary and novel contest, briefly to describe the general appearance of the country.

"It is one delightful to look upon, combining all the requisites of the picturesque, viz. wood, water, mountain, cliff, and a foreground gently undulating, partially cultivated, and of the richest soil. The mountain of Sarambo, about 3000 feet in height, is the principal feature in the scene, situated at a short distance from the left bank of the river. The remainder of the ground slopes gradually; and the town of Siniawan, likewise on the left bank, is close to the water, and at the foot of the eminence called Gunga Kumiel.

"The advance of the party last night was, as

I have said, disguised by firing, drumming, and shouting from the fleet and forts; and, in the deep stillness of the fine night, the booming of the guns, the clamour of the gongs, and the outcries raised from time to time, came on our ears like the spirit of discord breaking loose on a fair and peaceful paradise. About one o'clock the noises died away, and I enjoyed as quiet a slumber till daylight as though pillowed on a bed of down in the heart of Old England. About six I visited the three forts. The Chinese, Malays, and Dyaks were taking their morning meal, consisting of half a cocoanut-shell full of boiled rice with salt. The Dyaks were served in tribes; for as many of them are at war, it is necessary to keep them separate; and though they will not fight the enemy, they would have no objection to fall out with one another, and the slightest cause might give rise to an instant renewal of hostilities.

"About 9 A.M. a party proceeded to the elevation previously marked, within 300 yards of Balidah, and worked quietly till 2 P.M., by which time they had made considerable progress; and being then reinforced, they soon finished this new stockade, with a strong face towards their adversaries, and an outer fence. This erection, however, being below the brow of the hill, is useless as a post whence to assault Balidah; and to-morrow another stockade is to be made close to it on the summit, the present being intended to cover the working party at the next. The enemy, about 4 P.M., having discovered the stockade, opened a fire for half an hour; but finding it ineffectual, they sunk into their usual apathy. It is difficult to attribute this quietude to any other cause except weakness; and they are doubtless harassed by the want of Dyak light troops, as they are unable to oppose stockade to stockade. Our party, by these successful advances, seem to gain confidence; and it must soon come to an issue one way or other. To make it favourable, I have sent for two six-pounder cannonades, guns of vast calibre here, together with a small addition to our force. I had the curiosity to inquire of Macota the progress of his former campaign, when he had 1000 Malays with only a few Dyaks. He represented the enemy as active and daring then, and very different from their want of spirit now. They had, he declared, combats by sea and by land; stockade was opposed to stockade, and the fighting was constant and severe; but he never lost a man killed during the two months, and only boasted of killing five of the enemy! The principal danger in Malay warfare is the ' Mengamuk' (*Anglice*, running a-muck), which is the last resource of a desperate man.

" 27th.—The night passed quietly as usual. About 6 A.M. I started for the hills, and inspected each post in turn. They are about commencing another fort. I visited the spot to reconnoitre it; and the enemy opened a fire directly they perceived me, which we returned. They shot wretchedly ill; and the position is good, but exposed. About 10 A.M. they again began to fire from their fort, and detached thirty or forty men, who crept out between our forts in order to interrupt the work. The Malays, however, received them steadily; whilst the Chinese placed them between two fires, and, by a discharge from a tube, knocked down *one* man. The rebels shewed anxiety to possess themselves of their fallen comrade, whilst the opposite party shouted 'Cut off his head;' but he was carried off; and the enemy, when they had saved his body, fled in all directions, dropping a number of their small bamboo powder-flasks on the way. Some fierce alarms were given of an attack by water, and I went up the river to ascertain really whether there was any mischief to be expected; but there was no appearance of any adversary. A slack fire from the hill proclaimed that our work was going on there; and towards evening all was in repose.

"*28th.*—The stockade was completed in the evening, with ranjows stuck round the outer defence. It was excellently situated for battering Balidah; but Balidah, I fear, is too loosely constructed to be battered to the best advantage. During the day the Sow and Singè Dyaks joined, to the amount of about 150 men, and other tribes have been gradually dropping in; so that altogether there are not fewer than 500 of these men joined to our equipment. Most of them shew all the characteristics of a wild people; never resisting their masters, but so obstinate that they can always get their own way in every thing; opposing threats and entreaties by a determined and immovable silence. Many of them depend upon us for their food and salt, and their applications are endless. Three women of Singè are our regular pensioners; for their sex excludes them from the rations granted to the men. By these means we had many excellent opportunities of judging of their habits and temper. Amongst all these tribes the language differs but slightly— so slightly, indeed, that it is needless to note the variations in detail. They have the same superstition about particular birds, and I often heard this omen alluded to in conversation; but their birds are not the same as those of the sea Dyaks. ...... The chief of the Sarambo, explaining his reasons for leaving the rebels, urged the constant unfavourable omen of the birds as one. Often, very often, he said, when he went out, the bird cried, and flew in the direction of Siniawan, which will be explained by what I have before stated; for if they hear the bird to the right, they go to the left, and *vice versâ;* so that the bird may be considered as warning them from evil.

"The Sow Dyaks brought in the head of an unfortunate Malay whom they had decapitated in the jungle. This species of warfare is extremely barbarous, and in its train probably brings more evil than the regular campaigns of civilised nations. Not that it is by any means so fatal to human life directly; but it is the slow poison which wastes the strongest frame, the smouldering fire which does its work of destruction slowly but surely. Year after year it is protracted; few fall in open fight, but stragglers and prisoners are murdered; and whilst both weak parties, gradually growing weaker, hold their own ground, the country becomes a desert. First, trade stagnates, agriculture withers, food becomes scarce, all are ruined in finances, all half-starved and most miserable—and yet the war drags on, and the worst passions are aroused, effectually preventing the slightest concession, even if concession would avail. But each combatant knows the implacable spirit—the deep desperation—of the other too well to trust them; and if at length the fortunes of famine decide against them, they die rather than yield; for a Dyak can die bravely, I believe, though he will not fight as long as life has any prospect. This is also the case here: for the rebel chiefs know there is no pardon, and the Bandar is disgraced if he fails. It is indeed a slow process, but one of extermination.

"*29th.*—Our guns arrived with a welcome reinforcement. In the evening I dropped up the river to reconnoitre; but the adversary discovered us, as we were dressed in white clothes.

" 30*th*.—Fort not finished. All quiet.

" 31*st*.—Got the guns and ammunition up, and whilst fixing them opened a fire from one of our swivels to overbear the fire of the enemy. The little piece was well served; and, in a quarter of an hour, we silenced their fire entirely, and knocked about the timber considerably, making a breach which several men could enter together. Seeing the effect, I proposed to Macota to storm the place with 150 Chinese and Malays. The way from one fort to the other was protected. The enemy dared not shew themselves for the fire of the grape and canister, and nothing could have been easier; but my proposition caused a commotion which it is difficult to forget, and more difficult to describe. The Chinese consented, and Macota, the commander-in-chief, was willing; but his inferiors were backward, and there arose a scene which shewed me the full violence of the Malay passions, and their infuriated madness when once roused. Pangeran Houseman urged with energy the advantage of the proposal, and in the course of a speech lashed himself to a state of fury; he jumped to his feet, and with demoniac gestures stamped round and round, dancing a war-dance after the most approved fashion; his countenance grew livid, his eyes glared, his features inflamed; and for my part, not being able to interpret the torrent of his oratory, I thought the man possessed of a devil, or about to ' run a-muck.'

But after a minute or two of this dance, he resumed his seat, furious and panting, but silent. In reply, Subtu urged some objections to my plan, which was warmly supported by Illudeen, who apparently hurt Subtu's feelings; for the indolent, the placid Subtu leapt from his seat, seized his spear, and rushed to the entrance of the stockade, with his passions and his pride desperately aroused. I never saw finer action than when, with spear in hand, pointing to the enemy's fort, he challenged any one to rush on with him. Houseman and Surradeen (the bravest of the brave) like madmen seized their swords to inflame the courage of the rest—it was a scene of fiends—but in vain; for though they appeared ready enough to quarrel and fight amongst themselves, there was no move to attack the enemy. All was confusion; the demon of discord and madness was amongst them, and I was glad to see them cool down, when the dissentients to the assault proposed making a round to-night and attacking to-morrow. In the mean time our six-pounders were ready in battery, and it is certain the assailants might walk nearly to the fort without any of the rebels daring to shew themselves in opposition to our fire.

"*Nov.* 1*st.*—The guns were ready to open their fiery mouths, and their masters ready to attend on them; but both had to wait till midday, when the chiefs of the grand army, having sufficiently slept, breakfasted, and bathed, lounged up with their straggling followers. Shortly after day-light the forts are nearly deserted of their garrisons, who go down at the time to the water more like a flock of geese than warriors. The instant the main division and head-quarters of the army arrived at the battery, I renewed my proposal for an assault, which was variously received. If the Malays would go, the Chinese agreed; but the Malays had grown colder and colder. In order to encourage them, I opened a fire to shew the effect of our guns; and having got a good range, every ball, as well as grape and canister, rattled against and through the wood. I then urged them again and again, but in vain; that coward Panglima Rajah displayed that dogged resolution which is invincible—an invincible resolution to do nothing; and the cold damp looks of the others at once told the amount of their bravery! A council of war was called—grave faces covered timid hearts and fainting spirits. The Chinese contended with justice, that in fairness they could not be expected to assault without the Malays did the same; Abong Mia was not brave enough. The Datu agreed, and Panglima delivered himself of a wise harangue, to the effect that, 'the last campaign, when they had a fort, how had the enemy fired then?—stabbed them, speared them, &c., &c.; and without a fort, assaulting!—how could it be expected they should succeed? how unreasonable they should go at all!' But even his stolid head seemed to comprehend the sarcasm when I asked him how many men had been killed during all this severe fighting. However, it was clear that it was no battle. We were all very savage, and I intimated how useless my being with them was, if they intended to play instead of fight. 'What,' I asked, ' if you will not attack, are you going to do?' Oh, the wise councils of these wise heads! Abong Mia proposed erecting a fort in a tree, and thence going ' puff, puff,' down into Balidah, accompanying the words ' puff, puff' with expressive gestures of firing; but it was objected, that trees were scarce, and the enemy might cut down the tree, fort and all.[1]

[1] The following is an extract from an equally sapient proposition, published in the Chinese state-papers on the 14th January, 1840; it is headed, Memorial of Toang Wangyen to the Emperor, recommending plans for the extermination of barbarians : " Your minister's opinion is this : that we, being upon shore and they in their ships, it is not at all requisite to order our naval forces to proceed out a great distance to contend with them in battle. When the commercial intercourse of the said barbarians shall have been entirely put an end to, and their supplies grow scanty, it will be impossible for them to remain a long time anchored in the outer seas, and they will necessarily, as formerly, enter the inner waters in order to ramble and spy about them. We can then, by means of our naval vessels, tempt them and cause them to enter far in; and a previous arrangement having been made, we can summon the people who live along the coasts, such as are expert and able swimmers, and those who possess bravery and strength, to the amount of several hundreds of men: we can then cause them, during the night, to divide them-

THE RESULT.

"*2d.*—Till two o'clock last night, or thereabouts, I sat on our rampart and gazed upon the prospect around, shaded with gloom. The doctor was with me, and we ran over every subject—the past, present, and the future. Such a scene—a rude fort in the interior of Borneo; such a night, dark but starlight—leaves an indelible impression on the mind, which recurs to move it even after long years. The morning, however, found us ready, and no one else. The fort was left to ourselves; we waited and waited until 2 P.M., when I was made aware that all thoughts of attack were at an end. Macota, for very shame, stayed below; and I must say there was not a countenance that met mine but had that bashful and hang-dog look which expresses cowardice and obstinacy predominant, yet shame battling within. They were now resolved not to make the attempt; and I asked them casually whether they would fly a white flag, and hold a conference with the enemy. They caught at the alternative; the flag was hoisted; the rebels were ready to *meet me*, and it was agreed that we should assemble on the morrow. But no sooner was the arrangement made than a thousand objections were started, and any thing, even attack itself (though that was out of the question), was

selves into companies, and silently proceeding through the water, straightway board foreign ships; and overcoming the crews in their unprepared state, make an entire massacre of the whole of them."

held to be preferable. I need not dwell on this mixture of deceit and fear; in short, as they would do nothing themselves, they expected us to do nothing; and without the courage to carry on the war, they had not either wisdom or sorcery to bring it to a conclusion.

"3d.—Despatched an express during last night to the Rajah, and received an answer that he was coming up in person; but my resolve was taken, and I quitted the grand army, much to their evident surprise and vexation. Nevertheless, they were still friendly and polite, and very very lazy about bringing down our guns. This was, however, done at last, and we were ready for a start.

"4th.—Reached the ship at 2 P.M., saw Rajah, &c. &c.

"From the 4th to the 10th of November I may condense into the shape of a narrative. I explained to the Rajah how useless it was my remaining, and intimated to him my intention of departing; but his deep regret was so visible, that even all the self-command of the native could not disguise it. He begged, he entreated me to stay, and offered me the country of Siniawan and Sarāwak, and its government and trade, if I would only stop, and not desert him. I could at once have obtained this grant, but I preferred interposing a delay; because to accept such a boon when imposed by necessity, or from a feeling of gratitude for recent assistance, would have rendered it both suspicious and useless; and I was by no means eager to enter on the task (the full difficulties of which I clearly foresaw) without the undoubted and spontaneous support of the Rajah.

"*Jan. 8th*, 1841. — The following narrative extracted from my journal includes a period from the 10th of December to the 4th of January, and it is put into its present shape to avoid the tedium of detailing each day's proceedings. On the 10th of December we reached the fleet and disembarked our guns, taking up our residence in a house, or rather shed, close to the water. The Rajah's brother, Pangeran Budrudeen, was with the army, and I found him ready and willing to urge the proposals I made for vigorous hostilities on the other indolent Pangerans. We found the grand army in a state of torpor, eating, drinking, and walking up to the forts and back again daily; but having built these imposing structures, and their appearance not driving the enemy away, they were at a loss what next to do, or how to proceed. On my arrival, I once more insisted on mounting the guns in our old forts, and assaulting Balidah under their fire. Macota's timidity and vacillation were too apparent; but in consequence of Budrudeen's overawing presence, he was obliged, from shame, to yield his assent. The order for the attack was fixed as follows:—our party of ten (leaving six to serve the guns) were to be headed by myself. Budrudeen, Macota, Subtu, and all the lesser chiefs, were to lead their followers, from 60 to 80 in number, by the same route, whilst 50 or more Chinese, under their captain, were to assault by another path to the left. Macota was to make the paths as near as possible to Balidah, with his Dyaks, who were to extract the sudas and fill up the holes. The guns having been mounted and their range well ascertained the previous evening, we ascended to the fort at about eight A.M., and at ten opened our fire and kept it up for an hour. The effect was severe; every shot told upon their thin defences of wood, which fell in many places so as to leave storming breaches. Part of the roof was cut away and tumbled down, and the shower of grape and cannister rattled so as to prevent their returning our fire, except from a stray rifle. At mid-day the forces reached the fort, and it was then discovered that Macota had neglected to make any road, because it rained the night before! It was evident that the rebels had gained information of our intention, as they had erected a frieze of bamboo along their defences on the very spot which we had agreed to mount. Macota fancied the want of a road would delay the attack; but I well knew that delay was equivalent to failure, and so it was at once agreed that we should advance without any path. The poor man's cunning and resources were now nearly at an end. He could not refuse to accompany us, but his courage could not be brought to the point,

THE ATTACK. 173

and, pale and embarrassed, he retired. Every thing was ready—Budrudeen, the Capitan China, and myself, at the head of our men—when he once more appeared, and raised a subtle point of etiquette which answered his purpose. He represented to Budrudeen that the Malays were unanimously of opinion that the Rajah's brother could not expose himself in an assault; that their dread of the Rajah's indignation far exceeded the dread of death; and in case any accident happened to him, his brother's fury would fall on them. They stated their readiness to assault the place; but in case Budrudeen insisted on leading in person, they must decline accompanying him. Budrudeen was angry, I was angry too, and the doctor most angry of all; but anger was unavailing: it was clear they did not intend to do any thing in earnest; and after much discussion, in which Budrudeen insisted that if I went he should likewise go, and the Malays insisted that if he went they would not go, it was resolved we should serve the guns, whilst Abong Mia and the Chinese (not under the captain) should proceed to the assault. But its fate was sealed, and Macota had gained his object; for neither he nor Subtu thought of exposing themselves to a single shot. Our artillery opened and was beautifully served. The adverse troops advanced, but our fire completely subdued them, as only three rifles answered us, by one of which a seaman (Williams) was wounded in the hand, but not seriously. Two-thirds of the way the storming-party proceeded without the enemy being aware of their advance, and they might have reached the very foot of the hill without being discovered, had not Abong Mia, from excess of piety and rashness, begun most loudly to say his prayers. The three rifles then began to play on them; one Chinaman was killed, the whole halted, the prayers were more vehement than ever, and after squatting under cover of the jungle for some time, they all returned. It was only what I expected; but I was greatly annoyed at their cowardice and treachery —treachery to their own cause. One lesson, however, I learnt, and that was, that, had I assaulted with our small party, we should assuredly have been victimised! The very evening of the failure the Rajah came up the river. I would not see him, and only heard that the chiefs got severely reprimanded; but the effects of reprimand are lost where cowardice is stronger than shame. Inactivity followed; two or three useless forts were built; and Budrudeen, much to my regret and the detriment of the cause, was recalled.

"Amongst the straggling arrivals I may mention Panglima Dallam, with a number of men, consisting of the Orang Bentulu, Meri Muka, and Kayan, Dyaks from the interior. Our house—or, as it originally stood, shed—deserves a brief record. It was about twenty feet long, with a loose floor of reeds, and an attop roof. It served us for some time; but the attempts at theft obliged us to fence it in and divide it into apartments: one at the end served Middleton, Williamson, and myself; adjoining it was the store-room and hospital; and the other extreme belonged to the seamen. Our improvements kept pace with our necessities. Theft induced us to shut in our house at the sides, and the unevenness of the reeds suggested the advantage of laying a floor of the bark of trees over them, which, with mats over all, rendered our domicile far from uncomfortable. Our forts gradually extended at the back of the enemy's town, on a ridge of swelling ground; whilst they kept pace with us on the same side of the river on the low ground. The inactivity of our troops had long become a byword amongst us. It was indeed truly vexatious, but it was in vain to urge them on, in vain to offer assistance, in vain to propose a joint attack, or even to seek support at their hands; promises were to be had in plenty, but performances never!

"At length the leaders resolved on building a fort at Sekundis, thus outflanking the enemy and gaining the command of the river. The post was certainly an important one, and in consequence they set about it with the happy indifference which characterises their proceedings. Pangeran Illudeen (the most active amongst them) had the building of the fort, assisted by the Orang Kaya Tumangong of Lundu. Macota, Subtu, &c. were at the next fort, and by chance I was there likewise; for it seemed to be little apprehended that any interruption would take place, as the Chinese and the greater number of Malays had not left the boats. When the fort commenced, however, the enemy crossed the river and divided into two bodies, the one keeping in check the party at Pangeran Gapoor's fort, whilst the other made an attack on the works. The ground was not unfavourable for their purpose; for Pangeran Gapoor's fort was separated from Sekundis by a belt of thick wood which reached down to the river's edge. Sekundis itself, however, stood on clear ground, as did Gapoor's fort. I was with Macota at the latter when the enemy approached through the jungle. The two parties were within easy-speaking distance, challenging and threatening each other; but the thickness of the jungle prevented our seeing or penetrating to them. When this body had advanced, the real attack commenced on Sekundis with a fire of musketry, and I was about proceeding to the scene, but was detained by Macota, who assured me there were plenty of men, and that it was nothing at all. As the musketry became thicker, I had my doubts, when a Dyak came running through the jungle, and with gestures of impatience and anxiety begged me to assist the party attacked. He had been sent by my old friend the Tumangong of Lundu, to say they could not hold the post unless supported. In spite of Macota's remonstrances, I struck into the jungle, winded through the narrow path, and after crossing an ugly stream, emerged on the clear ground. The sight was a pretty one: to the right was the unfinished stockade, defended by the Tumangong; to the left, at the edge of the forest, about twelve or fifteen of our party, commanded by Illudeen, whilst the enemy were stretched along between the points, and kept up a sharp shooting from the hollow ground on the bank of the river. They fired, and loaded, and fired, and had gradually advanced on the stockade as the ammunition of our party failed; and as we emerged from the jungle, they were within twenty or five-and-twenty yards of the defence. A glance immediately shewed me the advantage of our position, and I charged with my Europeans across the padi-field; and the instant we appeared on the ridge above the river, in the hollows of which the rebels were seeking protection, their rout was complete. They scampered off in every direction, whilst the Dyaks and Malays pushed them into the river. Our victory was decisive and bloodless: the scene was changed in an instant, and the defeated foe lost arms, ammunition, &c. &c. whether on the field of battle or in the river, and our exulting conquerors set no bounds to their triumph.

"I cannot omit to mention the name of Si Tundo, the only native who charged with us. His appearance and dress were most striking, the latter being entirely of red, bound round the waist, arms, forehead, &c. with gold ornaments, and in his hand bearing his formidable Bajuck sword; he danced or rather galloped across the field close to me, and mixing with the enemy, was about to despatch a Hadji or priest who was prostrate before him, when one of our people interposed and saved him by stating that he was a companion of our own. The Lundu Dyaks were very thankful for our support, our praises were loudly sung, and the stockade was concluded. After the rout, Macota, Subtu, and Abong Mia arrived on the field; the latter with forty followers had ventured half way before the firing ceased, but the detachment, under a paltry subterfuge, halted, so as not to be in time. The enemy might have had fifty men at the attack; the defending party consisted of about the same number; but the Dyaks had very few muskets. I had a dozen Englishmen, Seboo, one of our boatmen, and Si Tundo. Sekundis was a great point gained, as it hindered the enemy from ascending the river and seeking any supplies.

"Macota, Subtu, and the whole tribe arrived as soon as their safety from danger allowed, and none were louder in their own praise; but nevertheless their countenances evinced some sense of shame, which they endeavoured to disguise by the use of their tongues. The Chinese came really to afford assistance, but too late. We remained until the stockade of Sekundis was finished, while the enemy kept up a wasteful fire from the opposite side of the river, which did no harm.

"The next great object was to follow up the advantage by crossing the stream; but day after day some fresh excuse brought on fresh delay, and Macota built a new fort and made a new road within a hundred yards of our old position. I cannot detail further our proceedings for many days, which consisted on my part of efforts to get something done, and on the others a close adherence to the old system of promising every thing and doing nothing. The Chinese, like the Malays, refused to act; but on their part, it was not fear, but disinclination. By degrees, however, the preparations for the new fort were complete, and I had gradually gained over a party of the natives to my views; and, indeed, amongst the Malays, the bravest of them had joined themselves to us, and what was better, we had Datu Pangeran, thirteen Illanuns, and the Capitan China allowed me to take his men whenever I wanted them. My weight and consequence was increased, and I rarely moved now without a long train of followers. The next step (whilst crossing the river was uncertain) was to take my guns up to Gapoor's fort, which was about 600 or 700 yards from the town, and half the distance from a rebel fort on the river's bank.

"Panglima Rajah, the day after our guns were in battery, took it into his head to build a fort on the river's side close to the town, in front and between two of the enemy's forts. It was a bold undertaking for the old man, after six weeks of uninterrupted repose. At night, the wood being prepared, the party moved down, and worked so silently that they were not discovered till their defence was nearly finished, when the enemy commenced a general firing from all their forts, returned by a similar firing from all ours, none of the parties being quite clear what they were firing at or about, and the hottest from either party being equally harmless. We were at the time about going to bed in our habitation; but expecting some reverse, I set off (to scale the hills) to the stockade where our guns were placed, and opened a fire upon the town and the stockade near us, till the enemy's fire gradually slackened and died away. We then returned, and in the morning were greeted with the pleasing news that they had burned and deserted five of their forts, and left us sole occupants of the right bank of the river. The same day, going through the jungle to see one of these deserted forts, we came upon a party of the enemy, and had a brief skirmish with them before they took to flight. Nothing can be more unpleasant to an European than this bush-fighting, where he scarce sees a foe, whilst he is well aware that their eyesight is far superior to his own. To proceed with this narrative, I may say that four or five forts were built on the edge of the river opposite the enemy's town, and distant not above 50 or 60 yards; here our guns were removed, and a fresh battery formed ready for a bombardment, and fire-balls essayed to ignite the houses.

"At this time Seriff Jaffer, from Singè, arrived with about seventy men, Malays and Dyaks of Balow. The river Singè being situated close to Sarebus, and incessant hostilities being waged between the two places, he, with his followers, was both more active and more warlike than the Borneons, but their warfare consists of closing hand to hand with spear and sword. They scarcely understood the proper use of fire-arms, and were of little use in attacking stockades. As a negotiator, however, the Seriff bore a distinguished part; and on his arrival a parley ensued, much against Macota's will, and some meetings took place between Jaffer and a brother Seriff at Siniawan, named Moksain. After ten days' delay nothing came of it, though the enemy betrayed great desire to yield. This negotiation being at an end, we had a day's bombardment and a fresh treaty brought about thus: Macota being absent at Sarāwak, I received a message from Seriff Jaffer and Pangeran Subtu to say that they wished to meet me; and on my consenting, they stated that Seriff Jaffer felt confident the war might be brought to an end, though alone he dared not treat with the rebels; but in case I felt inclined to join him, we could bring it to a favourable conclusion. I replied that our habits of treating were very unlike their own, as we allowed no delays to interpose; but that I would unite with him for one interview, and if that interview was favourable, we might meet the chiefs at once and settle it, or put an end to all further treating. Pangeran Subtu was delighted with the proposition, urged its great advantages, and the meeting by my desire for that very night, the place Pangeran Illudeen's fort at Sekundis. The evening arrived, and at dark we were at the appointed place, and a message was despatched for Seriff Moksain. In the mean time, however, came a man from Pangeran Subtu to beg us to hold no intercourse; that the rebels were false, meant to deceive us, and if any did come, we had better make them prisoners. Seriff Jaffer, after arguing the point some time, rose to depart, remarking that with such proceedings he would not consent to treat. I urged him to stay; but finding him bent on going, I ordered my gig (which had some time before been brought overland) to be put into the water; my intention being to proceed to the enemy's campong, and there hear what they had to say. I added, that it was folly to leave undone what we had agreed to do in the morning, because Pangeran Subtu changed his mind; that I had come to treat, and treat I would. I would not go away now without giving the enemy a fair hearing—for the good of all parties I would do it; and if the Seriff liked to join me, as we proposed before, and wait for Seriff Moksain, good; if not,

I would go in the boat to the campong. My Europeans, on being ordered, jumped up, ran out and brought the boat to the water's edge, and in a few minutes oars, rudder, and rowlocks were in her. My companions, seeing this, came to terms, and we waited for Seriff Moksain; during which, however, I overheard a whispering conversation from Subtu's messenger, proposing to seize him; and my temper was ruffled to such a degree, that I drew out a pistol, and told him I would shoot him dead if he dared to seize, or talk of seizing, any man who trusted himself from the enemy to meet me! The scoundrel slunk off, and we were no more troubled with him. This past, Seriff Moksain arrived, and was introduced into our fortress alone; alone and unarmed in an enemy's stockade, manned with two hundred men! His bearing was firm; he advanced with ease and took his seat; and during the interview the only sign of uneasiness was the quick glance of his eye from side to side. The object he aimed at was, to gain my guarantee that the lives of all the rebels should be spared; but this I had it not in my power to grant. He returned to his campong, and came again towards morning, when it was agreed that Seriff Jaffer and myself should meet the Patingis and the Tumangong, and arrange terms with them. By the time our conference was over, the day broke, and we descended to the boats to enjoy a little rest.

" On the 20th of December we met with the

chiefs on the river; and they expressed themselves ready to yield, without conditions, to the Rajah, if I would promise that they should not be put to death. My reply was, that I could give no such promise; that if they surrendered, it must be for life or death, according to the Rajah's pleasure; and all I could do was to use my influence in order to save their lives. To this they assented after a while; but then there arose the more difficult question, how they were to be protected until the Rajah's orders arrived. They dreaded both Chinese and Malays, especially the former, who had just cause for angry feelings, and who, it was feared, would make an attack on them directly their surrender had taken from them their means of defence. The Malays would not assail them in a body, but would individually plunder them, and give occasion for disputes and bloodshed. These apprehensions were almost sufficient to break off the hitherto favourable negotiations, had I not proposed to them myself to undertake their defence, and to become responsible for their safety until the orders of their sovereign arrived. On my pledging myself to this, they yielded up their strong fort of Balidah, the key of their position. I immediately made it known to our own party that no boats were to ascend or descend the river, and that any persons attacking or pillaging the rebels were my enemies, and that I should fire upon them without hesitation.

"Both Chinese and Malays agreed to the propriety of the measure, and gave me the strongest assurances of restraining their respective followers, the former with good faith, the latter with the intention of involving matters, if possible, to the destruction of the rebels. By the evening we were in possession of Balidah, and certainly found it a formidable fortress, situated on a steep mound, with dense defences of wood, triple deep, and surrounded by two enclosures, thickly studded on the outside with ranjows. The effect of our fire had shaken it completely, now much to our discomfort; for the walls were tottering, and the roof as leaky as a sieve. On the 20th of December, then, the war closed. The very next day, contrary to stipulation, the Malay Pangerans tried to ascend the river, and when stopped began to expostulate. After preventing many, the attempt was made by Subtu and Pangeran Hassim, in three large boats, boldly pulling towards us. Three hails did not check them, and they came on in spite of a blank cartridge and a wide ball, to turn them back. But I was resolved; and when a dozen musket-balls whistled over and fell close around them, they took to an ignominious flight. I subsequently upbraided them for this breach of promise, and Macota loudly declared they had *been greatly to blame;* but I discovered that he himself had set them on.

"I may now briefly conclude this detail. I ordered the rebels to burn all their stockades, which they did at once, and delivered up the greater part of their arms; and I proceeded to the Rajah to request from him their lives. Those who know the Malay character will appreciate the difficulty of the attempt to stand between the monarch and his victims; I only succeeded when, at the end of a long debate—I soliciting, he denying—I rose to bid him farewell, as it was my intention to sail directly, since, after all my exertions in his cause, if he would not grant me the lives of the people, I could only consider that his friendship for me was at an end. On this he yielded. I must own that during the discussion he had much the best of it; for he urged that they had forfeited their lives by the law, as a necessary sacrifice to the future peace of the country; and argued that in a similar case in my own native land no leniency would be shewn. On the contrary, my reasoning, though personal, was, on the whole, the best for the Rajah and the people. I stated my extreme reluctance to have the blood of conquered foes shed; the shame I should experience in being a party, however involuntarily, to their execution; and the general advantage of a merciful line of policy. At the same time I told him their lives were forfeited, their crimes had been of a heinous and unpardonable nature, and it was only from so humane a man as himself, one with so kind a heart, that I could ask for their pardon; but I added, he well knew that it was only from my previous knowledge of his benevolent disposition, and the great friendship I felt for him, which had induced me to take any part in this struggle. Other stronger reasons might have been brought forward, which I forbore to employ, as being repugnant to his princely pride, viz. that severity in this case would arm many against him, raise powerful enemies in Borneo Proper, as well as here, and greatly impede the future right government of the country. However, I gained my point, and was satisfied.

"Having fulfilled this engagement, and being moreover, together with many of my Europeans, attacked with an ague, I left the scene with all the dignity of complete success. Subsequently, the rebels were ordered to deliver up all their arms, ammunition, and property; and last, the wives and children of the principal people were demanded as hostages, and obtained. The women and children were treated with kindness, and preserved from injury or wrong. Siniawan thus dwindled away; the poorer men stole off in canoes and were scattered about, most of them coming to Sarāwak. The better class pulled down the houses, abandoned the town, and lived in boats for a month; when, alarmed by the delay and impelled by hunger, they also fled,—Patingi Gapoor, it was said, to Sambas; and Patingi Ali and the Tumangong amongst the Dyaks. After a time it was supposed they would return and receive their wives and children. The army gradually dispersed to seek food, and the Chinese were left in possession of the once-renowned Siniawan, the ruin of which they completed by burning all that remained, and erecting a village for themselves in the immediate neighbourhood. Seriff Jaffer and many others departed to their respective homes, and the pinching of famine succeeded to the horrors of war. Fruit being in season, helped to support the wretched people, and the near approach of the rice-harvest kept up their spirits."

CHAPTER IX.

Retrospect of Mr. Brooke's proceedings and prospects. Visit of a pirate fleet. Intercourse with the chief leaders, and other characteristic incidents. War-dances. Use of opium. Story of Si Tundo. Preparations for trading. Conditions of the cession of Sarāwak.

I HAVE gone into the details of this curious rebellion, and selected from my friend's memoranda more, perhaps, than the actual and present importance of the circumstances might seem to require; but I have done so under the impression that in developing the traits and lineaments of the native character, I am laying the foundation for a more accurate estimate of them and their bearing upon futurity. The difference between the Malay and the Chinese, between the sea and the land Dyak, and even between one tribe and another, presents a variety of elements out of which a consistent whole has to be compounded, and a new state of things to be established in Borneo. It is, therefore, of considerable interest to view these elements in their earliest contact with European mind and civilisation, and thence endeavour to shape out the course which is best calculated to ensure the welfare of all in the closer ties and more extended connexion which is springing out of this new intercourse. To enlarge the beneficial effects of trade and commerce, it is not enough to ascertain the products of a strange country, nor even the chief wants of its population; but to inform ourselves of their habits, feelings, and disposition, and so devise the wisest measures for supplying what is immediate, removing obstacles, and increasing demand by a continually growing improvement in government and general condition.

Following the war and receiving the investiture of the government of Sarāwak, Mr. Brooke was enabled, from the insight he had obtained into the diversified relations and habits of these people, and their objects and ways of thinking, to address himself clearly and at once to reform the evils which oppressed and the abuses which destroyed them. Had he not mixed with them and shared in this protracted contest, he must have begun rather as an experimentalist with a theory, which might be right or might be wrong. But he had acquired the necessary experience, and could proceed to put his finger where it was required to repress or to foster, without danger of mistake. It was extraordinary what his energy produced within a small compass of time. Security succeeded the utmost uncertainty, equal justice superseded tyrannical caprice, order arose out of confusion, and peace was gradually spread over the fruitful soil so lately polluted by the murderous warfare of heads-taking and imperishable feud. It is to be hoped that such an example will not be lost in the further prosecution of international and commercial policy in this interesting and important quarter of the eastern world. Piracy must be put down, slavery must be effaced, industry must be cherished and protected; and these objects we shall see, from the model afforded by our truly illustrious countryman, may be accomplished; and even farther, that there may not only be " a little war," but that its active participation and enlightened study may furnish the most judicious data on which to commence a mighty change, leading probably to the happiness of millions, and the foundation of colonial empire.

With these few retrospective remarks, I resume the sequel of my friend's Borneon Journal.

" Our subsequent adventures," he notes, " may be easily related. We lay for some days, after winding up our affairs, in order to have an agreement drawn out between the Rajah and myself; and during this time heard the bruit of a pirate-fleet being on the coast. In a day or two after, certain news arrived of their having taken two Sadung boats, bound from Singapore; and Datu Pangeran was, in consequence, despatched to communicate with them. He returned from Tanjong

Datu, bringing the fleet with him to the mouth of the river, whence they requested permission to visit Sarāwak, and pay their respects to the Rajah. I was consulted on the subject whether I would meet them; and as I preferred a pacific to a hostile rencontre, and had moreover a considerable curiosity to see these roving gentry, I consented without hesitation. Reports—a greater curse in Malay countries than elsewhere—stated their object to be the capture of the Royalist; as they had, it was averred, received positive accounts of her having fifty lacks of dollars on board, and that her figure-head was of solid gold. As, however, we had no such treasure, and the meeting was unavoidable and might be hostile, I put myself into a complete posture of defence, with a determination neither to shew backwardness nor suspicion. The day arrived, and the pirates swept up the river; eighteen prahus, one following the other, decorated with flags and streamers, and firing both cannon and musketry; the sight was interesting and curious, and heightened by the conviction that these friends of the moment might be enemies the next. Having taken their stations, the chief men proceeded to an interview with the Rajah, which I attended to witness. Some distrust and much ceremony marked the meeting; and both parties had numerous followers, who filled the hall of audience and the avenues leading to it; and as few of the Illanuns spoke Malay, the communication was rendered difficult and troublesome. The pirates consisted of Illanuns and Malukus from Gillolo. The Illanuns are fine athletic men, with a strong resemblance in appearance to the Bugis; their bearing was haughty and reserved, and they seemed quite ready to be friends or foes, as best suited their purpose. The Malukus are from a bay in Gillolo, and their country is now in possession of the Dutch; they are a darker and an uglier race, but their manners more supple and pliant. They were the principal talkers, whilst the Illanuns maintained a dignified silence.

"These Malukus, from their own account, since the capture of their rajah and the subjugation of their country, have led a wandering piratical life; they represent their force at about twenty-five boats, of which three are now joined by the Illanuns, as a matter of mere convenience. Beyond the usual formalities, this meeting had nothing to distinguish it; one party retired to their boats, whilst the other went to their respective houses, and every thing betokened quiet. In the evening I pulled through the fleet, and inspected several of the largest prahus. The entire force consisted of eighteen boats, viz. three Malukus and fifteen Illanuns; the smallest of these boats carried thirty men, the largest (they are mostly large) upwards of a hundred; so that, at a moderate computation, the number of fighting-men might be reckoned at from five to six hundred. The Illanun expedition had been absent from Magindano upwards of three years, during which time they had cruised amongst the Moluccas and islands to the eastward, had haunted Boni Bay and Celebes, and beat up the Straits of Makassar. Many of their boats, however, being worn out, they had fitted out Bugis prize prahus, and were now on their return home. They had recently attacked one of the Tambelan islands, and had been repulsed; and report said they intented a descent upon Sirhassan, one of the Southern Natunas group. These large prahus are too heavy to pull well, though they carry thirty, forty, and even fifty oars: their armament is one or two six-pounders in the bow, one four-pounder stern-chaser, and a number of swivels, besides musketry, spears, and swords. The boat is divided into three sections, and fortified with strong planks, one behind the bow, one amidships, and one astern to protect the steersman. The women and children are crammed down below, where the unhappy prisoners are likewise stowed away during an action. Their principal plan is boarding a vessel, if possible, and carrying her by numbers: and certainly if a merchantman fired ill, she would inevitably be taken; but with grape and canister fairly directed, the slaughter would be so great that they would be glad to sheer off before they neared a vessel. This is, of course, supposing a calm; for in a breeze, they would never have the hardihood to venture far from land with a ship in sight, and would be sorry to be caught at a distance. Their internal constitution is as follows:—one chief, a man usually of rank, commands the whole fleet; each boat has her captain, and generally from five to ten of his relations, free men; the rest, amounting to above four-fifths, are slaves, more or less forced to pursue this course of life. They have, however, the right of plunder, which is indiscriminate with certain exceptions; viz. slaves, guns, money, or any other heavy articles, together with the very finest description of silks and cloths, belonging to the chiefs and free men; and the rest obey the rule of 'First come first served.' No doubt the slaves become attached to this predatory course of life: but it must always be remembered that they are slaves and have no option; and it appears to me, that in the operation of our laws some distinction ought to be drawn on this account, to suit the circumstances of the case. The Datus, or chiefs, are incorrigible; for they are pirates by descent, robbers from pride as well as taste, and they look upon the occupation as the most honourable hereditary pursuit. They are indifferent to blood, fond of plunder, but fondest of slaves: they despise trade, though its profits be greater; and, as I have said, they look upon this as their 'calling,' and the noblest occupation of chiefs and free men. Their swords they shew with boasts, as having belonged to their ancestors who were pirates, renowned and terrible in their day; and they always speak of their ancestral heir-loom as decayed from its pristine vigour, but still the wielding of it as the highest of earthly existences. That it is in reality the most accursed, there can be no doubt; for its chief support are slaves they capture on the different coasts. If they attack an island, the women and children, and as many of the young men as they require, are carried off. Every boat they take furnishes its quota of slaves; and when they have a *full cargo*, they quit that coast or country and visit another, in order to dispose of their human spoil to the best advantage. Thus a cargo of slaves, captured on the east coast of Borneo, is sold on the west; and the slaves of the south find ready purchasers to the northward, and *vice versâ*. As the woolly-haired Papuas are generally prized by the natives, constant visits are made to New Guinea and the easternmost islands, where they are procured, and afterwards sold at high prices amongst any Malay community. The great nests of piracy are Magindano, Sooloo, and the northern part of Borneo; and the devastation and misery they inflict on the rest of the Archipelago are well known; yet are no measures adopted for their suppression, as every European community, be it English, Dutch, or Spanish, seems quite satisfied to clear the vicinity of its own ports, and never considers the damage to the native trade which takes place at a distance. To be attacked with success, they must be attacked on their own coasts with two or three steamers. A little money would gain every intelligence as to where they were preparing; and whilst the steamers were so worthily engaged in suppressing piracy, they might at the same time be acquiring information respecting countries little known, and adding to our stock of geography and science. A few severe examples and constant harassing would soon cure this hereditary and personal mania for a rover's life; and whilst we conferred the greatest blessing on the rest of the Archipelago, Magindano itself would be improved by the change.

"The Illanun Datus and the Gillolo chiefs visited the schooner constantly, and were always considerate enough to bring but few followers. We conversed much upon piracy in general, their mode of life, their successes, and their privations. They seemed to have but few fears of the Dutch or English men-of-war being able to take them, and during their three years' cruise had never been chased by any of them.

"After three or four days being in company with these worthies, *i. e.* the fleet of Illanuns and Malukus, the Royalist dropped down the river to Santobong, whilst Williamson and myself stayed yet a few days with Muda Hassim in his house. We had a week's incessant torrent of rain. Nothing could exceed the kindness of the Rajah during our stay, with his brothers of all ages as our constant companions. We had one day a dance of the Illanuns and Gillolos: they might both be called war-dances, but are very different. The performer with the Illanuns is decked out with a *fine helmet* (probably *borrowed* from our early voyagers) ornamented with bird-of-paradise feathers. Two gold belts, crossed like our soldiers' over the breast, are bound at the waist with a fantastical garment reaching half way down the thigh, and composed of various-coloured silk and woollen threads one above another. The sword or 'kempilan' is decorated at the handle with a yard or two of red cloth, and the long upright shield is covered with small rings, which clash as the performer goes through his evolutions. The dance itself consists of a variety of violent warlike gestures, stamping, striking, advancing, retreating, turning, falling, yelling, with here and there bold stops, and excellent as to *à-plomb*, which might have elicited the applause of the opera-house: but generally speaking, the performance was outrageously fierce, and so far natural as approaching to an actual combat; and in half an hour the dancer, a fine young man, was so exhausted that he fell fainting into the arms of his comrades. Several others succeeded, but not equal to the first; and we had hardly a fair opportunity of judging of the Maluku dance from its short continuance; but it is of a more gentle nature, advancing with the spear stealthily, casting it, then retreating with the sword and shield. The Maluku shield, it should be observed, is remarkably narrow, and is brandished somewhat in the same way as the single-stick player uses his stick, or the Irishman his shillelah; that is to say, it is held nearly in the centre, and whirled every way round. I procured some of the instruments, and found that the sword of the Malukus of Gillolo is similar to that of the Moskokas of Boni Bay, in Celebes. All these pirates are addicted to the *excessive* use of opium; but the effects of it are by no means so deleterious or so strongly marked as has been represented; and it must likewise be remembered that they are in other respects dissolute and debauched. Amongst the Chinese it would be difficult—nay, impossible—to detect the smokers of the drug. Here and there you may see an emaciated man; but out of a body of five hundred, some are usually emaciated and unhealthy. I do not mean to deny the bad effects of opium; but the stories of its pernicious results are greatly exaggerated where the habit exists in moderation. The Chinese themselves, when I spoke to them of the bad consequences, always argued that, taken moderately, it was a stimulus to industry and activity; but they allowed, at the same time, that excess was highly injurious.

" The time at length came for my departure, but I was pressed to stay one day after another, for our society was a relief to the usual monotonous tenor of their lives. The papers were signed which made me Resident of Sarāwak. I started to Santobong, and reached the vessel on the 13th of February; and after waiting two days in the vain hope of a lull or change of wind, we beat out of the channel."

Mr. Brooke did not remain long at Singapore. His principal object was to procure a vessel to trade between that place and Sarāwak. Trading, however, was not his forte; but he already felt the deepest interest in the welfare of those people. By accident—or, more properly, by Providence—he appears to have been sent to put a stop to an unnatural war, and to save the lives of the unfortunate rebels; and the benefit he had conferred on so many of his fellow-creatures, the good he had already done, and the infinity of good which he saw he still might do, made him anxious to return.

After some difficulty he succeeded in purchasing a schooner of 90 tons, called the Swift, which I recollected in the Malacca Straits as the Zephyr, then a cruiser in the East India Company's service. Having put a suitable cargo into her, he sailed with his squadron (Royalist and Swift) for Sarāwak early in April 1841.

The Rajah, already described as an indolent weak-minded man, had promised Mr. Brooke the government of the country; but among other obstacles with which he would have to contend in accepting it, I do not think my friend calculated on jealousy, low cunning, and treachery, or the dangerous enemy he had made in Pangeran Macota. He had been an eye-witness to his cowardice, and had more than once detected and exposed his cunning and trickery;—sins not to be forgiven, especially by a Malay. Notwithstanding this, firmness, courage, and straightforward honesty gained the victory, as the sequel will shew.

Among the characters with whom Mr. Brooke got acquainted during the rebel war was a young chief named Si Tundo, who was constantly by his side whenever there was danger. He was an Illanun, and had been sent from Sadung, with some thirteen of his countrymen, by Seriff Sahib, to offer his services to Macota, commander-in-chief of the Rajah's forces; and I resume Mr. Brooke's memoranda with the following interesting account of this poor fellow's fate:—" On my arrival at Sarāwak, we were received with the usual honours; and the first thing I heard was the decease of my poor companion, Si Tundo, of Magindano, who had been put to death by the Rajah's orders. The course of justice, or rather injustice, or perhaps, more justly, a mixture of both, is so characteristic of the people, that I am tempted to give the particulars. Si Tundo fell in love with a woman belonging to an adopted son of Macota, and the passion being mutual, the lady eloped from her master and went to her lover's house. This being discovered in a short time, he was ordered to surrender her to Macota, which he reluctantly did, on an understanding that he was to be allowed to marry her on giving a proper dowry. Either not being able to procure the money, or the terms not being kept, Si Tundo and a relation (who had left the pirate fleet and resided with him) mounted to Macota's hill, and threatened to take the woman and to burn the house. The village, however, being roused, they were unable to effect their purpose, and retired to their own residence. Here they remained for some days in a state of incessant watchfulness, and when they moved, they each carried their kempilan, and wore the krisses ready to the hand. The Rajah Muda Hassim, being well aware of the state of things, sent at this crisis to order Si Tundo and his friend to his presence; which order they obeyed forthwith, and entered the balei, or audience-hall, which was full of their enemies. According to Muda Hassim's account, he was anxious to save Si Tundo's life, and offered him another wife; but his affections being fixed on the girl of his own choice, he rejected the offer, only praying he might have the woman he loved. On entering the presence of the Rajah, surrounded by foes, and dreading treachery (which most probably was intended), these unfortunate men added to their previous fault by one which, however slight in European estimation, is here of an aggravated nature,—they entered the presence with their kempilans in their hands, and their sarongs clear of the kris-handle; and instead of seating themselves cross-legged, they only squatted on their hams ready for self-defence. From that hour their doom was resolved on: the crime of disrespect was deemed worthy of death, though their previous crime of abduction and violence might have obtained pardon. It was no easy matter, however, among an abject and timid population, to find executioners of the sentence against two brave and warlike men, well armed and watchful, and whom all knew would sell their lives dearly; and the subsequent proceeding is, as already observed, curiously characteristic of the people, and the deep disguise they can assume to attain their purposes. It was intimated to Si Tundo, that if he could raise a certain sum of money, the woman should be made over to him; and to render this the more probable, the affair was taken out of Macota's hands, and placed at the decision of the Orang Kaya de Gadong, who *was friendly* to the offenders, but who received his private orders how to act. Four men were appointed to watch their opportunity, in order to seize the culprits. It is not to be imagined, however, that a native would trust or believe the friendly assurances held out to him; nor was it so in the case of Si Tundo and his companion; they attended at the Orang Kaya de Gadong's house frequently for weeks, with the same precautions, and it was found impossible to overpower them; but the deceit of their enemies was equal to the occasion, and delay brought no change of purpose. They were to die, and opportunity alone was wanting to carry the sentence into effect. Time passed over, suspicion was lulled; and as suspicion was lulled, the professions to serve them became more frequent. Poor Si Tundo brought *all* his little property to make good the price required for the woman, and his friend added his share; but it was still far short of the required amount. Hopes, however, were still held out; the Orang Kaya advanced a small sum to assist, and other *pretended* friends slowly and reluctantly, at his request, lent a little money. The negotiation was nearly complete; forty or fifty reals only were wanting, and the opposite party were ready to deliver the lady whenever the sum was made good. A final conference was appointed for the conclusion of the bargain at the Orang Kaya's, at which numbers were present; and the devoted victims, lulled into fatal security, had ceased to bring their formidable kempilans. At the last interview the forty reals being still deficient, the Orang Kaya proposed receiving their gold-mounted krisses in pledge for the amount. The krisses were given up, and the bargain was complete, when the four executioners threw themselves on the unarmed men, and, assisted by others, overpowered and secured them. Si Tundo, wounded in the scuffle and bound, surrounded by enemies flourishing their krisses, remarked, 'You have taken me by treachery; openly you could not have seized me.' He spoke no more. They triumphed over and insulted him, as though some great feat had been achieved; and every kris was plunged into his body, which was afterwards cast, without burial, into the river. Si Tundo's relation was spared on pleading for mercy; and after his whole property, even his clothes, was confiscated, he was allowed to retire to Sadung. Thus perished poor Si Tundo, a Magindano pirate, with many, if not all, the vices of the native character; but with boldness, courage, and constancy, which retrieved his faults and raised him in the estimation of brave men. In person he was tall, elegantly made, with small and handsome features, and quiet and graceful manners; but towards the Malays even of rank, there was a suppressed contempt which they often felt, but could not well resent. Alas, my gallant comrade! I mourn your death, and could have better spared a better man; for as long as you lived, I had one faithful follower of tried courage, amongst the natives. Peace be with you in the world to come, and may the Great God pardon your sins and judge you mercifully!

" The case of poor Si Tundo proves that the feeling of love is not quite dead amongst Asiatics, though its power is obscured by their education and habits of polygamy; and that friendship and relationship may induce a man here, as elsewhere, to risk his life and sacrifice his property without any prospect of personal advantage. An old Magindano man, a sort of foster-father of Si Tundo's, when he saw me for the first time, clasped my arm, and repeatedly exclaimed, 'Si Tundo is dead, they have killed him;' adding, 'had you been here, he would not have been killed.' I was touched by the old man's sorrow and his expression of feeling."

Datu Jembrong was likewise an Illanun, and retired to Sadung when the rebel war had closed, and died after a few days' illness. Mr. Brooke writes: " Thus I have lost the two bravest men —men whom I would rather trust for fair dealing than any score of Borneons; for the Magindanos, though pirates by descent and education, are a far superior people to any in the Archipelago, with the exception of the Bugis. Whatever may be their vices, they are retrieved by courage to a certain degree; and where we find a manly character, we may presume that the meaner arts of *finesse* and treachery are less prevalent. Dampier and Forrest both give them an excellent character; and it is a pity that of late years little is known of them, and so little pains taken to hold a friendly intercourse either with them or the Sooloos."

The important changes which ensued on the return of Mr. Brooke to Saràwak, in the spring of 1841, now demand attention; and, as heretofore, I proceed to describe them from the data entrusted to my charge.

"In a former part of my journal," says Mr. Brooke, "I have mentioned briefly the occasions which led to my invitation, and the reasons which induced me to accept the offer of the Rajah Muda Hassim; but I will repeat these, in order to bring the narrative at once more distinctly before the memory. When I returned here for the second time, in August last year, it was with the determination of remaining for a few days only on my way to the northward; and nothing but my feeling for the miserable situation of Muda Hassim induced me to alter my intention. The rebellion, which he had come from Borneo to quell, had defied every effort for nearly four years; and the attacks he had made on the rebels had failed entirely and almost disgracefully. His immediate followers were few in number, and aid from the neighbouring countries was either denied, or withheld on trivial excuses; whilst the opposition of Pangeran Usop in Borneo paralysed the efforts of his supporters in the capital, and in case of non-success threatened his own power. The pride, the petty pride of the Malay prince bent before these circumstances, and induced him to state his difficulties to me, and to request my assistance. His failure was strongly dwelt on, and his resolution to die here rather than abandon his undertaking—to die disgraced and deserted! Under these circumstances, could I, he urged upon me, forsake him? could I, 'a gentleman from England,' who had been his friend, and knew the goodness of his heart, could I leave him surrounded and begirt with enemies? It was possibly foolish, it was perhaps imprudent, but accorded with my best feelings; and I resolved not to abandon him without at any rate seeing the probabilities of success; and it must always be remembered that in doing so, I had no ulterior object, no prospect of any personal advantage. I joined his miserable army, which, in numbers, barely exceeded that of the rebels strongly stockaded. I joined them at the outset of their campaign; and in a few days (ten days) witnessed such scenes of cowardice, treachery, intrigue, and lukewarmness amongst his followers, such a determination not to take advice or to pursue any active measures, that I left them and returned to my vessel. The Chinese I do not include in this representation; they were true and willing, but wretchedly armed; and very justly refused to be thrust forward into posts of danger, which the Malays in their own country refused to share. On my return to the vessel, I frankly stated how useless my presence was amongst men who would not do any thing I desired, yet would do nothing for themselves; and, under the circumstances, I intimated my intention of sailing. Here again I was pressed with the same entreaties; every topic was exhausted to excite my compassion, every aid was at my disposal; and lastly, if I would stay, and we were successful, the country was offered to me.

The only inquiry was, whether the Rajah had the right and authority to make over the country to me, and this I was assured he had. The government, the revenue (with slight deductions for the Sultan), and one of his brothers to reside here in order to ensure the obedience of the Malays, were all comprehended in his cession, freely and without condition. I might at this point of the negotiation have ensured *the title* to the government as far as a written agreement could give it; but for two sufficient reasons I declined all treaty upon the subject until the war was over. The first of these reasons was, that it would have been highly ungenerous to take advantage of a man's distress to tie him down to any agreement which, in other circumstances, he might not be willing to adopt; and by acting thus ungenerously, it would be tempting the Rajah to deceive me when the treaty came to be ratified. The second reason was equally cogent ; for a mere barren bond which I had no means to enforce was worse than useless, and no man would be nearer possession by merely holding a written promise. I may add, likewise, that I saw so many difficulties in the way of the undertaking, that I was by no means over-anxious to close with it; and previous to accepting and entering on so bold a project, I was desirous thoroughly to be assured of the good faith of the promiser. To the Rajah Muda Hassim's proposal I therefore replied, that I could not accept it whilst the war was pending, as I considered it wrong to take any advantage of his present situation; and that if he conferred authority on me in the camp, I would once more go up the river and assist him to the utmost of my power. It is needless to repeat any details of the war, except to say that I found every support from him, and the highest consideration, both in personal attentions and the bestowal of influence. He conquered, I may say without self-praise, through my means; and on the close of hostilities our negotiation about the country was revived. In its progress, I stated to him that Malay governments were so bad, that the high were allowed so much license, and the poor so oppressed, that any attempt to govern without a change of these abuses was impossible; and as a foundation of my acceptance was the proposition, that all his exertions must be employed to establish the principle that one man was not to take any thing from another, and that all men were to enjoy the produce of their labour, save and except at such times as they were engaged in working for the revenue. That the amount of the revenue was to be fixed and certain for three years, at a stated quantity of rice per family; in lieu of which, should a man prefer it, he might pay in money or in labour—the relative price of rice to money or labour being previously fixed at as low a rate as possible. That the officers, viz. Patingi, Bandar, and Tumangong, were to receive stated salaries out of this revenue, in order to prevent any extortion, either by themselves or in their name; and that they were to be answerable for the whole revenue under my superintendence. That the Dyaks were to be treated the same as the Malays, their property protected, their taxes fixed, and their labour free. At the same time I represented to him the difficulty of doing this, and that nothing but his power could effect it; as any foreigner, without his unlimited support and confidence, would have no chance of finding obedience from the numerous inferior Pangerans and their followers. This, with much more, was the theme of my conversation; to which was replied — *Imprimis*, That their customs and religion must not be infringed. That with regard to the violence and rapacity of the higher classes, and the uncertainty of taxation, which led to so much oppression, they were by no means any part of the Ondong Ondong in the law of Borneo, but gross abuses which had arisen out of lax government. That it was the wish of his heart to see these things mended; and that nothing should be wanting on his part to assist me in accomplishing objects so desirable, particularly with respect to the Dyaks, who were so grossly abused. On this, a written agreement was made out, merely to the purport that I was to reside at Sarāwak in order to ' seek for profit;' and on my remarking that this paper expressed nothing, he said I must not think that it was the one understood between us, but merely for him to shew to the Sultan at Borneo in the first place. I accepted this version of the story, though it looked suspicious; and on my part, out of our written agreement, which expressed nothing, I consented to buy a vessel, and bring down trade to the place, in return for which, I was assured of antimony-ore in plenty; and though I knew that profit was not to be expected, I was desirous to comply, as, without a vessel regularly trading here, it would be impossible to develop the resources of the country. Whilst I went to Singapore, the Rajah promised to build me a house, in which I was to take up my residence. I sailed accordingly, and returned within three months, having performed all my engagements; but on reaching Sarāwak, the first disappointment I experienced was, that the house was not commenced. I urged them to begin it, and after the most provoking delays at length got it finished. I mention this because it was the only instance in which good faith was kept.

"*August 3d.*—The two schooners Royalist and Swift having arrived at Sarāwak, I found myself with a heavy monthly expense, and was naturally anxious to despatch them as speedily as possible. I was assured that 6000 peculs of antimony-ore would be down immediately, and that whenever the people were set to work, any quantity might be procured without difficulty; which, indeed, I knew to be true, as Macota had loaded a ship, a brig, and three native vessels in six weeks. The procrastination therefore was the more provoking; but as I had determined to arm myself with patience, and did not anticipate foul play, I was content to wait for a time. The Swift being leaky and requiring repairs, was another inducement to me to lie by and land her cargo, which, ever since my arrival, the Rajah petitioned to have ashore, giving every pledge for a quick and good return. At length I consented to let him have the cargo into his own hands, on the assurance that the antimony-ore (*i. e.* the 6000 peculs which were ready?) should be brought down directly. Nothing could be more correct than the way they received the cargo, taking an account of each separate article, comparing each with the invoice, and noting down the deficiency; and no person could be more active than the Rajah himself, superintending from morning till dark in this interesting process. At this time, having agreed with him for the whole, as the easiest and best mode of dealing under the circumstances, I did not much trouble myself about the deposit; and my attention was first roused by the extreme apathy of the whole party directly the cargo was in their possession—overhauled, reckoned, and disposed of amongst them."

CHAPTER X.

Obstacles in coming to a satisfactory conclusion with Muda Hassim. The law of force and reprisal considered. Capabilities of Sarāwak. Account of Sarebus and Sakarran pirates. Excursion up the river. Visit to the Singè Dyaks. Description of Mr. Brooke's house at Sarāwak. Circumstances relating to the wreck off Borneo Proper.

DURING the succeeding pages of my friend's journal, one hardly knows which to admire most; his firmness, his cool courage, his determined perseverance, or his patience. On the other hand, it is difficult to decide whether the Rajah's indolence and ingratitude, or Macota's low cunning and treachery, are most disgusting. But I continue the narrative, and readers will judge for themselves.

"Yet," says Mr. Brooke, "I had confidence, and was loath to allow any base suspicion to enter my mind against a man who had hitherto behaved well to me, and had not deceived me before. From the time the cargo had been disposed of, I found myself positively laid on the shelf. No return arrived; no steps were taken to work the antimony-ore; no account appeared of the positive amount to be received: a promise was tendered; and all my propositions—nay, my very desire to speak of the state of the country—were evaded. I found myself clipped like Samson, while delay was heaped upon delay, excuse piled on excuse, and all covered with the utmost shew of kindness and civility. It was provoking beyond sufferance; but with several strokes which I considered important, I bore it with saint-like patience. I remonstrated mildly but firmly on the waste of my money, and on the impossibility of any good to the country whilst the Rajah conducted himself as he had done. I urged upon him to release the poor women whom he had kept confined for nearly five months; and I guaranteed the peaceful disposition of the people if it were done. I might as well have whistled to the winds, or have talked reason to stones. I was overwhelmed with professions of affection and kindness, but nothing ensued. I had trusted—my eyes gradually opened—I feared I was betrayed and robbed, and had at length determined to be observant and watchful, when an event occurred which finished the delusion, and woke me fully to the treachery, or at any rate the weakness, at work against me. My house was finished, and I had just taken possession of it, when I understood that an overwhelming body of Dyaks, accompanied by Malays, were proceeding up the river, with the avowed purpose of attacking a hostile tribe, but with the real design of slaughtering all the weak tribes in their way. Upwards of 100 boats, with certainly not fewer than 2500 men, had been at Sarāwak a week, asking permission for this expedition; and I was informed there was not the slightest chance of its being granted, when to my surprise I saw the expedition start. On being convinced that they really were going up the country, I instantly quitted the house and returned on board the Royalist, sending to know whether the Rajah had granted leave for their entrance into the interior. By him the whole blame of the transaction was thrown upon Macota and the Orang Kaya de Gadong; and he himself was said to be so ill that he could not be seen; but it was added, as I disliked the measure so greatly, the same parties who had sent the Dyaks up could recall them down, which indeed I had insisted on being done. They accordingly retrograded and left; after which I continued sulky on board, and the Rajah, shamming sick, sulked in his harem. That any man besides the Rajah himself would have been bold enough to grant the permission, I knew, from experience, was impossible. I accepted his denial as the groundwork of a reconciliation. In the mean time, as he continued indisposed, I intimated my intention of proceeding to Borneo in three days, and despatching the Swift at the same time to proceed to Singapore; part of her cargo, 750 peculs of antimony-ore, having been at length put on board. On this being made known to the Rajah, he forgot his sickness, and came out and proffered me a meeting to discuss affairs, which I postponed until the following day. In the mean time I took a candid view of my position, and considered the best means of extricating myself from my difficulties with as little trouble and inconvenience as possible to either party.

"I had lost much valuable time, spent much money, and risked my life and the lives of my crew, in order to render assistance to Rajah Muda Hassim in his distress; in return for which he had voluntarily offered me the country. The conditions of my acceptance had been discussed and mutually understood, and I had, in fulfilment of my part, brought vessel and cargo. Profit I did not much care about; the development of the country was my chief, I may say my only, aim; and on my arrival I had been delayed and cheated by false promises, which shewed too plainly that he neither meant to adhere to his former agreement, nor to pay for what he had on false pretences obtained. It may appear to many that no measures ought to be kept with one who had so behaved; but, for the following reasons, I resolved still to wait his pleasure. In the first place, it was barely possible that indolence, and not treachery, might have actuated him; and in the next, that if it was possible to arrange so as to get back the amount of the Swift's cargo, I was in duty and justice bound to use every endeavour before resorting to measures of force. As for the cession of the country, and all the good which must have resulted from it, I put these considerations altogether out of the question. I had been deceived and betrayed, and had met with the grossest ingratitude; but I had no claim, nor would any written agreement have given me one; and I was therefore constrained to submit without returning evil for evil. Every point weighed, I felt from every motive inclined, nay desirous, to avoid a rupture, or take an equivalent for my property by force. The Swift, with the part of her cargo received on board, after three months' detention, and no more even talked of, I therefore resolved, as already stated, to despatch to Singapore. My first intention on arriving here had been to send the Royalist back to that port and dispose of her; but a native rumour being afloat that the crew of a shipwrecked vessel were in Borneo Proper, I deemed it incumbent on me to visit that place and effect their release. I had used every means in my power since my arrival to induce the Rajah Muda Hassim to send one or two of his Pangerans and a letter from himself to the Sultan by the Royalist, in order to ensure that object; but although, day by day, I had received promises, they were never performed. Seeing now that this duty of humanity could no longer be delayed with propriety, I resolved to despatch the Royalist to Borneo, and myself to remain here, to endeavour, if I could, to obtain *my own.* Each vessel was to return as quickly as possible from her place of destination; and I then resolved to give two additional months to the Rajah, and to urge him in every way in my power to do what he was bound to do as an act of common honesty. Should these means fail, after making the strongest representations and giving amplest time, I considered myself free to extort by force what I could not gain by fair means.

"Having determined on these steps, I met the Rajah by appointment, and repeated all my grievances, and set strongly before him the injury done in consequence; and lastly, plainly told him that I only came and now only stayed in his country at his request, but that the property he had taken must be repaid, and subsequently to that, if he had any proposition to make, I would endeavour to meet his wishes. To all this I received *no one satisfactory answer*, and, from the shuffling on every complaint, I formed the worst opinion of his intentions.

"My determination, however, having been previously made, the result of this conversation had no effect upon me; and at the end of three days, the time I had limited, no letter for the Sultan being forthcoming, on the fourth morning the two schooners proceeded to sea, one for Borneo, the other for Singapore, whilst, with three companions, I remained in my new house.[1]

"I wish now to discuss a question which has often occupied my mind, and upon which I have been very desirous to arrive at a right conclusion. It is certain that a British subject cannot wrongfully attack or injure any prince or person in his own country without rendering himself liable to be punished by the laws of England. It is both right and just that it should be so, because in demi-civilised or savage countries the natives are often unable to protect themselves, and an attack upon them savours of piracy. On the other hand, if the native prince be the party to blame; if he fraudulently possess himself of property under false pretences, make promises which he breaks, and enter into agreements before witnesses which he never intends to fulfil; then, I ask, is a British

---

[1] I need hardly remark on the singular courage and disregard of personal safety and life itself evinced by my friend on this occasion. At issue with the Rajah on points of great temptation to him, beset by intrigues, and surrounded by a fierce and lawless people, Mr. Brooke did not hesitate to despatch his vessels and protectors, the one on a mission of pure humanity, and the other in calm pursuance of the objects he had proposed to himself to accomplish; and with "three companions," place himself at the mercy of such circumstances, regardless of the danger, and relying on the overruling Providence in which he trusted, to bring him safely through all his difficulties and perils.—H. K.

subject to submit to the loss, when the party defrauding him is able to pay and will not? I answer decidedly, he is not bound to submit to be cheated, and, if he have the means, he has the right to enforce repayment. It may be urged that trust ought not to be reposed; but trust is the ordinary course of trade, and cannot alter the question. Again, it may be said, Apply to the government; but it is well known and acknowledged that the government will not interfere in any case of the sort. Seek redress by law! there is no law to meet the contingency. Bear the loss, *i. e.* be betrayed, deceived, and cheated, and submit! It cannot be; for although the law may properly inquire into the circumstances, yet as it will not protect me here, or give me any redress for *fraud* or *murder*, it cannot punish if right be on my side. Am I quite sure that the right is on my side? It is, as far as I can judge; and having candidly stated every fact and circumstance, I am convinced there can be but one opinion on the subject. I am sure that if I seize property to the amount of that taken from me, I act justly, though perhaps not legally; yet I firmly believe legally likewise, although law and justice do not necessarily go always hand in hand. On the whole, there was the old sore rankling—the false promises, the gross deceit, the base ingratitude to a man who had done every thing to relieve this equivocating Rajah from disgrace, defeat, and perhaps death. But here I close this account for the present, to be resumed on the return of the Royalist from Borneo.

"*August 4th.*—Both retrospectively and prospectively the grounds for all these transactions were ever pressing on my mind and guiding my actions. The capabilities of the Sarāwak country were very great. It could abundantly supply the richest produce of the vegetable kingdom; it abounded in mineral wealth, and especially in a vast staple commodity of antimony-ore; with a considerable population of Dyaks, whose condition was decidedly improvable; a Malay population, by no means large, which was advantageous; and a Chinese population ready to immigrate with even a moderate prospect of protection. Besides these inducements, must be added its propinquity to the Pontiana river, and the trade which by that route might flow even from the centre of this little-known island. To crown all, there were the credit to myself in case of success, the amelioration of the native condition, however partial, and the benefit to commerce in general. These were the reasons that induced me to enter on this arduous task; and to these I may add a supplementary one, viz. that when I had struggled for a time, I might rouse the zeal of others, and find efficient support either from government or the mercantile body.

"I have in a former part of my journal mentioned the Illanun pirates, and my meeting with them here. On our return we heard of their being still on the coast, and from that time to this they have been ravaging and plundering between Tanjong Datu, Sirhassan, and Pontiana. Malays and Chinese have been carried off in great numbers; Borneo and Sambas prahus captured without end; and so much havoc committed, that the whole coast, as far as the natives are concerned, may be pronounced in a state of blockade.

"Besides the Illanuns, there are two other descriptions of pirates infesting these seas: one, the Dyaks of Sakarran and Sarebus, two predatory tribes already mentioned; the other called Balagnini, a wild people represented to come from the northward of Sooloo. I have not seen them; but their boats are said to be very long and swift, with sometimes outriggers; and one particular in their mode of attack is too curious to omit. In closing on their victims they use long poles, having a hook made fast at the extremity, with which, being expert, they hook their opponents at a distance and drag them overboard, whilst others are fighting with saligis and spears.

"I have before mentioned the arrival of one hundred Dyak boats at Sarāwak, to request permission from the Rajah to ascend the river and attack a tribe towards Sambas. What a tale of misgovernment, tyranny, and weakness, does this request tell! These Dyaks were chiefly from Sakarran, mixed with the Sarebus, and with them three boats of the Malo tribe, whose residence is towards the Pontiana river. The Sakarrans are the most powerful, the most predatory, and the most independent tribe on the N.W. coast, their dependence on Borneo being merely nominal. The latter are likewise predatory and numerous, but they are on good terms with all the coast tribes and with the Malays, whilst the Sarebus are against all, and all are against them. Speaking generally, they are a remarkably fine body of people, handsome, intelligent, powerful, well-made, beautifully limbed, and clear-skinned. They are somewhat fairer than the Malays and the mountain Dyaks; but in manners, customs, and language, exactly resemble the Sibnowans, except that the last, from misfortune, have become a peaceful tribe. The Sarebus and Sakarrans are only distinguishable by the numerous rings they wear in their ears. On one man I counted fourteen of brass, various sizes, in one ear only. They are rather fond of ornament, and wear grotesque caps of various coloured cloths (particularly red), some of them square, others peaked, and others like a cocked-hat worn athwart-ships, and terminating in sharp points on the top of the head. These head-dresses are ornamented with tufts of red hair or black human hair, shreds of cloth, and sometimes feathers; but what renders them laughable to look at is, that the hair is cut close to match the shape of the cap; so when a man displaces them, you find him bare of hair about the forehead and posterior part of the skull, cut into points over the ears, and the rest of the skull shewing a good crop of black bristles.

"The commanders of this party were yclept poetically by their own people, as *nommes de guerre*, the Sun and the Moon, *i. e. Bulan* for moon, and *Matari* for sun. The Sun was as fine a young man as the eye would wish to rest upon; straight, elegantly yet strongly made, with a chest and neck, and head set on them, which might serve Apollo; legs far better than his of Belvidere; and a countenance mild and intelligent. I became very good friends with both Sun and Moon, and gave them a great deal of good advice about piracy, which, of course, was thrown away.

"Their boats are built very long, raised at the stern, and the largest pulling as many as sixty paddles; but I should not think them fast, and any boat with a swivel might cut them up. The least average I could give the hundred boats is twenty-five men per boat, making, as already observed, 2500 in all. We counted ninety, and there were others down the reach we could not see; and they themselves stated their force to be 140 boats and 4000 men. The manners of these Dyaks were reserved, quiet, and independent, towards us. They stole nothing, and in trading for small quantities of rice, bees-wax, cotton, and their cloths, shewed a full knowledge of the relative value of the articles, or rather they priced their own at far above their proper worth. I may indeed say of all the Dyaks I have seen, that they are anxious to receive, but very loath to give; and when they have obtained cloth, salt, copper, beads, &c. to the amount of two or three dollars, as a present, will bring in a bunch of plantains or a little rice, and ask you *to buy*. The Sibnowans are the chief exceptions to this, and they are my pet tribe. The language of Sakarran and Sarebus is the same as the Sibnowan; and with all the word God, the *Allah Talla* of the Malays, is expressed by *Battara*, from which we may infer that their notion of the Deity, as probably was all the religion of these regions, was derived from the Hindoos.

" When this force of Dyaks was, contrary to the assurance given to me, sweeping up the river, I had just finished a late dinner. I was *angry enough*, and resolved instanter to leave the house, when who should come in, *as if by pure accident*, but Pangeran Budrudeen, the Rajah's brother. I controlled myself, spoke strongly withal but civilly, and sent him away wishing he had not come near me; and the boat being ready, I retired from the house to the Royalist. Their immediate recall was the consequence; for the Rajah having denied his permission, those who fathered the act dared not persist in it when I told them it was an act of disobedience. They tried to frighten me with the idea that the Dyaks would attack us; but as I felt sure we could blow them away in ten minutes, it had not the desired effect. They had in the mean time reached Leda Tanah, whence they were brought down again sulky enough, and did shew a slight inclination to see whether the people on board the Swift were keeping watch; for several of their boats dropped close to her, and one directly under the bowsprit, as silently as death; but on being challenged, and a musket levelled near them, they sheered off, and the next day finally departed. The poor Dyaks in the interior, as well as the Chinese, were in the greatest state of alarm, and thence I gained some credit amongst them for my interference on their behalf. The very idea of letting 2500 wild devils loose in the interior of the country is horrible; for though they have one professed object, they combine many others with it, and being enemies of all the mountain tribes, they cut them up as much as they can. What object, it may be inquired, can the Malays have in destroying their own country and people so wantonly? I must endeavour to explain, to the best of my belief and knowledge. The Malays take part in these excursions, and thirty men joined the Sakarrans on the present occasion, and consequently they share in the plunder, and share largely. Probably Muda Hassim would have got twenty shares (women and children); and these twenty being reckoned at the low rate of twenty reals each, makes four hundred reals, besides other plunder, amounting to one or two hundred reals more. Inferior Pangerans would of course partake likewise. Muda Hassim *must* have given his consent, must have been a participator in this atrocity, nobody being desperate enough to do such a thing without his orders. In fact, they dare not move up the river themselves without leave, much less send up the Dyaks. It is a hateful feature in this government, newly developed since the close of the war.

"*August 5th.*—One excursion I made up the river over our old ground, staying a week, visiting various places. Where the village of Siniawan once stood is now a small Chinese settlement, and their garden bespeaks the fertility of the soil. From Siniawan I walked over to Tundong, now the principal Chinese station. The scenery was beautiful all the way from Siniawan to Tundong —gently undulating ground rising into respectable hills, and backed by noble mountains, and valleys so quiet and still, and looking so fertile, that I sighed to think man's cultivating hand was not here. We paused, and rested at a farm of the Paninjow. Their mode of cultivation is the same as described by Marsden—cutting, clearing, planting, and abandoning after one or two crops. They seem likewise to prefer the upland to the wet ground. Tundong is quite a new settlement, situated close on the banks of the river, which is here quite narrow and shallow. The distance may be ten miles by water, as it took our boat four hours and a half to pull against stream. We spent the same time walking, but diverged from the road. Wherever the Chinese are, the sound of the axe and the saw is to be heard in the woods as you approach, and all are industriously employed. They have their carpenters, sawyers, blacksmiths, and housebuilders, whilst the mass work the antimony-ore, or are busy constructing the trench, where they find and wash the gold. With such inhabitants a country must get on well, if they are allowed fair play. I was quite tired, and stayed all night at Tundong. On the following morning I started for the Singè mountain, which is the residence of the Dyak tribe of the same name. The walk, including a rest, occupied nearly three hours, the latter part up-hill, and we reached the village a good deal knocked up from the heat of the sun and the badness of the way. Our entertainment was not of the best; yet the Singè were not inhospitable, but suspicious that we came to rob them. The rice and the fowls we required, although we paid for them at double their value, were reluctantly produced; while at the same time they shewed themselves anxious enough to obtain the salt we had brought to exchange, without giving the equivalent.

"The village is built on a shoulder of the mountain, not half way up, and only accessible by a ladder-like path on either side. It consists of about 200 miserable huts, and is as dirty and filthy as any place I ever was in, with numerous half-starved pigs and dogs running about it. The houses are small and mean, and detached from each other, unlike the other Dyaks, who inhabit one large house containing numerous partitions for families; here, however, they have one or two public halls or council-houses, which are built and thatched in a circular form, and in which their young men and bachelors sleep; here likewise are deposited the heads, of which they have more than enow, as above one hundred ghastly remnants of mortality ornamented the abode in which we slept. I could not on this occasion find out that they professed to take the heads of friends or strangers, though the latter may fall victims if on enemies' ground. They seem to have no idea of cannibalism or human sacrifice, nor did they accuse their enemies of these practices. They have a custom, that in case of sickness in a house, or child-bearing, the house is forbidden to the males and strangers, which is something similar to the tabboo of the South-Sea Islands. This plea was urged as a reason why the head man or Orang Kaya Parembam could not receive us in his dwelling. The Dyaks are always decorous in their behaviour, rarely give way to mirth, and never annoy by their curiosity. Towards the Malays they are extremely sulky and mulish; but they have good reasons, as the Malays are ever extorting from them, and threatening them with the anger of the Rajah or the incursion of the Sakarrans. The women wear the stays before mentioned, which are sewn on when they arrive at the age of puberty, and never removed save when *enceinte*. These Singè Dyaks, like the others, attend to the warning of birds of various sorts, some birds being in more repute than others. On starting for a hunting excursion we met one of them on the hill-side, who said, ' You will be fortunate : I heard the bird behind you.' Here, if a bird is before you, it is a sign that enemies are there too, and they turn back : if behind, they proceed in good spirits. They have a prejudice against the flesh of deer, which the men may not eat, but which is allowed to women and children. The reason given for this is, that if the warriors eat the flesh of deer, they become as faint-hearted as that animal. These may be called their superstitions, but religion they have none; and though they know a name for God, and entertain some faint notion of a future state, yet it is only in the abstract, for practically the belief seems to be a dead letter. At their marriage they kill fowls, as I have narrated ; but this is a ceremony, not a sacrifice. They have no priests nor idols, say no prayers, offer no offerings to propitiate the Deity ; and it is little likely therefore that human sacrifice should exist among them. In this respect they are different from any known people who have arrived at the same state of civilisation. The New Zealanders, the inhabitants of the South Seas, &c. &c., for instance, all bow to their idols, towards which the same feelings of reverence and devotion, of awe and fear, obtain as with more civilised beings in regard to the invisible Deity; but here are the mere words, barren and without practice.

"The day following our arrival at Singè we descended into the plains, amid their former rice-fields, to shoot deer. The place is called Pasar (bazaar or market), though it could scarcely ever have been one. The rice-cultivation was formerly very extensive, and the low ground all about the mountain is well cleared of wood by the industry of these Dyaks. But the country becoming unsettled and troubled, and roving parties of strange Dyaks landing on the coast near Onetong, cut off the people employed in the fields, and they consequently were abandoned. We took up our quarters in a ruinous little deserted hovel, and in the evening walked over the neighbouring district, where the cocoa-nut and betel-trees mark its former state of prosperity. The sago is likewise planted in considerable quantity, and serves for food when rice falls short. Deer, the large deer of Borneo, abound, and in a walk of a few miles we saw from fifteen to twenty, and from their tracks they must be very numerous indeed. The walking was difficult, owing to the softness of the ground,

where we often sunk in up to our thighs, and
generally to our knees : and a short distance in
this sort of wading in stiff mud serves to knock a
man up. I was fortunate enough to kill one of the
deer, and have no doubt that with more favourable
light a man might get many. The night's repose
in the hut was broken and uncomfortable, and our
people were busy for several hours curing the flesh
of the animal, which is done as follows :—first it
is slightly salted, and then burnt over a quick
wood-fire in slices or lumps, and thus keeps for
many days, and is very palatable. Seriff Hussein
(formerly of Siniawan) was my companion on this
excursion. He had three followers, whilst I had
three Javanese with me, besides my Bugis boy
Sika, who walks with the best of us. The morning after killing the deer we ascended the Singè
again by a desperately steep path; and after resting an hour or two, walked to our boats, and
descended the stream to Siniawan. The night
was marked by torrents of rain, thunder, and lightning, which left the roads so bad that I resigned
my intention of walking up to Sarambo, and in the
evening dropped down to Leda Tanah, and tried
unsuccessfully for another deer. We saw some,
but could not get near them. Here likewise are
plenty of rice-fields deserted, but which little labour would bring again into cultivation. The day
following we rejoined the schooner, and, as usual,
found every thing at a stand-still on shore.

"I may here mention our house, or, as I fondly styled it, our palace. It is an edifice fifty-four feet square, mounted upon numerous posts of the Nibong palm, with nine windows in each front. The roof (*atap*) is of Nipah-leaves, and the floor and partitions are all of plank: furnished with couches, tables, chairs, books, &c. the whole is as comfortable as man would wish for in this out-of-the-way country; and we have, besides, a bathing-house, cook-house, and servants' apartments detached. The view from the house to the eastward comprises a reach of the river, and to the westward looks towards the blue mountains of Matang; the north fronts the river, and the south the jungle; and but for the uncertainty of our affairs, I would have had a garden ere this, and found amusement in clearing and improving. Farewell, I fear, to these aspirations; our abode, however, though spacious, cool, and comfortable, can only be considered a temporary residence, for the best of all reasons—that in the course of a year it will tumble down, from the weight of the superstructure being placed on weak posts. The original plan was to have had a lower story, but about this I am now indifferent. The time here passes monotonously, but not unpleasantly. Had we but the animation of hope, and the stimulus of improvement, time would pass rapidly, though without a companion to converse with.

"*August 6th.*—The Royalist, as I mentioned before I reverted to the subject of the pirate fleet, started for Borneo Proper, to inquire respecting the crew of an English vessel, reported to have been shipwrecked. Pangeran Sulieman brought the intelligence from Borneo, but he knew very few particulars; and having been here four months before my arrival, the chances were that with the change of the monsoon they had sailed for Manilla. As, however, he assured me he had seen European men and women, and a numerous Lascar crew, I thought it right, at all events, to ascertain the fact; and in case of their being there still, to endeavour to obtain their release. For this purpose I was very desirous of procuring a letter from Muda Hassim to the Sultan, conveyed by a Pangeran of rank; which, in addition to my own application, would most likely ensure the object in view. This, however, though promised, I could not accomplish; delay coming upon delay, and the plague of my own affairs also intervening, postponed my intention till I could see the Swift fairly off for Singapore. The Royalist then went out with her on the Sunday, July 25th, proceeding to Borneo to demand the crew, if there: and the other to Singapore. On the 2d of August I was surprised by the receipt of a letter brought from Sadong, and bearing date the 10th of July. The gentleman who writes it can best tell his own story.

'Island Sirhassan, off Tan Datu,
'July 10th, 1841.

'A boat leaves this to-morrow for Sarāwak; perhaps this may fall into the hands of Mr. Brooke, or some of my countrymen, which, should I not succeed in getting to Singapore, I trust will lose no time in letting the authorities know, so that steps may be taken for the release of the remaining thirty-six British subjects now at Borneo; which I fear nothing but one of H. M. ships will effect. The pirates are cruising in great force between Sambas and this, and have taken thirteen Borneo prahus, or more; they know that there are Europeans in the prahu, and have expressed a wish to take them. Our situation is not very enviable. The bearer of this has just escaped from them. I have been living ashore with Abduramon, a native of Pulo Pinang, who knows Mr. Brooke, and has been very kind to me. Trusting penmanship and paper will be excused,

'I remain, &c. &c.
'G. H. W. GILL.'

"On the reverse was the following attestation, which threw more light on the circumstances:—

'I, G. H. Willoughby Gill, late chief officer of the ship Sultana, of Bombay, do hereby certify that the said ship was totally destroyed by lightning, thirty miles N.E. of the Bombay shoal, coast of Palawan, on the 4th of January, 1841. Part of the crew, forty-one in number, succeeded in reaching Borneo on the 16th of January, in a state of starvation and misery not to be described; the remainder are reported to have landed on the coast of Borneo per long boat:—Captain John Page; G. H. W. Gill, chief officer; Alexander Young, second officer; one gunner; five sea-cunnies; two carpenters; twenty-three natives and Lascars; two Nakodas. Passengers:—Mrs. Page (of a daughter, 31st of March); Mr. and Miss de Souza; Mrs. Anderson, servant; one Ayah; in all forty-two souls. The Sultan has permitted myself, Mr. and Miss de Souza, with three servants, to proceed to Singapore in one of his prahus, where I hope to succeed in procuring the release of the remainder of my companions from their present very uncomfortable situation. I dare not say more. Mr. de Souza and myself left on the 24th of May, and put in here dismasted on the 20th of June; since then have been detained by a fleet of piratical prahus, which arrived on the 24th, and left 9th of July. Should nothing prevent, we expect to be ready by the 15th; but am very doubtful of ever getting to Singapore, as I fear they are on the look-out for us outside.'

"This is the contents of the paper, which arriving after I had retired to rest, effectually banished sleep from my pillow. The 'uncomfortable situation,' coupled with 'I dare say no more,' gives the worst suspicions of their treatment in Borneo; whilst the chance of the party at Sirhassan falling into the hands of the pirates is extremely shocking. I instantly, on the receipt of the letter, sent to the Rajah to request that he would despatch a boat for Sirhassan, with a person competent to treat with the pirates; and on the morning of the 3d I succeeded in despatching a boat to Songi, in the Sadong, to get some of the Datu Pangerans' people, who are Illanuns; but up to this time they have not returned. I can only hope these poor people at Sirhassan will be wise enough to stay there, instead of risking a capture by the pirates. Should the Royalist return shortly, and have obtained the crew, we may fight our way to that place and release the party, who, I have little doubt, are still detained there. If the Royalist is long away, and the captain goes in search of the missing boat's crew, we may yet have the Illanuns from Sadong here in time to despatch. As for myself, I am tied, and have not the means at present of locomotion; my situation is an anxious one. The Swift must have been liable to fall in with this great force of pirates on her way to Singapore, and will be again liable on her return. The doubt and uncertainty about the poor fellows in Borneo and Sirhassan, and the wretched condition of my own affairs, all cause unpleasant reflections to my mind; yet I yield not, but will fight it out.

"I have just brought up my history to the present time; and, like a log on the water, must wait for events to develop themselves.

"*7th.*— A report arrived this morning, that the Sirhassan party sailed for Singapore on the 3d of the moon; and as Mr. Gill says they would be ready for sea about the 15th of last month, I consider it likely to be true. I trust they may escape the pirates, and safely reach their destination."

CHAPTER XI.

Return of the Royalist from Borneo Proper, with intelligence of the sufferers from the wreck of the Sultana. Effect of the arrival of the Diana on the negotiations for their release. Outrage and oppression of Macota. Fate of the Sultana and her crew. Mr. Brooke made Rajah of Sarāwak. Liberation of rebel prisoners. State of Dyak tribes. Court of justice opened. Dyak burials, and respect for the dead. Malay cunning and treachery.

WHILE waiting events, Mr. Brooke amused himself by writing down such accounts of the interior as he was enabled to collect, from time to time, from the natives visiting Sarāwak; as well as a brief description of the constitution and government, as enacted in Borneo Proper. But as my object now is to trace the progress of my friend up to the time when he embarked on board the Dido, I shall refer to these matters hereafter.

" *Tuesday, August* 17*th,* 1841.—Three weeks the Royalist has now been absent, and I begin, in spite of my determination to the contrary, to be somewhat uneasy about her. Suspense is certainly more difficult to bear than misfortune, for the certainty of an event arouses within us some of our best feelings to resist it; but suspense lets loose our imagination, and gives rise to that sickening feeling of 'hope deferred,' so truly characterised in the Scriptures.

"18*th*.—The Royalist arrived near Sarāwak, having come into the river on the 16th, and in one tide from the Morotaba entrance as far as the Paduman[1] rocks. They reported that they had not effected the release of the prisoners, were very rudely treated, the boat detained at a fort near the entrance of the Borneo river, all communication denied with the Europeans, a letter for them seized from the native crew, and provisions and water refused. In addition to this, a letter from the Sultan, addressed to me, stated to the effect, that the crew of the Sultana having entered into a treaty with him, the merchant and mate (Messrs. de Souza and Gill) had gone to Singapore to fulfil that agreement. The captain having a wife in the family-way, preferred staying in Borneo, as the vessel was a small one; and therefore the Sultan did not grant my request on this occasion; and further, that having an agreement, he did not wish to be deceived regarding it. This was a falsehood from beginning to end, as will be clear by comparing it with Mr. Gill's statement, though I fear the poor men have been rash enough to enter into some arrangement to ransom themselves."

[1] Now called Samarang.

On the 19th August the Swift arrived; but the journal was laid by until the 24th October; when it thus recommences:—

"I may now continue my narrative of events which have happened since I last used my pen, together with such fresh details of my present intentions, and such additional knowledge, as has been acquired. After the arrival of the Swift, I still adhered to my former resolution of waiting patiently for a settlement. I made several strong remonstrances, and urged for an answer to a letter I had addressed to Muda Hassim, in which was recapitulated our entire negotiation. This letter was acknowledged to be perfectly true and correct; and the Rajah, in the conference which followed, again pledged himself to give me the country; saying he always intended to do so, but was involved in difficulties of the nature of which I could not be aware. Thus so far things went well, and there appeared, indeed, a frankness in his manner which had formerly pleased me, but had long been in abeyance.

"On the return of the Royalist from Borneo, I had assured them that a government vessel would be sent to demand the captives; but, taking this assurance for a mere boast, they paid little attention to it, and were therefore excessively frightened when, a week after the Swift, the Diana steamer entered the river. I had the pleasure of calming their fears, and was too generous to push matters to a settlement during the two days the steamer remained.

"Muda Hassim now expressed himself desirous of sending some Pangerans to Borneo, and I wished him likewise to do so on account of the reflective power of the steamer, which, in that case, would have shone upon him. With his usual delay, however, he failed to be ready, and these Pangerans did not quit the river for two days afterwards, when they proceeded in a native prahu. I accompanied the steamer to the mouth of the river; and wishing them success, pulled back to the capital of Sarāwak.

"*Oct. 30th.*—The Swift was slowly laden with antimony-ore, worked by the Chinese; and I gradually robbed the Royalist of furniture for my house on shore. But I had no intention of allowing either vessel to sail until the time arrived which I had fixed on for the final adjustment of my affairs. By degrees, however, I learned many of the difficulties of poor Muda Hassim's situation, and much of the weakness of his character. The dissensions in Borneo, the intrigues of Macota, the rapacity of his own people and their total want of fidelity, the bribes from the Sultan of Sambas, the false representations of numerous Borneo Pangerans who asserted the immense profit to be derived from the country, the dilatory movements of the Chinese, some doubts of my good faith, and, above all, the natural tenacity of power,—all conspired to involve the Rajah in the utmost perplexity, and would, but for counterbalancing circumstances, have turned the scale against me. Muda Hassim knew Macota to be false and in league with the Sultan of Sambas; and he felt that he had no power, and that if he broke with me, it would be extremely difficult to support himself against the former rebels. He was fond of me, and trusted me more than he trusted any one else; and pecuniary considerations had no doubt some weight; for with all Macota's promises he could not get sufficient ore to repay one quarter of his debt to me. However, all these conflicting considerations, instead of inducing Muda Hassim to take one course, only served to encourage his dilatory temper, and although puzzled, ashamed, and fearful, he could not decide.

"At this period a robbery was committed up the river by some of Macota's followers on a Chinese hadji, a converted Mahomedan. They beat the old man, threw him into the water, and robbed him of a tael of gold. The beating and attempt at drowning were certain; for the Chinese hadji was so ill for several days under my care, that he was in considerable danger. He complained to me loudly of Macota; and from other sources I gained a pretty accurate account of that gentleman's proceedings. By threats, by intrigue, by falsehood, and even by violence, he had prevented or driven all persons from daring to visit or come near me whether aboard or ashore. He was taxing the poor Dyaks, harassing the Siniawans, leagued with the Borneo Pangerans to plunder and get all he possibly could. Every Dyak community was watched by his followers, and a spear raised opposite the chief's house, to intimate that no person was to trade or barter except the Pangeran. The mode of plunder is thus perpetrated. Rice, clothes, gongs, and other articles are sent to a tribe at a fixed price, which the Dyaks dare not refuse, for it is at the risk of losing their children! The prices thus demanded by Macota were as follows: one gantong of rice for thirty birds-nests. Twenty-four gantongs here is equal to a pecul of rice—a pecul of rice costs one dollar and a half; whereas thirty birds-nests weigh one catty, and are valued at two rupees, so that the twenty-fourth part of one and a half dollars is sold for two rupees. Was it surprising that these people were poor and wretched? My astonishment was, that they continued to labour, and indeed nothing but their being a surprisingly industrious race can account for it; and they are only enabled to live at all by secreting a portion of their food. Yet war and bad government, or rather no government, has had the effect of driving more than half the Dyak tribes beyond the limits of Sarāwak.

"The rapacity of these Malays is as unbounded as it is short-sighted; for one would think that the slightest degree of common sense would induce some of the chiefs to allow no one to plunder except themselves. But this is so far from being the case, that when their demand has been enforced, dozens of inferior wretches extort and plunder in turn, each according to his ability; and though the Dyak is not wanting in obstinacy, he can seldom withstand these robberies; for each levy is made in the name of the Rajah, or some principal Pangeran; and the threat of bringing the powerful tribe of Sakarrans or Sarebus to deprive them of their heads, and wives and families, generally reduces them to obedience. Whilst on this subject, I may as well mention a fact that came later to my knowledge, when several of the Dyak chiefs, and one of particular intelligence, Si Meta by name, assured me that each family paid direct revenue from thirty to fifty pasus (tubs) of padi, besides all the other produces, which are extorted at mere nominal prices.

".To return to my relation, the Chinese hadji recovered, and I determined to punish the aggressors; for which purpose I seized an Illanun said to be concerned, but who was innocent. In the mean time the steamer returned from Borneo, and once more put in here for wood and water. She brought Captain and Mrs. Page, Mr. Young, the second officer, and all the rest of the crew, save only a few who had landed at the north part of Borneo, and there been seized and sold as slaves, and brought afterwards as slaves to Borneo Proper.

As the shipwreck and detention is curious, I may here relate it as nearly as I can.

"The Sultana, a fine ship of 700 tons, the day previous to being struck by lightning, found the French frigate Magicienne aground and deserted on the Bombay-shoal; Captain Page boarded her, and discovered every thing as it had been left by the crew—provisions, water, &c. in abundance! The day after, the Sultana met with a worse fate, being struck, and the cotton in the hold, fore and aft, fired by the electric fluid. They had scarcely time to hoist out the boat when the flames burst forth, and they quitted her very short of provisions, and saving only some money and jewels. Captain Page bore up for the wreck of the French frigate, intending to refit his long-boat aboard her, and take provisions and arms to last them to Singapore; but on making her there was so great a wash of the sea on the lee part of the reef, that it was totally impossible to reach the Magicienne. Under these unfortunate circumstances they bore up once more, still intending to prosecute the voyage to Singapore, and made the land to the southward of Palawan; and being then short of water and provisions, landed on a small islet off Balabac, or Balambangan. Here they procured a few shell-fish and some very bad water; but seeing some natives in prahus on a neighbouring islet, and being unarmed and apprehensive, they lighted large fires in the evening to mislead these people, and, as night advanced, silently put to sea, and made the best of their way along the coast. With a heavy sea, and often high wind, they reached as far as Labuan, off the entrance of the Borneo river; and here, being in the utmost want, and reduced to an allowance of half a biscuit and a cup of water per day, they were forced to put into Borneo Proper, not without hopes of being well used, and enabled to buy provisions and stores sufficient to carry them to Singapore or Sambas. I have omitted to mention that, on making the land the first time, they parted from the cutter, in consequence of the tow-rope breaking in the night; but as they were then within sight of Borneo, and the wind fair, there was no doubt of its making the land somewhere. This, indeed, it did at Malludu Bay, where the native crew were seized and sold as slaves.

"The arrival of Captain Page in his long-boat caused, as may well be imagined, considerable sensation in the campong; and they reached the Sultan's house, thinking it the best place to seek shelter and protection. In this, however, they were soon undeceived; for neither the one nor the other was granted; but a message sent that they must deliver up all their property into the Sultan's hands, as otherwise he was afraid they would be plundered by his people. Accordingly, having possessed himself of their money, some jewels, their boat, &c., he gave them a miserable shed to live in. Here they passed the time, and were gradually robbed of every thing they had in the world, even to the baby-linen which Mrs. Page had prepared for an expected infant. Sometimes, indeed, when Captain Page refused to yield to the Sultan's demands, their provisions were stopped till they could no longer hold out; and in this way they were compelled to sign bonds for considerable sums, with the understanding that till procured and paid they should be detained.

"In this sad situation Mrs. Page was confined of a daughter on the 31st March; and this miserable life continued from the 4th of January, 1841, to August of the same year. Their first ray of hope was the Royalist coming to fetch them: the steamer followed, and they were released.

"After a stay of two or three days, the steamer once more sailed; though I would fain have persuaded Captain Congleton to search for the piratical fleet, of which I had excellent information; but he considered himself not authorised, or, in other words, he declined the responsibility.

"As there was a chance that Mr. Gill and the de Souzas were either at Sirhassan or Tambelan, the steamer decided to touch at the latter place; and a native chuliah (brig) was directed to call at the former. I afterwards learned that the pirates were then at Sirhassan; but as the brig knew nothing about Sirhassan, it is probable she never went there. In the evening the Diana sailed;

and I reached Sarāwak about two o'clock in the morning.

"I now return to my concerns. The Chinese hadji, whom I had protected, continued to reside with my servants, till one evening we were alarmed at an attempt to poison my interpreter, a native of the name of Mia. Arsenic had certainly been put into his rice; but as the servants endeavoured to point suspicion on this hadji, and as I learned, at the same time, that they did not agree with the old man, I cleared him in my own mind, and rather leant to the opinion of Mia having placed the arsenic in the plate himself for the express purpose of accusing the hadji. Connecting this event with all Macota's former intrigues, I determined to bring matters to a crisis, and test at once the strength of the respective parties. Accordingly, after complaining of the matter previously mentioned to the Rajah, I landed a party of men, fully armed, and loaded the ship's guns with grape and canister; after which I once more proceeded to Muda Hassim, and whilst I protested my kindness towards him, exposed Macota's machinations and crimes, his oppression and his deceit, and threatened him with an attack, as neither Muda Hassim nor myself were safe whilst he continued practising these arts. Muda Hassim was frightened; but how Macota felt I cannot say, as he never moved out of his house, and it was long afterwards before he was seen. From my knowledge, however, of his temperament, I can well conceive that he was reduced to a pitiable state of terror. The Siniawans took my part directly; and their chiefs came to me to say that 200 men were all ready whenever I pleased to call for them. The Chinese and the rest of the inhabitants took no side; and Macota did not get a single follower besides his immediate slaves, perhaps about twenty in number. After this demonstration, affairs proceeded cheerily to a conclusion. The Rajah was active in settling; the agreement was drawn out, sealed, and signed; guns fired, flags waved; and on the 24th September, 1841, I became the governor of Sarawak, with the fullest powers."

Being now regularly established in his government, Mr. Brooke, with his usual activity and circumspection, applied himself to the discharge of the onerous duties it imposed upon him; and his first acts were such as equally displayed his wisdom, firmness, and humanity. His journal runs thus:

"*Nov. 3d.*—I have a country; but, oh, how beset with difficulties, how ravaged by war, torn by dissensions, and ruined by duplicity, weakness, and intrigue! Macota's underhand dealings, after the conclusion of my agreement with Muda Hassim had been ratified, soon brought letters from his Sambas friends, *i. e.* one from the Sultan, one from the Tumangong, and one from another Pangeran—an immense effort of conspiracy and correspondence! Of these letters the Sultan's alone was curious; for the rest only dealt in professions of devoted attachment to the person and interests of Muda Hassim. But the Sultan, for want of some better plea, made use of the following singular specimen of reasoning, viz. that the Chinese Kunsi were indebted to him a sum of money which they had agreed to pay him in antimony-ore; the agreement was not to pay him in gold, or money, or other commodity—only in antimony-ore; therefore he wanted antimony-ore. To this it was properly replied, that an arrangement had been made with me, and that the Chinese could not agree to give antimony-ore without his (Muda Hassim's) consent.

" My first object, on holding the reins of government, was to release the unfortunate women confined for a whole year by the Rajah. This, indeed, was not only necessary to inspire confidence in my just intentions, but was dictated by humanity. I found Muda Hassim not averse to take the measure *now* that he had really resolved to adhere to my advice; and consequently I had the sincere satisfaction, within a few days, of liberating upwards of a hundred females and young children, and of restoring them to their husbands and fathers; this act being somewhat alloyed by Muda Hassim detaining twelve females, and among them *two wives*. I urged as strongly as I could, but without success, the advisability of releasing the whole; and I was obliged at last to content myself with the mass, and yield the few whom I could only have got *by force,* or the utter abrogation of our infant treaty. When I pressed the affair, it was answered, that except for me, *none* would have regained their liberty; and that the release was an act of great kindness and unexampled confidence towards me; that what had been done was perfectly accordant with their customs; and that the women detained were for the Rajah's brothers—so far, indeed, from being intended as an injury to the women, it was a great honour and advantage. I explained the circumstances to the Patingi and Tumangong, and they acquiesced in the decision—allowing the custom—and said they had gained so much more than they had ever hoped for, that they could submit to the rest.

"The next step was to assemble the Siniawans, who, since the close of the war, would run away, and whom it was found impossible to keep here. Some had retired to Sambas; some (amongst them Patingi Ali) had gone to Sariki; and others had built a village on the borders of the Sambas territory. The whole aim and object of Macota's government was to get these people back; and those who were already here were constantly plying backwards and forwards to recall their companions; but as soon as they succeeded in getting one family, another absconded. Confidence alone could restore them; and I therefore intimated to the Patingi and Tumangong that there was no occasion for their seeking them; that I by no means desired their return; and that any of their people who wished to leave the country were at liberty to do so whenever they felt inclined. This had the desired effect, in a short time, of bringing back the fugitives from Pankalon Nibong; and they continued daily to arrive from Sambas.

"My next measure was to inquire into the state of the Dyaks, to gain their confidence, and, as much as it was within my power, prevent the oppressions of the Malays. It was necessary, likewise, to fix a rate of tax to be levied yearly; and the prospect seemed fair, as the chief people of the following tribes had come in, and agreed that such a tax on rice, amounting to sixteen gantongs, would be required from each man, and that for the rest they would be obliged to labour; that they could trade at pleasure; that no man could demand any thing from them; that their wives and children were safe; and that, in case any trouble arose, they were to let me know, and I would myself come to their assistance. The tribes were Lundu, Sarambo, Bombak, Paninjow, and Sow. The only other tribe on the right-hand river were the Singè, a powerful and stiff-necked people, with good reason to be shy; but when once they are treated justly, their strength will be advantageous, and give them confidence to resist oppression.

"The story told me by the three heads of the Sow Dyaks brought tears into my eyes, as they each in turn related their grievances. One of them, a remarkably intelligent person, addressed me nearly in the following terms:—' From former times we have been the subjects of the Patek of Borneo. The Borneons are the elder brothers, we the younger; and the custom of old was, that we should pay revenue and find protection. But they forgot what was right, and departed from the custom, and robbed the Dyaks and oppressed them. We have done no wrong: we listened to the commands of the Patingi who was put over us by the Patek. If he did wrong, he should be punished; but we have suffered because we obeyed the commands of the officer legally appointed. You might, sir, a few years ago, have sought in this river, and not have found a happier tribe than ours. Our children were collected; we had rice in plenty, and fruit-trees; our hogs and fowls were in abundance; we could afford to give what was demanded of us, and yet live happily. Now we have nothing left. The Sadong people and the Sakarran Dyaks attacked us: they burnt our houses, destroyed our property, cut down our fruit-trees, killed many of our people, and led away our wives and young children into slavery. We could build another house; we could plant fruit-trees and cultivate rice; but where can we find wives? Can we forget our young children? We have asked the

Patek to restore them; we have asked Pangeran Macota to restore them: they have told us they would, but have not; we cannot trust them; their words are fair, but in their hearts they do not mean to help us. We have now no one to trust but you—will you help us? Will you restore our wives and children? If we get our families, you will never repent it: you will find us true.'

"What could I answer? I could not deceive them, as I knew not how to obtain their object; I therefore told them I feared it was impossible; but I would try, and they themselves should go and try at the same time. Poor unhappy people, who suffer for the crimes of others! God knows, I will aid you to the utmost of my power.

"*Nov. 5th.*—To-day the greatest, and I hope the final, struggle of the opposing faction was developed by the arrival of a brig from Sambas, with two of the Sultan's sons on board—Macota in high spirits, and my party looking rather desponding; and, in fact, I cannot trust them against Sambas. For good or for bad, for success or for failure, for life or for death, I will act justly, and preserve the high hand over Macota.

"After the steps I have mentioned, I determined to open a court for the administration of justice, wherein I should preside, together with such of the Rajah's brothers as liked to assist me. As for a jury, or any machinery of form or law, it was rejected, because it must be inefficient, if not corrupt; and the only object I aimed at was, keeping witnesses out of ear-shot of each other, hearing the evidence, deciding as appeared best, and in future punishing. This simple plan ensured substantial redress; and it gave all the people confidence in me, and a notion of what was right.

"The first case was a follower of the Rajah's, of the name of Sunudeen; and a greater villain could not exist, either in this or any other land. It was as follows: A man from Samarahan, named Bujong, had undertaken to marry his daughter to a Sarāwak man called Abdullah; but Abdullah proving a dissolute character, and greatly in debt, Bujong broke off the engagement before the proper authorities, and returned the presents which Abdullah, according to custom, had made. Abdullah, it appeared, was indebted a small sum to Matassim (Mahommed Orsin), and, between Sunudeen and Matassim, they resolved to lay the debt on Bujong's shoulders; in other words, to plunder Bujong under false pretences. Accordingly, Sunudeen, with his comrade, went to Samarahan; and, in his capacity of follower of the Rajah, demanded the debt due by Abdullah to Matassim. Bujong having no money, Sunudeen proceeded and seized his nephew, a boy, and a slave-man belonging to him, as *his slaves*. Poor Bujong resisted, and recovered his nephew, but yielded his slave; he appealed, however, to the Orang Kaya de Gadong's sons, and they failing, a Nakodah stated the case secretly to me. I investigated it, and ordered the return of the slave in my presence, which was obeyed. This may give an idea of the state of the country, and the power of every petty scoundrel hanging about the Rajah to rob and plunder at pleasure.

"*7th.*—I have before mentioned that the Dyaks of Sibnow bury their dead; but I always found a reluctance on their part to shew me their place of sepulture. Once, indeed, chance led me to the burial-ground of part of that tribe settled at Simunjang; but as they seemed restless to get away, I only took a hasty survey. The reason, I have lately learnt, for this is, that in their graves they deposit the golden ornaments and other property of the person deceased, amounting frequently to a considerable value in the precious metals, brass swivels, gongs, &c.

" The tribe now at Lundu were formerly settled on the Samarahan river for many years; and their burial-place there contained the ashes of the parents and grand-parents of the present chief, who, with his followers, were not long ago driven to Lundu; and their former settlement being deserted, it has been the employment of some of the rascals here to rob these graves of their contents, and to desecrate the repose of the dead. The Orang Kaya of Lundu complained to me sadly but mournfully on this account, and said that if he could not find redress from the Rajah, he must obtain it himself by taking the heads of those who had disinterred the bones of his ancestors. His whole manner convinced me that they hold the burying-places in great respect; and my advice to remove the wealth and bones to a place of security at Lundu, was rejected on the ground that they could not disturb the remains of those whom they had once deposited in the earth.

"Whilst there is so much of right feeling and manly principle in the actions of these Dyaks, the miserable race who pretend to be their superiors have no single virtue or good intention. I do not, however, mean to confound the inhabitants of Sarāwak, or the other rivers, with those of Borneo Proper. The latter are thoroughly corrupt and profligate. The former are Malays, but have their good qualities, and certainly do not possess the spirit of intrigue which seems the life, the only moving principle, of the Borneons. It may truly be said of the latter, that they would tell a lie when the truth would serve them better. They will employ duplicity and treachery on every slight occasion; defeat their own purpose by their meanness, and yet continue in the same crooked paths. They will conspire without any object, or one too mysterious to arrive at; and whilst they raise a cloud of doubts in the mind of the poor, their own equals look on and detect the game. Yet, after all, they gain but little individually; because so many are practising the same arts at the same time, with equal skill; and the country is so exhausted by their oppressions and rapacity, that in the end there is nothing to be got by their tricks and manœuvres. It is a strange state of society, and it is only wonderful how it can exist; but they have their reward in being poor and ill-provided, though living in the midst of a marvellously fertile and luxurious country.

"*December 31st.*—The last day of the year, in which I must bring up the arrears of my account.

"The Sambas brig left only yesterday, after exhausting every effort of intrigue, and every artifice which Malays can invent, to compass their ends.

"With the Sambas brig came Seriff Hussein, a relation of the Sultan of Pontiana, and half Arab, half Bugis, by descent. He came with the avowed purpose of entering into the most friendly communication with me, and residing here, provided I gave him any encouragement. His real motive (if he has one) not being obvious, I, in the mean time, treated him with all kindness; and he is an intelligent and pleasing person, and, moreover, connected with the Siniawans, who have a good opinion of him.

CHAPTER XII.

Reflections on the new year. The plundered village, and other wrongs. Means for their suppression. The new government proceeds to act. The constitution. Preparation for an expedition against the Sea Dyaks. Form of a treaty. Wreck of the Viscount Melbourne. Administration of justice. Difficulties and dangers. Dyak troubles. Views and arrangements of the Chinese. Judicial forms. Wrongs and sufferings of the Lundus.

"*Jan. 1st*, 1842.—The past year is in the bosom of eternity, into which bourne we are all hurrying. Here we have no merry-making, no reunion of families, no bright fires or merry games, to mark the advent of 1842; but we have genial weather, and are not pinched by cold or frost. This is a year which to me must be eventful; for at its close I shall be able to judge whether I can maintain myself against all the circumstances and difficulties which beset me, or whether I must retreat, broken in fortune, to some retirement in my native land. I look with calmness on the alternative; and God knows no selfish motives weigh on me; and if I fail, my chief regret will be for the natives of this unhappy country. Let the year roll on, let the months pass; and whatever they bring—whether it be life or death, fortune or poverty—I am prepared; and in the deep solitude of my present existence, I can safely say that I believe I could bear misfortune better than prosperity. In this, probably, I am not singular; for there is something in prosperity which, if it does not make us worse, makes us more foolish and more worldly; which decks passing time with wreaths of gay flowers, and gilds the things of this life with tinsel hopes and wishes, to the exclusion of the pure gold of reflection for the life to come. What are all these gewgaws, these artificial flowers, these momentary joys, these pleasures of the sense, before the war of time?—Nothing! And yet, if exertion can benefit our race, or even our own country; if the sum of human misery can be alleviated; if these suffering people can be raised in the scale of civilisation and happiness,—it is a cause in which I could suffer, it is a cause in which I *have* suffered and *do suffer:* hemmed in, beset, anxious, perplexed, and the good intent marred by false agents, surrounded by weakness, treachery, falsehood, and folly, is suffering enough; and to feel myself on the threshold of success, and only withheld by the want of adequate means, increases this suffering. Hail, however, 1842! Come good, come ill, still hail! and many as are the light hearts which have already greeted thee, mine will be more ready to bow to the decrees of Providence which thy twelve months will develop.

"*Jan. 3d.*—I have mentioned that the Sanpro

had been attacked from Sadong; and I now learn that, at the time, the men were out of the village, and thus the women and children alone suffered; twenty-two have been carried away into slavery. The village was burnt, after being plundered; and the unfortunate people have since been living in the jungle, with only such food as they could get there. The head of the tribe and about six of his followers came down the river on a raft to ask assistance from me, and I had the story from them. They were relieved as far as my means admitted, and returned far happier than they came. The very same day arrived news that six men of the Sows were cut off by a wandering party of the Sakarrans.

"This leads me naturally to consider the means by which these atrocities may be prevented. I propose first to send letters to Seriff Sahib of Sadong, Seriff Muller of Sakarran, and Seriff Jaffer of Singè, stating that I wish to be on good terms with my neighbours, but am determined to attack any place which sends Dyaks to rob in my country; and that I call on them to restrain their subjects from making incursions here. In case this warning is neglected, I must strike one blow suddenly, as a further warning; and keep a good look-out at sea to destroy any Dyak fleet that may be prowling outside. A good-sized boat, with a six-pounder and a swivel or two, will effect the latter object; backed by two or four light fast-pulling boats, with musketry, which, when the Dyak prahus fly, may keep pace with them and thin their pullers, till the heavier boat can come up. To carry one of their campongs, I must have twenty-five Europeans, and from some thirty to fifty Bugis, who, coming from Singapore, may proceed at once to Sadong, or rather, the campong Tangi. Seriff Sahib is a great freebooter, and despatches his retainers to attack the weak tribes here, for the sake of the slaves; calculating on the Rajah's presumed weakness, that he can do so with impunity: he may find himself mistaken.

"Seriff Muller is a brother of Seriff Sahib, and lives at Sakarran, which powerful Dyak tribe are always willing to be sent by either brother on a forage for heads and slaves. It is certain, however, that they could never come from the Sadong side without Seriff Sahib's permission; and on the late attack on Sanpro they were accompanied by a party of Malays.

"Seriff Jaffer is by no means mixed up with these brothers, and there is no love lost between them; nor would he, I think, do any thing to annoy me. This is the foreign policy.

"The domestic policy is as disturbed as the foreign. The Rajah weak; Macota intriguing; and my ministers—viz. the Patingi (Abong Mia), the Bandar, and Tumangong—all false and foolish. Macota's men with me, however, are the Siniawans.

"*Jan. 6th.*—The Sambas brig returned, having been baffled and beat about, and nearly lost at sea, unable to weather Tanjong Datu. The crew say she was one hour under water. She now remains here to wait the change of the monsoon, and her intriguing Pangerans return by land.

"*8th.*—Seriff Hussein returned from Sambas, having been nearly stabbed whilst there. The assassins, it was understood, were here, and I endeavoured to apprehend them; but having heard of the Seriff's arrival, they made off.

"*10th.*—This day the first laws and regulations are to be promulgated in Sarāwak; and as the event is a rare one, I here inscribe a copy for the benefit of future legislators; observing, that there is an absolute necessity for mildness and patience, and that an opposite course would raise such a host of enemies as to crush every good seed; for, as it is, the gentlest course of justice brings down much odium, and arouses intense dislike amongst a people who have had no law but their own vile intrigues to guide or control them.

"Two cases have lately come to notice, which will serve as examples of their singular crimes.

"One poor man owed another sixteen reals, and the debtor was away trading for a few days, when the creditor sold the daughter (a free woman) for thirty reals, to a person of influence.

"The second case, a respectable man, or a respectably born man, owed a Pangeran fifty peculs of ore, and proposed to make over to him, in payment, a slave woman and her four children. The woman *had been* a slave of his grandfather's, but was adopted as his daughter, and enfranchised publicly; yet by intimidation, they were nearly getting her and her offspring. Here the Pangerans and Nakodahs bully a man into silence and acquiescence; and they dare not, as yet, bring their complaints to me. But I hear these things, call the parties together, and often prevent the commission of a premeditated crime; by which means I save myself from the odium of punishing.

"There is great difficulty in acting at once with temper and firmness, and to appear the benefactor rather than the tyrant. It is, indeed, an arduous and troublesome task; but *I think I see a ray of light to encourage me.*

"Here are the regulations, which I had printed at Singapore in the Malayan language:—

"'James Brooke, esquire, governor (rajah) of the country of Sarāwak, makes known to all men the following regulations:—

"'1st. That murder, robbery, and other heinous crimes will be punished according to the ondong-ondong (*i. e.* the written law of Borneo); and no person committing such offences will escape, if, after fair inquiry, he be proved guilty.

"'2d. In order to ensure the good of the country, all men, whether Malays, Chinese, or

Dyaks, are permitted to trade or labour according to their pleasure, and to enjoy their gains.

"'3d. All roads will be open, that the inhabitants at large may seek profit both by sea or by land; and all boats coming from others are free to enter the river and depart, without let or hindrance.

"'4th. Trade, in all its branches, will be free, with the exception of antimony-ore, which the governor holds in his own hands, but which no person is forced to work, and which will be paid for at a proper price when obtained. The people are encouraged to trade and labour, and to enjoy the profits which are to be made by fair and honest dealing.

"'5th. It is ordered, that no person going amongst the Dyaks shall disturb them, or gain their goods under false pretences. It must be clearly explained to the different Dyak tribes, that the revenue will be collected by the three Datus, bearing the seal of the governor; and (except this yearly demand from the government) they are to give nothing to any other person; nor are they obliged to sell their goods except they please, and at their own prices.

"'6th. The governor will shortly inquire into the revenue, and fix it at a proper rate; so that every one may know certainly how much he has to contribute yearly to support the government.

"'7th. It will be necessary, likewise, to settle

the weights, measures, and money current in the country, and to introduce doits, that the poor may purchase food cheaply.

"'8th. The governor issues these commands, and will enforce obedience to them; and whilst he gives all protection and assistance to the persons who act rightly, he will not fail to punish those who seek to disturb the public peace or commit crimes; and he warns all such persons to seek their safety, and find some other country where they may be permitted to break the laws of God and man.'

"*Jan.* 11*th.*—I have frequently said that all law and custom have been long banished from this country; but I may here retrace the customs which once obtained, the best of which I wish to restore.

"The inhabitants were all considered the property of the Sultan—serfs rather than slaves—and were divided into four classes. Imprimis, the Dyaks (the aborigines); the Bruni, or people of the soil, probably the descendants of the first Malay emigrants; the Awang-Awang, the meaning of which I am ignorant of; and the Hamba Rajah, or rajah's slaves. There is every reason to believe the Dyaks are an aboriginal people; but between the Bruni and Awang-Awang it is difficult to decide the priority. The Hamba Rajah speaks for itself.

"These three distinctions have been long confounded by intermarriage; and the names rather than the reality are retained. The governors of the country are the Patingi, a Bandar, and a Tumangong, who are appointed from Borneo. Each of the classes was formerly ruled by its particular officer, and the Dyaks were appropriated likewise among them; the Patingi holding the tribes on the right-hand river, the Bandar to the left, and the Tumangong on the sea-coast. The annual revenue paid to Borneo was 300 reals; but they were subject to extra demands, and to the extortions of the powerful chiefs.

"The government of the Dyaks I have already detailed; and though we might hope that in a more settled state of things they would have been more secure from foreign pillage, yet they were annually deprived of the proceeds of their labour, debarred from trade, and deprived of every motive to encourage industry. The character of their rulers for humanity alone fixed the measure of their suffering, and bad was the best; but it seems to be a maxim amongst all classes of Malays, that force alone can keep the Dyaks in proper subjection; which is so far true, that force alone, in the hopelessness of resistance, could induce a wild people to part with the food on which they depend for subsistence. At a distance I have heard of and pitied the sufferings of the negroes and the races of New Holland—yet it was the cold feeling dictated by reason and humanity; but now, having witnessed the miseries of a race superior to either, the feeling glows with the fervour of personal commiseration : so true is it that visible misery will raise us to exertion, which the picture, however powerfully delineated, can never produce. The thousands daily knelled out of the world, who lie in gorgeous sepulchres, or rot unburied on the surface of the earth, excite no emotion compared to that conjured up by the meanest dead at our feet. We read of tens of thousands killed and wounded in battle, and the glory of their deeds, or the sense of their defeat, attracts our sympathy; but if a single mangled warrior, ghastly with wounds and writhing with pain, solicited our aid, we should deplore his fate with tenfold emotion, and curse the strife which led to such a result. Among the thousands starving for want of food we trouble not ourselves to seek one ; but if the object is presented before our eyes, how certain a compassion is aroused! To assist is a duty; but in the performance of this duty, to be gentle and feeling is godlike; and probably, between individuals, there is no greater distinction than in this tender sympathy towards distress. Poor, poor Dyaks! exposed to starvation, slavery, death! you may well raise the warmest feelings of compassion— enthusiasm awakes at witnessing your sufferings! To save men from death has its merit; but to alleviate suffering, to ameliorate all the ills of slavery, to protect these tribes from pillage and yearly scarcity, is far nobler; and if, in the endeavour to do so, one poor life is sacrificed, how little is it in the vast amount of human existence!

"18th.—A Chinese boat with four men was chased into the river by four Dyak prahus, and escaped with difficulty. On the intelligence reaching me, I, with some trouble, mustered three canoes, and we proceeded down, about one o'clock in the morning, in search of the enemy. After rowing in the dark for some hours, we discovered a light gliding up the river, and gave chase, but did not succeed; and at daybreak returned, wet and tired, without seeing any thing more, when we learnt that the chase was a Sarāwak boat, which, mistaking us for Dyaks, as we did them, pulled with all speed home, and gave the alarm of being nearly captured.

"In the evening I ordered a fine boat to be prepared for the war with Sarebus and Sakarran, which appears to me inevitable; as it is impossible, laying all motives of humanity aside, to allow these piratical tribes to continue their depredations, which are inconsistent with safety, and a bar to all trade along the coast. Eighty prahus of Sarebus and Sakarran are reported to be ready, and waiting for further reinforcements before putting to sea.

"19th. — Information of three more of my Dyaks being cut off in the interior by the predatory tribes!

"20th.—Opened the subject of restoring the old Patingi, Bandar, and Tumangong, and found Muda Hassim quite willing, but wishing to wait till he hears from Borneo; at the same time telling me that I might employ them in their respective situations. This matter I consider, therefore, settled; and as these men are natives, and have the command of all the common people, and are, moreover, willing to serve under me, I conceive it a great advance in my government. Since my return here they have proved themselves faithful and ready; but though true in adversity, will they continue equally so in prosperity? I hope the best from them, especially as their circumstances will be easy; and I will endeavour to pay them as much as I can. Pay well, and men may be trusted. Either way, it is a great advance; for every change will not occur immediately; and, in the mean time, I shall be strengthened by incomers, especially Chinese, so that the parties may be balanced, and each look to me as the link which holds them together. The government must be a patchwork between good and evil, abolishing only so much of the latter as is consistent with safety. But never must I appear in the light of a reformer, political or religious; for to the introduction of new customs, apparently trivial, and the institution of new forms, however beneficial, the disgust of the semi-barbarous races may be traced. People settled like myself too often try to create a Utopia, and end with a general confusion. The feeling of the native which binds him to his chief is destroyed, and no other principle is substituted in its stead; and as the human mind more easily learns ill than good, they pick up the vices of their governors without their virtues, and their own good qualities disappear, the bad of both races remaining without the good of either.

"We are in active preparation to fit out a fleet to meet the piratical Dyaks. The Rajah has a fine prahu, which I have taken in hand to repair, and I have purchased a second; and the two, with three or four small canoes, will be able to cope with a hundred or a hundred and fifty Dyak boats. The largest of these boats is worth a description. Fifty-six feet in length and eight in breadth; built with a great sheer, so as to raise the bow and stern out of the water, and pulling thirty paddles, she is a dangerous customer when mounting four swivels and carrying a crew of twenty men with small arms. She is called the 'Snake,' or 'Ular.' The second boat, somewhat shorter and less fast, is named the 'Dragon;' her complement of paddles twenty, and her fighting-men twenty, make one hundred and forty in two boats. The long canoes carry fifteen men each, which will bring the force up to one hundred and eighty-five; and one boat of the Rajah's will complete two hundred men, of whom nearly one hundred are armed with muskets.

"To shew the system of these people, I may

mention, that one of the principal men proposed to me to send to Sakarran and Sarebus, and intimate that I was about to attack Siquong (a large interior tribe), and invite them to assist. 'They will all come,' he said : 'nothing they will like so well; and when they are up the Samarahan river, we will sally forth, attack, and destroy them at one blow.' My answer was, that I could not deceive; but if they did come, I would attack them.

" *Feb. 1st.*—Matari, or ' the Sun,' the Sakarran chief I have already mentioned, arrived with two boats, and paid me several visits. He assured me he wanted to enter into an agreement, to the effect, that neither should injure the other. To this treaty I was obliged to add the stipulation, that he was neither to pirate by sea nor by land, and not to go, under any pretence, into the interior of the country. His shrewdness and cunning were remarkably displayed. He began by inquiring, if a tribe, either Sakarran or Sarebus, pirated on my territory, what I intended to do. My answer was, ' To enter their country and lay it waste.' But he asked me again, ' You will give me, your friend, leave to steal a few heads occasionally ?' 'No,' I replied, ' you cannot take a single head ; you cannot enter the country : and if you or your countrymen do, I will have a hundred Sakarran heads for every one you take here.' He recurred to this request several times : 'just to steal one or two!' as a schoolboy would ask for apples. There is no doubt that the two tribes of Sakarran and Sarebus are greatly addicted to head-hunting, and consider the possession as indispensable. The more a man has, the greater his honour and rank; nor is there any thing without to check or ameliorate this barbarous habit; for the Malays of all classes, on this coast, take the same pride in heads as the Dyaks themselves, with the exception that they do not place them in their houses, or attach any superstitious ideas to them.

"I asked Matari what was the solemn form of agreement amongst his tribes; and he assured me the most solemn was drinking each other's blood, in which case it was considered they were brothers; but pledging the blood of fowls was another and less solemn form.

"On the 26th of January the Royalist's boat, with Captain Hart and Mr. Penfold, second mate, of the Viscount Melbourne, arrived here. The reason, it appears, of the Royalist coming was, to seek the missing crew of the Viscount Melbourne, a large ship wrecked on the Laconia shoal. The captain in the launch, with some Coolies; the first and third mates, with Colonel Campbell of the 37th, M.N.I., in a cutter; the second mate, Mr. Penfold, and the surgeon, in the second cutter; a fourth boat with twenty-five Lascars, and the jolly-boat, making in all five boats, left the vessel well provisioned, and steered in company for the coast, which they made somewhere between Borneo and Tanjong Barram. The fourth boat was missed the night they made the land; and being all at anchor, and the weather fine, it was strongly suspected that the twenty-five Lascars deserted with her.

"The other four boats proceeded a day or two, when the first cutter, with Colonel Campbell on board, went in the evening in search of water; and though the rest shewed lights all night, returned no more. They were, on the following day, attacked by a prahu, which fired into them and severely wounded one man, and succeeded in capturing the jolly-boat; but finding nothing in her, set her on fire—Lascars and all. The crew, however, was rescued, and she was abandoned; and the two remaining boats, in course of time, arrived at Singapore. The Royalist was taken up by government to seek the missing boats, and just touched here for an hour or two, the boat coming up whilst the vessel kept the sea.

"*Feb. 9th.*—Mr. Williamson returned from Sanpro, where I sent him to watch a party of natives who had gone amongst the Dyaks; the Panglima Sadome, of the tribe of Sanpro, came with him, and brought the lamentable account of the death of eight more Dyaks, cut of by the Sakarrans. It frets me dreadfully; however, on the whole I see a vast improvement, and a degree of confidence in me arising amongst the Dyaks, greater than I expected.

"14th.—I have now entered on the most difficult task, and the one most likely to cause an ultimate failure in my undertaking, but which is indispensably necessary. I mean, the administration of justice. As long as my laws are applied to the people of the country, there is no trouble; but directly *equal* justice is administered, it causes heartburn and evasion; the Rajahs and Pangerans are surrounded by a gang of followers who heretofore have robbed, plundered, and even murdered, without inquiry being made. It was enough that a follower of the Rajah was concerned, to hush up all wrongs; and any of the oppressed who were bold enough to lodge a complaint were sure to rue it. All the rascals and ruffians who follow the great men find this species of protection the best and the only reward; and as the slaves are looked upon as personal property, any punishment inflicted upon them is likewise inflicted upon their masters. I have all along foreseen these obstacles, and the necessity of at once combating them — whether successfully or not signifies little; but they must be encountered, and the result left to the Almighty.

"Equal justice is the groundwork of society; and unless it can be administered, there can be no hope of ultimate improvement. The country may have bad laws; but such laws as it has must be enforced, gently and mildly as may be towards the superiors, but strictly towards the guilty; and all crimes coming under my cognisance must meet with their punishment. These remarks are preliminary to two cases, in which the Rajah's followers have been concerned.

"The first of these was a man stealing sago, which is stored without the houses at the water's edge; he was convicted. The other occurred some time since, but has only just been traced. A party at night gutted a house, getting a booty of upwards of 200 reals; the goods have been discovered; but the three followers of the Rajah have absconded since the affair has been blown; whether to return or not is uncertain. There can be no doubt, however, that they have been sent away to keep clear of the consequences, by one of the Rajah's brothers named Abdul Khadir, who, when they were off, accused two accomplices, people of the country!

"Another most shameful mode of exaction and tyranny is practised by these Borneo people, particularly their Nakodahs. It consists in lending small sums of money to the natives (that is, Sarawak people), and demanding interest at the rate of fifty per cent per month; by this means a small sum is quickly converted into one which is quite out of the power of the poor man to pay; and he, his wife, and children, are taken to the house of the creditor to work for him, whilst the debt still accumulates, and the labour is endless. I intend to strike at this slavery in disguise, but not just yet; the suppression of robbery, the criminal department of justice, being more immediately important.

"15th.—I may, in continuation of yesterday, mention another instance in illustration of this oppressive system. Si Pata (a Siniawan), son of the Tumangong, lost in gambling to Nakodah Ursat eighteen reals, which in eighteen months has now arisen to a debt of 170 reals; but all prospect of payment of such an accumulated sum being impossible from a poor man, Nakodah Ursat consigns the debt to Pangeran Abdul Khadir, who can demand it by fair means or by foul; and if Si Pata cannot pay, make his father pay. Thus a gambling transaction is run up to ten times its original amount, and a whole family involved in distress by these iniquitous proceedings. Such things must not be; and odious as they seem to an European, and indignant as they make him, yet he must not proceed with the strong hand. Reflection, too, teaches us that vice is comparative; and in forming a judgment, we must not forget a man's education, the society in which he lives, the absence of restraint, and the force of example from childhood; so that what would be heinous in a Christian long under a settled government, is light by comparison in a Malay, who is a nominal professor of Islam, and brought up with the idea that might makes right, and has no one external cause to deter him from crime.

"*March* 12th.—On the whole getting on very well, but with many reasons for vexation, and more for anxiety. The chief of these is, whether Mr.

Bonham will come here, as I have suggested, or rather pressed. Another feature of inquietude is from the Chinese of Sipang, who certainly aim at greater power than I shall allow them, and perhaps, some day or other, it will come to a struggle.

"Petty troubles I do not reckon, though there are enow on all sides, and for the last few days I have felt as if sinking under them; but that is not my usual temperament. I now look impatiently for intelligence. Blow, fair breezes, and waft Royalist here!

"*25th.*—A period of wearing uncertainty since my last, having news neither of the Royalist nor of Mr. Bonham, and kept on the *qui vive* by a schooner or two at the entrance of the river. The plot thickens in and around; and for the sake of keeping up a register of events in something like order, I will here mention the leading features. Seriff Sahib, of Sadong, pretends to be friendly, but is treacherous in his heart, as is his brother, Seriff Muller of Sakarran. We have been quite clear of Dyaks, and our own tribes enjoying rest and peace; and one tribe from without, namely Serang, has come in and claimed my protection. The only tribe at all troublesome is the Singè, the chief of which (the Orang Kaya Parembam) is decidedly opposed to me, and swears by Macota. I am given to believe, however, that the majority of his people do not agree with him; and I shall dispossess him of his dignity, and substitute a friendly chief.

The Singè Dyaks are the most powerful and numerous in my territory, and the only ones who have not been attacked and plundered by the Sakarrans.

"At Lundu are the Sibnowan Dyaks, under the Orang Kaya Tumangong; and the Lundu Dyaks, once a flourishing tribe, now, by ill-treatment of all sorts, reduced to twenty persons. I may mention, among my other difficulties, that many, nay most, of the Dyak tribes are held as *private property:* any rascally Borneon making a present to the Sultan, gets a grant of a Dyak tribe, originally to rule, now to plunder or sell; and in this way the portion of the Sibnowans settled at Lundu are under Bandar Sumsu; but, being a resolute people, he cannot do them much wrong. This Bandar Sumsu has lately been disturbing the Lundu Dyaks in the following manner: a Sibnowan Dyak lived with the Lundu Dyaks, which gave him an opening to demand of the Lundus the sum of fifty reals (100 rupees), which was paid; but unluckily the Sibnowan died in the course of a few months, still with the Lundus, and a further sum of eighty reals, or 160 rupees, was demanded, which not being raised, the daughter of one of the head people was seized and sold for the sum of a Chinaman!

"Pangeran Macota has likewise been injuring these poor people, though I shall find it difficult to bring it home to him. His agent, Bandar Dowud (a man involved in debt), took fifteen Dyak cloths and sold them, or rather forced them to take them, at an exorbitant rate; in a month or two after, he returns and demands 200 reals over and above the large price already paid for articles worth seven or eight reals; the poor Dyaks not being able to pay, he seizes the chief's daughter (a married woman), and demands four other women in lieu of the sum. Happily for the poor Dyaks, this news came to my ears, and I sent to Lundu in haste. They had all fled, having *stolen* their two women, one from each Bandar, and carried them away. On the Patingi and Tumangong reaching Lundu, they found two of the tribe, one the Pangeran, the other the father of the girl sold to the Chinaman, after a long search in the jungle. These two men I have now with me, and wait for the Orang Kaya Tumangong before going into the case. The Pangeran is the same Dyak whose conversation I have detailed at large on my first visit to the place. He is a man of intelligence; and this tribe (if it may yet be so called) has always borne the character of being the most hospitable and generous amongst the Dyaks. I may at some future time revert to them.

"There is a rumour of war between the Sarebus and Sakarran Dyaks, in consequence of the former tribe seizing a Balow woman on the territory of the latter, and refusing to restore her. Let these two predatory tribes employ and weaken one another, and it will be well for us and all the other people of this country, and they will afterwards be the more easily brought into subjection.

"From Borneo we have news, but as uncertain as every thing else regarding the capital. A hundred vessels, it is reported, are coming to attack them; and they, in consequence, are building *a fort*. The Royalist had been there and departed.

"Pangeran Usop, it is said, was about to come here, when the arrival of the Royalist induced him to postpone his design.

"There is every reason to believe that the Chinese of Sambas, particularly Montrado, are extremely dissatisfied; and a report yesterday states that a man sent by the Sultan to demand gold had been killed by them, and that the Sultan's letter to the Kunsi, after being defiled, was publicly burned. Our own Chinese of Sipang are certainly intriguing with Sambas; and, as the Rajah well expresses it, 'their clothes-box is here, but their treasure-chest is at Sambas.'

"It is impossible to say what quantity of gold the Kunsi may get; but their pretence that they *get none* must be false, when every common Malay obtains from half to one bunkal per month.

"To counteract the chance of evil, I have intimated that the Simbock Kunsi are to come here; and on the whole, they (of Sipang) have taken it more quietly than I expected. They are not in a state for war; but they have vague notions and intentions, provided they can keep out opposition, to make this place subservient to them, as it would indeed be, provided they were allowed to strengthen themselves whilst the other parties remained stationary. But 'divide and rule' is a good motto in my case; and the Chinese have overlooked the difference between this country and Sambas. There they have numerous rivers in the vicinity of their settlements—here but one; and, the Dyak population being against them, starvation would soon reduce them to terms. The Royalist arrived about the end of March, and sailed again on the 9th April.

"I have before mentioned the difficulty of administering justice; and experience teaches me that the risk to myself, on this score, is more to be apprehended than on any other. The forms I have not much alluded to; and the following is as nearly as possible the Malay custom:—The Rajah's brothers and myself sit at one end of the long room in my house; at the sides are the Patingis and Tumangong, and other respectable people; in the centre the parties concerned; and, behind them, any body who wishes to be present. We hear both parties; question, if necessary; and decide—and from this decision there is no appeal. One only condition I insist upon; and that is, that in any intricate case, or whenever I dread confederacy, I do not allow the witnesses to hear each other. The laws of evidence, in a *free country*, prohibit any leading questions being put to witnesses: here, for the purposes of justice, it is indispensable; for the people, being ruled by fear, and apprehensive of consequences, often falter before the face of the accused, and their testimony has to be wrung from them. To decide also according to the technicalities of construction would be here ridiculous, and defeat the ends of justice. The people are rude and uncivilised; their oppressors crafty and bold, who have no hesitation about lying, and bringing others to lie for them. Oaths are a farce to them. The aggrieved are timid, vacillating, and simple, and cannot readily procure even necessary evidence; for their witnesses are afraid to speak. Under these circumstances, I look at the leading features of the case, the probability, the characters, the position of the parties, and determine according to my judgment. It is not, indeed, a very difficult task; for the disputes are generally glaring, and, when bolstered up, usually fail in their most important links; and at a touch of cross-questioning, the witnesses, resolved to tell the same story, fall into opposite ones. In one case, about a slave, three witnesses had resolved on the sex; but, questioned separately as to size and age, all disagreed. They were not prepared. One represented her a woman grown and marriageable; another, as high as my walking-stick; the third, a little child.

"I have now on hand a serious matter, of robbery to a large extent, and three of the Rajah's followers are implicated. Would it were over and well!—but done it must be. How little can those at a distance know my difficulties—alone, unaided, the unceasing attention by day, the anxiety and sleeplessness by night, the mountain of doubt upon mountain piled, and the uncertainty of necessary support or assistance!

"The Pangeran of the Lundu Dyaks lived with me three weeks, and I was able to do him substantial justice; and hope for the future that his life, and that of the remnant of his tribe, may be rendered more endurable.

"His residence with me was doubly advantageous, as it enabled me to ascertain his character, and him to see something of our habits and manners. The impression on my part was highly favourable; for I found him a quiet, intelligent man, and a keen observer; and I believe the impression he received was equally favourable. The *poetry* of the Dyak expressions is remarkable; and, like most wild people, they seem to delight in oratory, and to be a good deal swayed by it. For hours I have talked with the Pangeran, listened to his history, heard his complaints, sympathised in the misfortunes of his tribe, and shuddered at the wrongs and sufferings they have endured. 'We are few,' he exclaimed, 'and therefore our oppressions are aggravated; the same demands are made upon us as though we were many, and we have not the means of resisting or complying. We fly to the jungle; we are like deer—we have no home, no perch. Our wives and children are taken from us; our sufferings are very great.' On another occasion he said, 'I have felt my sufferings to be so great, that I wished to die, if Jovata would permit it. I wished to die; for I remembered how happy we were once, and how miserable now.' I could dwell largely on these, and such language and descriptions, which appear to me highly pathetic and touching—at least I found them so in reality; and I cannot forbear adding one or two more such, highly characteristic.

" 'Our home,' said the Pangeran, 'was a happy one; none who came to us wanted. The fruit on the trees was saved; the fish in the river near us was never destroyed. Rice was plenty; if it was scarce, we kept it, and fed ourselves upon vegetables, that we might give it to those who visited our habitation. The fish, the fruit, and the rice were preserved,[1] that the men of the sea (Malays) might eat of them; yet they had no pity on us. We were free men, yet they treated us worse than slaves. We are now but few; and unless you protect us, we shall soon cease to be.' Again: 'The Tumangong was severe to us; and when Macota came, he said the Tumangong was a bad man, and

---

[1] This I found, on inquiry, to be strictly true—a most amiable trait!—B.

he would shield us; but he was much worse than the Tumangong. Now, you say you will cherish us; we believe you; but you are at a distance, and perhaps may not be able.' Further: 'Pangeran Macota kept me nine months in his house, and wanted to make me a slave; but I escaped, and travelled through the woods, and swam the rivers, till I came to my own country. He thought the Dyak had no eyes except in the jungle; he thought he had no ears except to listen to the bird of omen; he thought he had no wit except to grow rice; but he saw, and heard, and understood, that whilst his words were sweet, his heart was crooked, and that, whether they were men of the sea or Dyaks, he deceived them with fair sayings; he said one thing to one man, and another to a second; he deceived with a honied mouth. I saw and understood it all whilst I lived in his house. How could I trust him afterwards?' These expressions were concluded by significantly twisting his two fore-fingers round each other, to shew the intrigues that were carried on. I grew very fond of this poor naked savage; for if honesty and a kind heart entitle a man to our esteem, he is worthy of it.

"I had a long conference with Si Nimook, the Sow Dyak, and hope to recover his wife. Amidst all the wealth and all the charity of England, how well bestowed would a small portion be for the purpose of restoring one hundred and fifty women and children to their husbands and parents, and releasing them from slavery! A small rill from the plenteous river would cheer this distant misery, and bestow the blessing of fertility on the now barren soil of these poor Dyaks. Oh, that I had the brass to beg—to draw out a piteous tale so as to touch the heart!"

CHAPTER XIII.

Ascent of the left-hand river to the Stabad. Remarkable cave in the Tubbang. Diamond works at Suntah. Return. Infested by Dyak pirates. A meeting of prahus and fight. Seriff Sahib's treatment of the Suntah Dyaks. Expedition against the Singè. Their invasion of the Sigos, and taking heads. The triumph over these trophies. Arms and modes of war. Hot and cold council-houses. Ceremonies in the installation of the Orang Kaya Steer Rajah. Meeting of various Dyak tribes. Hostile plans of Seriff Sahib, and their issue. Resolves to proceed to Borneo Proper.

THE next portion of Mr. Brooke's Journal details another excursion up the country, and then proceeds to describe the early incidents of his infant government. As he advanced on his way, affairs began to assume more important aspects; and yet they could hardly be painted with greater force or interest than in his simple notes.

"*April 25th.*—Ascended the left-hand river, in order to introduce the Kunsi Simbock to their new territory; passed the night on a pebbly bank; moon at full, bright and unclouded, tinging the luxuriant foliage, and glancing on the clear rapid stream. Four distinct and distant races met on this lonely and lovely spot—English, Chinese, Malays, and Dyaks! What a scope for poetry and reflection—the time, the clime, the spot, and the company!

"26th.—After our morning meal and bath, entered the small river Stabad, which, according to report, runs from a source two or three days' journey farther into the interior. At present it is so obstructed by fallen trees, that we were forced to return, after ascending about four miles. We left our boats near its entrance, and walked to the small but steep mountain, Tubbang. Its length may be about 400 feet. After mounting, by a winding path, about half-way up towards the top, we arrived at the entrance of a cave, into which we descended through a hole. It is fifty or sixty feet long, and the far end is supported on a colonnade of stalactites, and opens on a sheer precipice of 100 or 150 feet. Hence the spectator can overlook the distant scene; the forest lies at his feet, and only a few trees growing from the rock reach nearly to the level of the grotto. The effect is striking and panoramic; the grotto cheerful; floored with fine sand; the roof groined like Gothic, whence the few clear drops which filter through form here and there the fantastic stalactites common to such localities. The natives report the cave to be the residence of a fairy queen; and they shew her bed, pillow, and other of her household furniture. Within the cave we found a few remnants of human bones; probably some poor Dyak who had crawled there to die.

"Having finished our survey of the place, and wandered sufficiently about the mount, we re-embarked, and dropped a short way down the river, and started again into the jungle to look for antimony-ore, but without success, our guide having forgotten the road. After a couple of hours' wandering, the latter part in a heavy storm of rain, we reached the boats; and I thence ascended to Suntah, where we were all glad to house ourselves, as the deluge continued.

"*27th.*—I will say nothing of my works at Suntah, except that they run away with my money, are badly conducted by my Chinese hadji, and, above all, that I have great reason to suspect the integrity and steadiness of this said hadji. I must therefore make up my mind either to change him when the business is finished, or to watch him very narrowly; for the honesty of a diamond-worker, like the virtue of Cæsar's wife, must be above suspicion, or he must be watched closely; but how?

"*28th.*—Descended the river, and, arriving at Sarāwak, found both work and cause for inquietude. The Rajah had heard of Dyak pirates, and despatched four boats, two large and two small: the Snake, weakly manned by the Tumangong's people, and the rest led by Pangerans (who neither work nor fight) and a wretched crew, chiefly Borneons. Mr. Crimble, taking my servant Peter and four Javanese, went most imprudently in the second of the large boats. The whole, being despatched in haste (foolish haste), insufficiently provided in every respect, may fall into trouble, and involve me in very unpleasant circumstances.

"The other cause for uneasiness is the attack of a Chinese boat at the mouth of the river. The boat that attacked her is a small one, with eight or ten men, which came out of Sadong, and had been lying here for a week or more. She is commanded by a Pangeran named Badrudeen, has some Illanuns on board, and is bound on a piratical cruise. As she descended the river, she met with the small China boat, likewise from Sambas, with eight men, which she treacherously assailed, desperately wounding one man and severely another; but the China boat's consort heaving in sight, the pirate pulled away. I must redress this, if it be in my power; and have ordered the Datus to gather men to follow the rascals, as it is probable they will be lurking not far from hence. In the mean time it gave me great pain dressing the hurts of these poor Chinese, one of whom I think must die, being cut along the back and side—across the body from the side nearly to the backbone—a ghastly gaping wound, besides having his arm slashed through. The other man is very severely, and perhaps, without medical attendance, mortally, hurt, having his arm half cut through at the muscular development between the shoulder and elbow—poor fellow! I must say for the Chinese, they seem very grateful for any attention shewn them.

"29th.—My birthday. Men collected, and tomorrow we start for Telang Telang. This morning, much to my relief, our fleet returned, after an encounter with thirteen Dyak boats. About one o'clock on the 28th, pulling into a bay between Morotaba and Tanjong Poe, they came unexpectedly on them. One Borneon boat had lagged behind; the Pangeran who commanded deserted the second, and sought refuge with the Tumangong, trying to induce him to fly; and the crew of the third, a large boat with my two Europeans on board, was, by their account, in a state of fear, which totally incapacitated them from acting. All rose, none would pull; all shouted, none would serve the guns; all commanded, none obeyed; most were screaming out to run; all bellowing out, in hopes of frightening the enemy; none to direct the helm. The Tumangong, with only seventeen men in all, insisted on advance; and the Borneons, encouraged by threats from the Europeans, and the good example of the Javanese, did not fly. The two boats opened their fire; the Dyaks retreated in confusion and alarm; but from the tumult, the noise, and the rocking of the boat, Mr. Crimble could only fire three times with the bow six-pounder cannonade, and from other guns loaded with grape and canister, whilst the rascally Borneons never fired at all. The Dyaks suffered loss, and left behind them clothes, rice, fish, cooking-pots, swords, &c.; and, considering the state of the Borneons, it was lucky the dread of our prowess put them to flight so easily. Crimble assured me that, with a Siniawan crew, he could have destroyed half their force. The Dyaks behaved very well, pulling off with great steadiness and without noise.

"*June 20th.*—The events of the month may be compressed into a narrative comprising the internal and external.

" The internal state of the country is decidedly improving and flourishing, and bears the aspect of gradually increasing prosperity, Justice has been strictly administered. Robberies, which a few months ago were of nightly occurrence, are now rarely heard of; and that vile intriguing to make poor people slaves, from debt or false claims, is entirely stopped.

" The people who had scattered at the close of the war have been collected, and are building their houses a short way up the river at the Campong Jekiso, which, when finished, will be a neat-looking village.

" The Pangeran Macota is intriguing; but as he is sure to do that, it need not be insisted upon.

" Muda Hassim is true and agreeable, and entirely reconciled to the Patingi and Tumangongs; so far, indeed, nothing can be better than our internal state : there is peace, there is plenty; the poor are not harassed, and justice is done to all.

" The Dyaks of the interior are improving and

content, and gaining courage daily to complain of any wrong that may be offered them. To the sena, or forced trade, I have almost put a stop, by confiscating the goods wherever met with; and this plan once acted on, the Dyaks have not been slow to bring me bundles of bidongs (Dyak cloths), iron, and the like.

"The tribes that continue unsettled are the Suntah and Singè: the affairs of the latter I will mention hereafter.

"Suntah has been for a long time under the government of Seriff Sahib of Sadong, and through his *paternal* charge has dwindled away from four hundred to fifty or sixty families. Shortly after my assuming the reins of government, he despatched (according to custom) a mixed party of Malays and Dyaks, and falling on my helpless tribe of Sanpro, killed some, and carried away twenty women and children into captivity. I was not strong enough to resent the injury; but wrote him a strong letter, demanding the women, and telling him he was not to send, under any pretext, into my country. The women I did not get; but I heard that the communication frightened him; for, of course, they deem I am backed by all the power of my country. Whilst the Royalist still lay here, I heard that his people were raising the revenue from the Suntah Dyaks; but it must be remarked, that the Suntah are on the edge of my territory, having left the former location. As this was done in the face of my caution not to intermeddle without my consent, I resolved at once to put the matter to the issue; and having armed four boats, went up and seized all the rice and padi collected for my neighbours' use. The Suntah Dyaks were and are alarmed to a pitiable degree; for they fear Seriff Sahib with good reason; and yet my being on the spot gave them no option of evading my demand. Thus the matter was brought to a crisis; and having taken the revenue (as it was called) for the poor Dyaks themselves, I shall be able to keep them from starvation, to the verge of which, so early in the season, they are already reduced. The Dyaks remain unsettled; but I am now in hopes of bringing them to the interior of the Quop, which is further within our own territory. Muda Hassim wrote to Seriff Sahib to tell him the Dyaks were no longer his, but mine; and Seriff Sahib, sore-hearted, conspired against us, and held for some time a higher tone than his wont.

"I shall now narrate my proceedings at the mountain of Singè, from which I have just returned. The mountain, with its groves of fruit-trees, has been already described; and as a preface to my present description, I must particularise the circumstances of the Dyak tribe of Singè. The tribe consists of at least 800 males, the most ignorant, and therefore the most wild, of the Dyaks of my country; and, from their position, they have never been overcome or ruined, and are therefore a rich community, and proportionately independent. Their old chief is by name Parembam, and the Panglima, or head-warrior, his younger brother, by name Si Tummo. These men have for a very long time ruled this tribe; and the elder has certainly acquired from the Malays a portion of cunning and intrigue, and lost the general simplicity of the native Dyak character. He is unquestionably a man of ability. His sway, however, on the mountain, has for a long time been unpopular; and a large proportion of the people, dissatisfied with his extortions, have been attached to a younger chief, by name Bibit. Some time past, finding it impossible to manage this old chief, Parembam, and being convinced that the change might readily be made, I called Bibit, and made him chief, or Orang Kaya of the tribe. Parembam neither was nor is inclined to give up his authority without a struggle; and though the mass adhere to the new chief, by title 'Steer Rajah,' yet Parembam's long-established customs, his great wealth, and his talents, render him a dangerous old man to the younger leader. One quality, however, Parembam is deficient in, as well as his brother the Panglima, and that is *bravery;* and on this much depends in a Dyak tribe. Steer Rajah, on the contrary, has always been renowned in war, and is the envied possessor of many heads. The Dyaks have amongst them a fashion which they call bunkit, or vaunting; for instance, in the present case Steer Rajah and Parembam dared each other to go on excursions to procure heads, *i. e.* against their enemies—this is bunkit. One of Steer Rajah's followers went accordingly, and quickly procured the head of a hostile warrior far out of my territory; and on the return of the party, Parembam in turn sent forty men to Simpoke, which is a tribe attached to Samarahan, and on our immediate border. Close to the Dyaks of Simpoke live a party of the Sigo Dyaks, who belong to me; and this party of Parembam's, confounding friends and enemies, killed some of the Sigo Dyaks—how many is not certain. The Sigos, taking the alarm, cut off their retreat, and killed two of the Singè Dyaks; and many besides were wounded by sudas and ranjows, and, all broken, fled back to their own country. Thus, though they obtained five heads, they lost two, and those belonging to their principal warriors. This news reaching me, I hurried up to the hill, and arrived just after part of the war-party had brought the heads.

"I may here remark, that I have positively forbid the Dyak tribes within my territory to war one upon the other; and this, therefore, was a serious offence against me on the part of Parembam. At once to aim at more than this restriction would be fruitless, and even risk my ability to effect this first step on the road to improvement. I likewise came up here to go through the ceremony of installing the Orang Kaya Steer Rajah in his office; and thus I have had an excellent opportunity of seeing their customs and manners. What follows will be a personal narration, or nearly so, of what I have seen; and it applies, with slight difference, to almost all the interior tribes.

"On our ascending the mountain, we found the five heads carefully watched, about half a mile from the town, in consequence of the non-arrival of some of the war-party. They had erected a temporary shed close to the place where these miserable remnants of noisome mortality were deposited; and they were guarded by about thirty young men in their finest dresses, composed principally of scarlet jackets ornamented with shells, turbans of the native bark-cloth dyed bright yellow, and spread on the head, and decked with an occasional feather, flower, or twig of leaves. Nothing can exceed their partiality for these trophies; and in retiring from the 'war-path,' the man who has been so fortunate as to obtain a head hangs it about his neck, and instantly commences his return to his tribe. If he sleep on the way, the precious burden, though decaying and offensive, is not loosened, but rests on his lap, whilst his head (and nose!) reclines on his knees. The retreat is always silently made until close to home, when they set up a wild yell, which announces their victory and the possession of its proofs. It must, therefore, be considered, that these bloody trophies are the evidences of victory—the banner of the European, the flesh-pot of the Turk, the scalp of the North American Indian—and that they are torn from enemies, for taking heads is the effect and not the cause of war. On our reaching the Balei, or public hall, of the Orang Kaya Steer Rajah, I immediately called a number of their chiefs together, and opened a conference with them on the subject of Parembam having attacked and killed the Dyaks of Sigo. They *all* disapproved of it most highly, asserting that the Sigos were their younger brothers; that no sufficient cause had ever existed; that Parembam had acted badly, and must pay to purchase *peace*. Were they, I asked, willing to force Parembam into payment? They were. Would they insist on the heads being restored to the Sigos, and receive those of their own people? They would!

"It may be observed, that their causes for war, as well as its progress and termination, are exactly the same as those of other people. They dispute about the limits of their respective lands; about theft committed by one tribe upon another; about occasional murders; the crossing each other on the war-path; and about a thousand other subjects.

"When a tribe is on a warlike excursion,

it often happens that their track (or 'trail') is crossed by another tribe. Those who strike the trail guard it at some convenient spot, apprehending the party to be enemies; they plant ranjows in the path, and wait till the returning party are involved amongst them to make an attack. If enemies, and they succeed, all is well; but if friends, though no attack be made, it is a serious offence, and mostly gives occasion to war, if not paid for. The progress of the contest consists in attacking each other by these surprises, particularly about the time of sowing, weeding, and cutting the rice-crops. When one party is weaker, or less active, or less warlike than the other, they solicit a peace through some tribe friendly to both, and pay for the lives they have taken: the price is about two gongs, value $33\frac{1}{2}$ reals, for each life: thus peace is concluded. This is the custom with these Dyaks universally; but it is otherwise with the Sarebus and Sakarran. But Sarebus and Sakarran are not fair examples of Dyak life, as they are pirates as well as head-hunters, and do not hesitate to destroy all persons they meet with.

"Parembam, having been called before me, declared that these heads belonged to the Simpoke Dyaks, and that they had not attacked the Sigos. As I was not quite certain of the fact, I thought it unjust to proceed against him till I had stronger proof.

"On the following morning the heads were brought up to the village, attended by a number of young men all dressed in their best, and were carried to Parembam's house amid the beating of gongs and the firing of one or two guns. They were then disposed of in a conspicuous place in the public hall of Parembam. The music sounded and the men danced the greater part of the day; and towards evening carried them away in procession through all the campongs except three or four just about me. The women, in these processions, crowd round the heads as they proceed from house to house, and put sīrih and betel-nut in the mouths of the ghastly dead, and welcome them! After this they are carried back in the same triumph, deposited in an airy place, and left to dry. During this process, for seven, eight, or ten days, they are watched by the boys of the age of six to ten years; and during this time they never stir from the public hall—they are not permitted to put their foot out of it whilst engaged in this sacred trust. Thus are the youths initiated.

"For a long time after the heads are hung up, the men nightly meet and beat their gongs, and chant addresses to them, which were rendered thus to me: 'Your head is in our dwelling, but your spirit wanders to your own country.' 'Your head and your spirit are now ours: persuade, therefore, your countrymen to be slain by us.' 'Speak to the spirits of your tribe: let them wander in the fields, that when we come again to their country, we may get more heads, and that we may bring the heads of your brethren, and hang them by your head,' &c. The tone of this chant is loud and monotonous, and I am not able to say how long it is sung; but certainly for a month after the arrival of the heads, as one party here had had a head for that time, and were still exhorting it.

"These are their customs and modes of warfare; and I may conclude by saying that, though their trophies are more disgusting, yet their wars are neither so bloody, nor their cruelties so great, as those of the North American Indian. They slay all they meet with of their enemies—men, women, and children; but this is common to all wild tribes. They have an implacable spirit of revenge as long as the war lasts, retort evil for evil, and retaliate life for life; and, as I have before said, the heads are the trophies, as the scalps are to the red men. But, on the contrary, they never torture their enemies, nor do they devour them; and peace can always be restored amongst them by a very moderate payment. In short, there is nothing new in their feelings, or in their mode of shewing them; no trait remarkable for cruelty; no head-hunting for the sake of head-hunting. They act precisely on the same impulses as other wild men: war arises from passion or interest; peace from defeat or fear. As friends, they are faithful, just, and honest; as enemies, bloodthirsty and cunning, patient on the war-path, and enduring fatigue, hunger, and want of sleep, with cheerfulness and resolution. - As woodmen they are remarkably acute; and on all their excursions carry with them a number of ranjows, which, when they retreat, they stick in behind them, at intervals, at a distance of twenty, fifty, or a hundred yards, so that a hotly-pursuing enemy gets checked, and many severely wounded. Their arms consist of a sword, an iron-headed spear, a few wooden spears, a knife worn at the right side, with a sīrih-pouch, or small basket. Their provision is a particular kind of sticky rice, boiled in bamboos. When once they have struck their enemies, or failed, they return, without pausing, to their homes.

"To proceed with my journal. My principal object in coming up the hill was, to appoint the Orang Kaya Steer Rajah as the chief, besides Pagise as Panglima, or head warrior, and Pa Bobot as Pangeran, or revenue officer. It was deemed by these worthy personages quite unfit that this ceremony should take place in the public hall or circular house, as that was the place wherein the heads are deposited, and where they hold councils of war.

"With the Dyaks, all council is divided into hot and cold; peace, friendship, good intentions, are all included under the latter head—war, &c.

are under the former. Hot is represented by red, and cold by white. So, in every thing, they make this distinction; and as the public hall is the place for war-councils and war-trophies, it is hot in the extreme, unfit for friendly conference. A shed was therefore erected close to the Orang Kaya's house, wherein the ceremony was to take place. About nine in the evening we repaired to the scene; loud music, barbarous, but not unpleasing, resounded, and we took our seats on mats in the midst of our Dyak friends. A feast was in preparation; and each guest (if I may call them such) brought his share of rice in bamboos, and laid it on the general stock. As one party came up after another, carrying their burning logs, the effect was very good; and they kept arriving until the place and its vicinity was literally crammed with human beings. A large antique sīrih-box was placed in the midst; and I contributed that greatest of luxuries, tobacco.

"The feast, in the mean time, was in preparation, some of the principal people being employed in counting the number who were to eat, and dividing the bamboos into exactly equal portions for each person. About six inches was allotted to every man; and it took a very long time to divide it, for they are remarkably particular as to the proper size and quantity of each share. The bamboos of rice being, however, at length satisfactorily disposed, the Orang Kaya produced as his share a large basin full of sauce, composed of salt and chilis, and a small stock of sweetmeats; and then the ceremony of his installation commenced as follows: —

"A jacket, a turban, a cloth for the loins, and a kris (all of white) were presented to the chief as a token of sejiek dingin, or cold, *i. e.* good. The chief then rose, and, taking a white fowl and waving it over the eatables, repeated nearly the following words: — (The commencement, however, is curious enough to dwell upon: the opening is a sort of invocation, beginning with the phrase, 'Samungut, Simungi.' Samungut is a Malay word, Simungi signifying the same in Dyak: the exact meaning it is difficult to comprehend; but it is here understood as some principle, spirit, or fortune, which is in men and things. Thus the Dyaks, in stowing their rice at harvest, do it with great care, from a superstitious feeling that the Simungi of the padi will escape. They now call this principle to be present — that of men, of pigs (their favourite animal), of padi, and of fruits. They particularly named my Simungi, that of my ancestors, of the Pangeran from Borneo, of the Datus and of their ancestors, and of the ancestors of their own tribe. They call them — that is, their Simungi — to be present. They then call upon Jovata to grant their prayer, that the great man from Europe, and the Datus, might hold the government for a length of time) — 'May the government be cold' (good); 'May there be rice in our houses;' 'May many pigs be killed;' 'May male children be born to us;' 'May fruit ripen;' 'May we be happy, and our goods abundant;' 'We declare ourselves to be true to the great man and the Datus: what they wish we will do, what they command is our law.' Having said this and much more, the fowl was taken by a leading Malay, who repeated the latter words, whilst others bound strips of white cloth round the heads of the multitude. The fowl was then killed, the blood shed in a bamboo, and each man dipping his finger in the blood, touched his forehead and breast, in attestation of his fidelity. The fowl was now carried away to be cooked: and when brought back, placed with the rest of the feast, and the dancing commenced. The chief, coming forward, uttered a loud yell ending in 'ish,' which was oftentimes repeated during the dance. He raised his hands to his forehead, and, taking a dish, commenced dancing to lively music. Three other old chief men followed his example; each uttering the yell and making the salute, but without taking the dish. They danced with arms extended, turning the body frequently, taking very small steps, and little more than lifting their feet from the ground. Thus they turned backwards and forwards, passed in and out of the inner rooms, and frequently repeating the yell, and making the salutation to me. The dish, in the mean time, was changed from one to the other: there was little variety, no gesticulation, no violence; and, though not deficient in native grace, yet the movements were by no means interesting. The dance over, the feast commenced; and every thing was carried on with great gravity and propriety. I left them shortly after they began to eat, and retired, very fagged, to my bed, or, rather, to my board; for sitting cross-legged for several hours is surely a great infliction.

"I may add to this account that, whilst writing it, the Dyak land-tribes of Siquong, Sibaduh, and Goon, sent their deputies to me. These people are not under any Malay government, and it is now for the first time they have trusted themselves as far as Sarāwak. They have an objection to drinking the river-water, and expressed great surprise at the flood-tide. Their confidence is cheering to me, and will, I trust, be advantageous to themselves. Their trade in rice is very considerable; and towards Sambas they exchange eight or ten pasus of rice for one of salt.

"Our conference was pleasing. They desired protection, they desired trade. 'They had all heard, *the whole world had heard*, that *a son of Europe* was a friend to the Dyaks.' My visitors drank Batavia arrack with great gusto, declaring all the time it was not half so good as their own: however, at a pinch any thing will do. Some other Dyaks met these strangers; they were not adversaries, and so they chewed sīrih, and drank grog in company, but amongst enemies this may not be; they can neither eat nor drink in company, without desiring a reconciliation. I may add, that the Siquong tribe consists of at least four hundred families, and forty public halls, or baleis, for heads. A Dyak family cannot be estimated at fewer than twelve people, which will give four thousand eight hundred or five thousand people. Sibaduh and Goon may be about seventy-five families; besides these, Si Panjong and Sam Penex want to come in to me, which will give one hundred and one more families. What might be done with these people, if I had a little more power and a little assistance!

"I was going to close my account of the Dyaks; but I had scarcely penned the last sentence, when a large party of Singè Dyaks and five Dyaks of Sigo arrived—thus all these enemies meeting. In the conference which followed, the Singè allowed they were wrong in attacking Sigo, and laid all the blame on the old chief, Parembam. They likewise allowed it to be just that Parembam should be forced to pay, and conclude a peace. With the Goon and Sibaduh Dyaks they had long been at enmity; but they agreed to make peace if Sibaduh would pay two gongs, formerly demanded, as the price of peace. The Sibaduh, however, did not allow the justice of the demand; but the parties were reconciled so far as that each promised to maintain a truce, and to eat together; and the Singès declared they would not attack the Sibaduhs on account of the two gongs, but obtain them in a friendly conference. I have (being hurried) briefly mentioned these circumstances, which took a long time to settle, as the Dyaks are very fond of speechifying, which they do sitting, without action or vivacity, but with great fluency, and using often highly metaphysical and elegant language. It was a great nuisance having fifty naked savages in the house all night, extended in the hall and the anterooms. They finished a bottle of gin, and then slept; and I could not avoid remarking that their sleep was light, such as temperance, health, and exercise bestow. During many hours I heard but one man snore; whilst half the number of Europeans would have favoured me with a concert sufficient to banish rest.

"I shall now briefly mention our *foreign policy* for the last few months.

"For a time we were annoyed with incessant reports of their coming to attack us in force; but though scarcely believing they would be bold enough, I took precautions, pushed on the completion of our boats, built a fort, and made a fence round the village. These precautions taken, and fifteen boats in the water, ready for action, I cared very little, though the news reached me that Byong the Sarebus chief had hung a basket on a high tree which was to contain my head.

"*Sadong*.—Our relations with Seriff Sahib were very unsettled; and by the bullying tone of the people of Singè I thought it probable he might be induced to measure his strength, backed by the Sakarran Dyaks, against us. I have already mentioned his attack upon my Dyaks of Sanpro, and the second dispute about the Suntah Dyaks; in the first of these he came of with impunity; in the second I met him with success, and out-manœuvred him, and wrested the Dyaks from him. Shortly after the transactions at Suntah, a boat of Sakarran Dyaks came to Sarawak nominally *to trade*, but in reality to tamper with the fidelity of the Datus and others. They proposed to the Tumangong to join Seriff Sahib, stating that they were sent by him to try all the people here. 'They had been ruined here; Seriff Sahib would restore them their property; and if they left Muda Hassim, James Brooke, and the Chinese, they could afterwards easily make a prey of the Dyaks and Chinese, with Seriff Sahib's assistance, and get plenty of slaves.'

"The plan proposed for the removal was as follows: Seriff Sahib, with forty Malay boats, and the Sakarrans with one hundred boats, were to request permission from Muda Hassim to attack the Dyak tribe of Siquong; and under this pretence were to come up the river, when the Datus were to join, with their wives and children, and all were to take flight together. The Tumangong told me this as soon as he heard it himself; and, to make sure, I sent Patingi Gapoor to fish their story out of them, which he did most successfully. Being assured of the fact, I called the Dyaks, and before some dozens of our people and one or two persons from Singè, taxed them with their guilt. They were obliged to confess, and insisted upon it that Seriff Sahib had sent them, &c. Many urged me to put these Dyaks to death; but the reluctance we all have to shedding blood withheld me, and I had no desire to strike at a wren when a foul vulture was at hand. I dismissed the emissaries scot-free; and then both Muda Hassim and myself indited letters to Seriff Sahib; that of Muda Hassim being severe but dignified. Before they were despatched, an ambassador arrived from Singè with letters both to the Rajah and myself, disclaiming warmly all knowledge of the treachery, swearing *the most solemn* oaths in proof of his truth, and declaring that so far from having committed so shameful an action, he had never even dreamed of such a thing in his worst dreams, as he hoped that God would save him. Our letters were sent before his ambassador was received; and a second disclaimer, like the first, quickly reached us. Of course it was my policy, whatever my opinion might be, to receive his offers of friendship, and to believe all he said; and therefore the matter ended, and ended so far well, that Seriff Sahib lowered his former tone; and certainly, whatever he may desire in his heart, or *dream* of, he wants to be well with us here, and, I can see, fears us. I am content, because I really wish for peace, and not war; Muda Hassim is content, because he has humbled Seriff Sahib, and acted decisively; and the Seriff is content, as the fiend in the infernal regions. I leave it to all gentle readers to form their own opinion of his truth or treachery; but I must hint to them my private opinion that he did send agents to tempt, and would have gained the Datus if he could; and as for his oaths, my belief is, he would swear a basketful of the most sacred before breakfast to support a lie, and yet not lose his appetite! The Datus were too old, and knew him too well, to be caught in his trap.

"Seriff Sahib has now sent a fleet of boats up the Sarebus river; but the result I do not yet know.

"To conclude our foreign policy, I must mention Borneo Proper.

"My great object is to reconcile Muda Hassim and the Sultan, and to restore the former to Borneo, before the coming of Mr. Bonham on his diplomatic mission. To effect this, I have resolved to proceed myself; and Muda Hassim, equally anxious, has letters and two of his brothers ready to accompany me. If we can gain this object, I shall be firmly established, and relieved from the intriguing, mean, base Borneons. And it will be an advantage to the government measure, in as far as they will be enabled to form their arrangements with all instead of a single faction of the Borneo Pangerans. From all I hear, Muda Hassim is more powerful than either the Sultan or Pangeran Usop; and that if he appeals to arms, am assured he will carry his point, and become the sovereign of Borneo virtually, if not nominally.

"The Royalist now waits for us at the mouth of the river, which I hope to reach on the 14th, this being the 12th July. Heigh for the sea once more; but yet, though I go, I take my cares with me; and but for the necessity, the absolute necessity, of bringing the Borneo question to a crisis, good or bad, I would fain stop where I am. For even during one short month's absence I fear my poor people will suffer from the intrigues of the rascally Borneo Pangerans. In this I do not include Muda Hassim, who, with a most amiable private character, and with integrity and good faith, desires to do right, as far as his education and prejudices will permit. It is sad to reflect that this very prince, who really wishes to do good, and to conduce to the comfort of his people, should, from want of energy, have been so fearful an oppressor, through the agency of others; and it is not here alone that vile agents for vile purposes are plentiful."

CHAPTER XIV.

Visit of Captain Elliott. Mr. Brooke sails for Borneo Proper. Arrival. Visited by leading men. Condition of the country. Reception by the Sultan. Objects in view. The different chiefs, and communications with them. The Sultan and his Pangerans. Objects of the visit accomplished. Return to Sarāwak. Ceremonies of the cession. Sails for Singapore.

AFTER Mr. Brooke's return from his expedition against the Singè Dyak chief Parembam, he was visited by his friend Captain Elliott, of the Madras engineers, whose acquaintance I had the pleasure of subsequently making at Singapore. He is, as Brooke describes him, "a man of science and education, and the best of good fellows." During his stay at Sarāwak, he established his observatory, and all its apparatus; and a shed (now converted into a goat-house) will always retain the appellation of "the Observatory." Mr. Brooke and Captain Elliott appear to have made some very amusing and agreeable excursions up the different rivers, an account of which is given in the journal, which I shall pass over, as I am anxious to follow my friend through with his government up to the time of my meeting him at Singapore.

"*Thursday, July* 14*th*.—We were to have started on this most lucky day at ten o'clock, but what with innumerable preparations and delays, it was near six before the Rajah was ready to dismiss the procession; and my alarm became considerable that, Friday (an unlucky day) having commenced by the native reckoning, we should again be postponed till Sunday. However, by making six o'clock five, and keeping back the watches to suit our purpose, our departure was achieved. The state spears and swords were brought forth. The letters for the Sultan, in their brass tray covered with embroidered cloth, were duly mounted, with the greatest reverence, on the head of Bandar Sumsu; and nothing remained but to take leave. The Rajah addressed a few words to his brothers, requesting them to tell the Sultan that his heart was always with him; that he could never separate from him, whether far or near; and that he was, and always had been, true to his son. Budrudeen then rose, and approaching the Rajah, seated himself close to him, bending his head to the ground over his hand, which he had grasped. The Rajah hastily withdrew his hand, and clasping him round, embraced, kissing his neck. Both were greatly agitated and both wept, and I could have wept for company, for it was no display of state-ceremony, but genuine feeling. It is seldom, very seldom, they shew their feelings; and the effect was the more touching from being unexpected; besides, it is a part of our nature (one's better nature) to feel when we see others feel. Pangeran Marsale followed; both brothers likewise parted with Muda Mahammed in the same way, and they certainly rose in my opinion from this token of affection towards each other. My adieus followed; we all rose; the Rajah accompanied us to the wharf; and as we embarked, I could see the tears slowly steal from his eyes. I could not help taking his hand, and bidding him be of good cheer; he smiled in a friendly manner, pressed my hand, and I stepped into my boat. Our gongs struck up; the barge, decorated with flags and streamers, was towed slowly along against the flood-tide; the guns fired from the wharf, from the Chinese houses, and from our fort, and we passed along in all the pomp and pride of *Sarāwak state*. It was dusk when we got down to the first reach, and there we brought up to wait for the ebb."

I shall omit that part of my friend's journal containing his remarks and observations along the coast between Sarāwak and the entrance of the Borneo river. On the 21st July his narration continues thus:—

"I must now leave geography, and turn to politics. On casting anchor we acted on a plan previously formed, and sent off the gig, with Seriff Hussein and Nakodah Ahmed, to the city, to intimate my arrival, and that of the Rajah's brothers, with letters from Muda Hassim. I trusted to their dread of, and curiosity about, the English expedition to ensure my reception; but I gave particular directions, in case the Sultan asked about me, that my ambassadors were to say I was here; that I had been corresponding about the English coming; that I was not a man in authority, or belonging to the East India Company; and that they were sure I should not land unless he invited me to come and see him. To shew eagerness would have raised suspicion; backwardness excites the contrary feeling, and a desire to entertain some intercourse.

"*July 22d.*—At the unconscionable hour of 2 A.M., a mob of Pangerans came on board, in number not fewer than fifty, and with a multitude of followers. They awoke us out of our first sleep, and crowded the vessel above and below, so that we could scarce find room to make our toilette in public, whilst the heat was suffocating us. However, we did manage it, and sat talking till daylight. Our visitors were chiefly relations or adherents of Muda Hassim, and some of the first men in the country. Pangeran Budrudeen and Pangeran Marsale were in their glory, and happy; and it was evident at once that our affairs were likely to succeed to our hearts' content. All were anxious and eager in inquiries about Muda Hassim, and wishing his return. The Sultan, Pangeran Usop, Pangeran Mumin, and others declared, 'Borneo could never be well till he came back.' In short, it was clear that the country was in distress and difficulty from within: trade ruined, piracy abounding, the mouth of the river unsafe, their forts insulted by the pirates, the communication with their dependencies cut off, food dear, and the tobacco, which comes from the northward, not to be had. Every thing conspires to forward Muda Hassim's views and mine; and, during this conversation, it was evident they were looking to me as a friend.

"At daylight a boat from the Sultan arrived to carry up the letters; but Budrudeen and his brother resolved to proceed first, in order to make sure of an honourable reception for the chop. At 7 o'clock there was a stir. I saw them over the side with delight, and gave them a salute with pleasure. Breakfast done, I was too happy to lie down, and slept till past midday, having then only to wait for Budrudeen's return.

"*23d.*—Budrudeen came at 3 P.M., bringing with him good news of the most favourable reception from all parties, all wishing for reconciliation and the return of Muda Hassim. To-morrow, boats are to come for the letters, which are to be conveyed in state. The day following I am to go up, and am likewise to be received in all honourable form.

"*24th.*—At 7 A.M. the state-boat, a shabby concern, decorated with yellow flags, arrived, and at eight the letters were borne away under a salute. Thus we had a second time the satisfaction of getting rid of the mob at an early hour.

"*25th.*—At 9½ A.M. I started with Williamson in the gig, with the long-boat, in company, carrying the presents. On approaching the town, before the ebb had run long, it appeared to be a very Venice of hovels, a river Cybele rising from the water. For those who like it, the locality is not ill chosen. The hills recede from the river and form an amphitheatre; and several other rivers or streams flowing in, cause a muddy deposit, on which the houses are built. At high-water they are surrounded; at low water, stand on a sheet of mud. On nearing it, we were encompassed by boats which preceded and followed us, and we passed the floating market, where women, wearing immense hats of palm-leaves, sell all sorts of edibles, balanced in their little canoes, now giving a paddle, now making a bargain, and dropping down with the tide, and again regaining their place when the bargain is finished. The first impression of the town is miserable. The houses are crowded and numerous, and arriving at the palace does not present a more captivating aspect, for, though large, it is as incommodious as the worst. Our presentation was exactly similar to that of our first meeting with Muda Hassim at Sarāwak, only the crowd was much greater. We had been seated but a few minutes when Pangeran Usop arrived, and directly afterwards the Sultan.

He gave us tea, leaf-cigars, and sīrih, and, in short, shewed us every attention; and, what was best of all, did not keep us very long. Our apartment was partitioned off from the public hall, a dark-looking place, but furnished with a table brought by us, and three rickety chairs, besides mattresses and plenty of mats. We were kept up nearly all night, which, after the fatigues of the day, was hard upon us.

"Further observation confirmed us in the opinion that the town itself is miserable, and its locality on the mud fitted only for frogs or natives; but there is a level dry plain above the entrance of the Kiangi river, admirably suited for a European settlement; and across the Kiangi is swelling ground, where the residents might find delightful spots for their country-houses. The greatest annoyance to a stranger is the noisome smell of the mud when uncovered; and all plated or silver articles, even in the course of one night, get black and discoloured. The inhabitants I shall estimate moderately at 10,000, and the Kadien population are numerous amid the hills.

"*27th.*—Our objects in coming to Borneo were threefold. Firstly, to effect a reconciliation between the Sultan and Muda Hassim; secondly, to gain the Sultan's approval and signature to my holding Sarāwak; and thirdly, to release the Klee-ses [Hindoostanees] of the shipwrecked vessels the Sultana and Lord Melbourne. The first object was gained at once, as the Sultan seemed really overjoyed at being good friends with his uncle; and Pangeran Usop, from whom we anticipated difficulty, stepped forward directly to aid us, whilst Pangeran Mumin was not averse. I will not now stop to sketch the characters of these worthies, as I shall hereafter have a better knowledge of them; but I may remark, *en passant*, that it was evident, even to my inexperience, that no two of them were on good terms, and all probably united in a feeling that Muda Hassim's return would be a personal as well as public advantage. The other principal Pangerans, namely, Tizudeen (the Sultan's natural brother), Kurmaindar (the father of the country), Bahar (the Rajah's brother-in-law), Tizudeen second (the Rajah's natural brother), were all for Muda Hassim; and the population, as far as I could learn, decidedly desirous of his being restored to them.

"Each day I had several interviews with the Sultan, in his surow or private room; and he assured me of his fondness for Muda Hassim, his wish to have him near him again, and the great benefit it would be. Moreover, he was pleased to express great personal regard for me, and every five minutes I had to swear 'eternal friendship,' whilst he, clasping my hand, kept repeating 'amigo *suya*,' 'amigo *suya*,' meaning, *my* friend, *my* friend. At the same time he professed great readiness to give me Sarāwak—inquired the amount of revenue

—seemed satisfied, and said, 'I wish you to be there; I do not wish any body else; you are my amigo, and it is nobody's business but mine; the country is mine, and if I please to give you all, I can.' His majesty is very proud of displaying his very small smattering of Spanish or Portuguese; and almost all the higher people having acquired a few words, shews there must have been a communication at no very distant date. I was also warned not to care for any of the other Pangerans,—not, indeed, to have any thing to say to them.

"With this advice I took the liberty to dispense; and sent to Pangerans Mumin and Usop to intimate my wish to visit them. The former pleaded that his house was unfit to receive me; but the latter immediately sent a most polite message, that any time, either by day or night, he should be happy to see me; and accordingly I went. The house *and style* are the best in Borneo. I was politely and kindly greeted; and I soon found that I was with a man of sense and quickness. There was a little diplomacy at first on his part; but as I proceeded direct to my object, he at once laid it aside. In fact, candour is the basis of our right influence with the natives; and as I desired to make Pangeran Usop my friend, I went candidly to work, and immediately told him all that I had already told the Sultan. The amount of my conversation was as follows: The first topic being the anticipated visit of the English, 'Were the English coming?' 'Was Mr. Bonham coming?' were the first questions; and, 'With what intent?' I replied, that the English were certainly coming, but with no evil intentions; that it was true they were offended by the ill usage the captain and people of the Sultana had met with; yet that I had endeavoured to put it in the best light, and had urged that a friendly communication for the future was better than a retrospect which might give rise to unpleasant feelings: I was sure that the English desired a friendly intercourse; and I hoped, though I could not say, that they would look to the future, and not to the past. I had, I added, no authority; but my friendship for the Sultan induced me to inform him what I had heard abroad. When Mr. Bonham came, he would be able to tell them all; but I could say now that I thought he would demand a treaty between Singapore and Borneo for the mutual protection of trade, and the care of individuals of each nation who were shipwrecked or otherwise sought protection at either place.

"On the whole, it is certain that the feelings of Borneo are decidedly friendly, and equally certain that the persons of influence will receive us in their warmest manner, and grant us every thing, if we resort only to measures of conciliation. It never can be too often repeated, that conciliation is the only policy with Malays, and particularly the Borneons, who have very vague and confused ideas of our power. A harsh truth, a peremptory demand, they have never heard in their lives, and they will not hear it for the first time and remain friendly; for all who have the least acquaintance with the native character know their acute sense of false shame. To demand, therefore, of the chief here to acknowledge our superiority would, I am sure, be met with a haughty refusal. In a few years, if we proceed mildly to establish a beneficial influence, they will fall into our views without reserve; for, as I have often before stated, their government is in the last stage of destruction and decay.

"The reconciliation of Muda Hassim was soon complete; and as to the Kleeses of the Lord Melbourne, twenty in number, they were at once surrendered to me, with a request that I would forward them to Singapore as quickly as I could. The boat of the Lord Melbourne was likewise given to me. I had some scruples about three Kleeses of the Sultana, who had been sold at Malludu Bay, bought there by an Arab Seriff, and brought here. By all their laws and customs they were his slaves, purchased at a distance, and, as I had no right to claim them (supposing even that to be just), and was resolved not to leave them in captivity, I paid a fair price for them, at the rate of twenty-five dollars per man. I regret to add, there is one other man not in the place; and one is gone to Tutorga —about a day's journey hence.

"*28th.*—I may here draw a brief sketch of the principal personages of this most primitive court, beginning with its worthy head, the Sultan.

" The Sultan is a man past fifty years of age, short and puffy in person, with a countenance which expresses very obviously the imbecility of his mind. His right hand is garnished with an extra diminutive thumb, the natural member being crooked and distorted. His mind, indexed by his face, seems to be a chaos of confusion; without acuteness, without dignity, and without good sense. He can neither read nor write; is guided by the last speaker; and his advisers, as might be expected, are of the lower order, and mischievous from their ignorance and their greediness. He is always talking, and generally joking; and the most serious subjects never meet with five minutes' consecutive attention. The favourable side of his character is, that he is good-tempered and good-natured; by no means cruel; and, in a certain way, generous, though rapacious to a high degree. His rapacity, indeed, is carried to such an excess as to astonish a European, and is evinced in a thousand mean ways. The presents I made him were unquestionably handsome; but he was not content without begging from me the share I had reserved for the other Pangerans; and afterwards, through Mr. Williamson, solicited more trifles, such as sugar, penknives, and the like. To crown all, he was incessantly asking what was left in the vessel; and when told the truth,—that I was stripped as bare as a tree in winter,—he frequently returned to the charge. In the middle of the night, when our boat came up with some gifts for him, he slipped out his royal person, that he might see what packages there were. I must say, however, that this was not intended for me to know; and, personally, he did not behave very ill towards me, only dunning me occasionally. In regard to the Sarāwak revenue, he was eager in his inquiries; and was very ready, on the strength of his thousand dollars, and my generosity, to give me a list of things which amounted to 10,000 dollars in value. I may note one other feature which marks the man. He requested, as the greatest favour,—he urged, with the earnestness of a child, —that I would send back the schooner before the month Ramban (Ramadan of the Turks); remarking, 'What shall I do during the fast without soft sugar and dates?' What effect the exaggerated promises of Mr. de Souza must have had on such a temper, may readily be imagined; and what the evil influence of such a prince on the country, need not be stated; for, like other fools, he is difficult to guide where the object is right, and facile whenever it promises any immediate advantage. I will only add, that during my intercourse of six days, he has given me the impression that he is not in his right mind; and, at any rate, that flattery and bad counsel have deprived him of the little wit he might probably originally have possessed.

"Of Pangeran Mumin, the De Gadong and the Sultan's son-in-law, I know little; and he is, in secret, a most determined opposer of mine; but I believe he, as well as most, are desirous of being good friends with the English, and will readily listen to any overtures which promise increase of trade. He seemed to me a shrewd, cunning man, fit for a Nakodah.

"Pangeran Usop is a man of middle age, short, active, and intelligent, and, I may add, ambitious. Pangeran Muda Hassim will throw himself into the arms of the English, from his partiality, and from the hope of a better order of things, and the eventual succession to the throne, to which he stands next,—the present Sultan having no legitimate children.

"Two of my objects were thus achieved at once; and the Kleeses (twenty-three) were, much to their satisfaction, despatched to the vessel in the Melbourne's gig. My own affair of Sarāwak meets with some opposition from Mumin, who is decidedly friendly to Macota. The Sultan, however, is steady to me, gabbles daily and hourly of his intentions; and Pangeran Usop likewise pushes on my suit with his influence, at the same time giving me this one piece of good advice, viz. that Muda Hassim must be induced to return to Borneo, for that two persons (Muda Hassim and myself) cannot govern together; and he added, 'If Muda Hassim returns, you will have a fine trade at Sarāwak; but whilst he is there, no native prahus will visit the place.' This is true: I have no fear of ultimate success in my suit; but delay is formidable, and I have already intimated that I propose making my *congé* on the 2d of August.

"30*th*.—I have little more to add about Borneo, save my plaint against our dungeon, though the said dungeon be honourably situated behind the throne, and within the royal apartments. Just below the town are several rills of the finest water; and the natives report that they issue from a small but deep lake at a very short distance. Beneath one of these spouts we each evening took a most delicious bath in water as cold as it is limpid. I am no great bustler at any time; but since being here, I have purposely abstained from all manifestation of curiosity, and never desired or requested to see much; it rouses suspicion, and suspicion rouses distrust, and distrust draws the kris. On the contrary, by being backward at first, you become subsequently a sort of domesticated animal, and privileged to use your eyes and limbs. Most Europeans do themselves great injury by searching the mountains and the waters, breaking the rocks, shooting the birds, and gathering the plants. The natives can never believe they would take so much trouble without being well paid by the value of the treasures found, or employed by the East India Company to espy their land, in order that the said company might seize it at their convenience.

"31st.—A conclave of Pangerans, when it was finally resolved to grant the country of Sarāwak to me as Rajah or governor.

"*August 1st*, 1842.—An important day in my history, and I hope one which will be marked with a white stone in the annals of Sarāwak. The letters to Muda Hassim being finished and signed, the contract giving me the government of Sarāwak came under discussion, and was likewise completed by ten at night, signed, sealed, and witnessed. Thus I have gained every object for which I came to Borneo; and to-morrow, God willing, I take my leave.

"'The miserable state of Borneo I have already mentioned; and it is now a saying of the Balagnini pirates, that 'it is difficult to catch fish, but easy to catch Borneons.' Externally and internally they are equally wretched, and torn by factions; yet, on the whole, I am not inclined to judge harshly of the poorer order of them. They are a good-tempered, very hospitable, and unwarlike people, the victims of their Rajahs; the oppressed, but not the oppressors. In this character, however, I do not reckon the Pangerans and their followers; and it is from these that Europeans take their estimate of the people generally, and consequently truly account them, from that standard, to be a wretched sample of humanity,—mean, thievish, arrogant, insolent, and ready for any wickedness. The Pangerans themselves are only a step better: but even here I must make a little allowance; for I believe their crimes arise more from their poverty and impunity than from any inherent viciousness.

"*3d.*—The Pangerans Budrudeen and Marsale, and a host more, came on board this night, and kept us up as usual.

"*4th.*—Another mob arrived the middle of last night. I retreated from them, being far from well, and got some sleep. At 2 P.M. the letters came on board; were received with honours; and as soon as we could rid ourselves of our troublesome visitors, we dropped outside Tanjong Sapo, and sailed the following day.

"The Kleeses sold at Malludu were bought by Ambun, and reported to the authorities that a European woman was detained there. I made particular inquiries of the Borneon Pangerans, and they said they had always understood that such was the case. Unhappy lady, if she be a lady! Is it a compassionate part to release her after many years of captivity?

"*14th.*—Anchored off the Morotaba, having had nothing but calms, light winds, and squalls.

"*15th.*—Got part of the way up the river, and 8 P.M. dropped our anchor; and in about an hour later two boats started for Sarāwak. The night was moonlight, with a cold breeze; and, after a pleasant pull, we arrived, and created as much sensation as we could desire. But it was better, and I was gratified with the intelligence that every thing had gone on well during our absence. At break of day I went, fagged, to bed. So ended our mission to Borneo.

"On the evening of the 18th the Sultan's letters were produced in all the state which could possibly be attained. On their arrival they were received and brought up amid large wax torches, and the person who was to read them was stationed on a raised platform; standing below him was the Rajah, with a sabre in his hand; in front of the Rajah was his brother, Pangeran Jaffer, with a tremendous kempilan drawn; and around were the other brothers and myself, all standing—the rest of the company being seated. The letters were then read, the last one appointing me to hold the government of Sarāwak. After this the Rajah descended, and said aloud, 'If any one present disowns or contests the Sultan's appointment, let him now declare.' All were silent. He next turned to the Patingis, and asked them; they were obedient to the will of the Sultan. Then came the other Pangerans,—' Is there any Pangeran or any young Rajah that contests the question? Pangeran Der Macota, what do you say?' Macota expressed his willingness to obey. One or two other obnoxious Pangerans who had always opposed themselves to me were each in turn challenged, and forced to promise obedience. The Rajah then waved his sword, and with a loud voice exclaimed, 'Whoever he is that disobeys the Sultan's mandate now received, I will separate his skull;' at the moment some ten of his brothers jumped from the verandah, and, drawing their long krisses, began to flourish and dance about, thrusting close to Macota, striking the pillar above his head, pointing their weapons at his breast. This *amusement*, the violence of motion, the freedom from restraint, this explosion of a long pent-up animosity, roused all their passions; and had Macota, through an excess of fear or an excess of bravery, started up, he would have been slain, and other blood would have been spilt. But he was quiet, with his face pale and subdued, and, as shortly as decency would permit after the riot had subsided, took his leave. This scene is a custom with them; the only exception to which was, that it was pointed so directly at Macota. I was glad, at any rate, that all had gone off without bloodshed.

"*22d.*—I found that though matters had been quiet during my absence, repeated efforts had been made to disturb the country. First, it was positively stated and industriously circulated that I was certain to be killed in Borneo; and next, a report was propagated that 6000 Chinese were on their march from Sambas, with evil intentions. These rumours did not serve any object, and my return has set them at rest; but I regretted to hear that the Singè Dyaks had, contrary to my positive prohibition, killed a Dyak of Sanpro.

"Other affairs are prosperous. Macota is to be sent out of the country, and the Rajah himself talks of returning to Borneo; and both these events will please me greatly.

"*January 1st*, 1843.—Another year passed and gone; a year, with all its anxieties, its troubles, its dangers, upon which I can look back with satisfaction—a year in which I have been usefully employed in doing good to others.

"Since I last wrote, the Dyaks have been quiet, settled, and improving; the Chinese advancing towards prosperity; and the Sarāwak people, wonderfully contented and industrious, relieved from oppression, and fields of labour allowed them.

"Justice I have executed with an unflinching hand; and the amount of crime is certainly small —the petty swindling very great.

"The month of January was a dreary month. A sick man in the house, and very little medicine; and what was worse, the Royalist did not make her appearance. Yet both these troubles disappeared nearly together; for M'Kenzie got well, and the schooner, bringing with her Dr. Treacher, arrived. She had been detained undergoing some necessary repairs. The accession of a medical man is particularly valuable.

"I have nothing to say about the country, except that I have given Pangeran Macota orders to leave, which he is obeying in as far as preparing his boat; and I hope that in six weeks we shall be rid of his cunning and diabolically intriguing presence.

"The Rajah Muda Hassim, his brothers, and the tag-rag following, I also hope soon to be rid of; for although they behave far better than they did at first, it is an evil to have wheel within wheel; and these young Rajahs of course expect, and are accustomed to, a license which I will not allow.

"Budrudeen is an exception—a striking and wonderful instance of the force of good sense over evil education.

"The rest of the people go on well; the time revolves quietly; and the Dyaks, as well as the Malays and Chinese, enjoy the inestimable blessing of peace and security. At intervals a cloud threatens the serenity of our political atmosphere; but it speedily blows over. However, all is well and safe; and so safe that I have resolved to proceed in person to Singapore.

"My motives for going are various; but I hope to do good, to excite interest, and make friends; and I can find no season like the present for my absence. It is now two years since I left

Singapore, 'the boundary of civilisation.' I have been out of the civilised world, living in a demi-civilised state, peaceably, innocently, and usefully.

"*Feb.* 8*th*.—After ten days' delay at the mouth of the river, got out."

APPENDIX.

No. I.

Natural History.

Mr. Brooke's Report on the Mias. (From the Transactions of the Zoological Society.)

JAMES BROOKE, ESQ. TO MR. WATERHOUSE.

Singapore, 25th March, 1841.

MY DEAR SIR,—I am happy to announce the departure of five live orang-outangs by the ship Martin Luther, Captain Swan; and I trust they will reach you alive. In case they die, I have directed Captain Swan to put them into spirit, that you may still have an opportunity of seeing them. The whole of the five are from Borneo: one large female adult from Sambas; two, with slight cheek-callosities, from Pontiana; a small male, without any sign of callosities, from Pontiana likewise; and the smallest of all, a very young male with callosities, from Sadung. I will shortly forward a fine collection of skulls and skeletons from the north-west coast of Borneo, either shot by myself or brought by the natives; and I beg you will do me the favour to present the live orangs and this collection to the Zoological Society. I have made many inquiries and gained some information regarding these animals, and I can, beyond a doubt, prove the existence of two, if not three, distinct species in Borneo.

First, I will re-state the native account; secondly, give you my own observations; and thirdly, enter into a brief detail of the specimens hereafter to be forwarded.

1st. The natives of the north-west coast of Borneo are all positive as to the existence of two distinct species, which I formerly gave you by the names of the *Mias pappan* and *Mias rombi;* but I have since received information from a few natives of intelligence that there are three sorts, and what is vulgarly called the Mias rombi is in reality the *Mias kassar,* the rombi being a distinct and third species. The Mias pappan is the *Simia Wurmbii* of Mr. Owen, having callosities on the sides of the face: the natives treat with derision the idea of the Mias kassar, or *Simia morio,* being the female of the Mias pappan or Simia Wurmbii; and I consider the fact can be established so clearly that I will not trouble you with their statements: both Malays and Dyaks are positive that the female of the Mias pappan has cheek-callosities, the same as the male; and if on inquiry it prove to be so, the existence of three distinct species in Borneo will be established. The existence of the Mias rombi is vouched by a few natives only, but they were men of intelligence, and well acquainted with the animals in the wild state. They represent the Mias rombi to be as tall as the pappan, or even taller, but not so stout, with longer hair, a smaller face, and no callosities either on the male or female; and they always insisted that it *was not* the female of the pappan.

The Mias kassar or Simia morio is the same colour as

the Mias pappan, but altogether smaller, and devoid of callosities either on the male or female adults.

By the native statements, therefore, we find three distinct species, viz. the Mias pappan or Simia Wurmbii, the Mias kassar or Simia morio, and the Mias rombi, which is either the *Simia Abelii,* or a fourth species. The existence of the Sumatran orang in Borneo is by no means impossible; and I have already compared so many of the native statements, that I place more confidence in them than I did formerly, more especially as their account is in a great measure borne out by the skulls in my possession. I had an opportunity of seeing the Mias pappan and the Mias kassar in their native woods, and killing one of the former and several of the latter species. The distribution of these animals is worthy of notice, as they are found both at Pontiana and Sambas in considerable numbers, and at Sadung on the north-west coast, but are unknown in the intermediate country which includes the rivers of Sarāwak and Samarahan. I confess myself at a loss to account for their absence on the Sarāwak and Samarahan rivers, which abound with fruit, and have forests similar and contiguous to the Sadung Linga and other rivers. The distance from Samarahan to Sadung does not exceed twenty-five miles; and though pretty abundant on the latter, they are unknown on the former river. From Sadung, proceeding to the northward and eastward, they are found for about 100 miles, but beyond that distance do not inhabit the forests. The Mias pappan and Mias kassar inhabit the same woods, but I never met them on the same day; both species, according to the natives, are equally common, but from my own experience the Mias kassar is the most plentiful. The Mias rombi is represented as unfrequent and rarely to be met with. The pappan is justly named *Satyrus,* from the ugly face and disgusting callosities. The adult male I killed was seated lazily on a tree, and when approached only took the trouble to interpose the trunk between us, peeping at me and dodging as I dodged. I hit him on the wrist, and he was afterwards despatched. I send you his proportions, enormous relative to his height; and until I came to actual measurement my impression was that he was nearly six feet in stature. The following is an extract from my journal relating to him, noted down directly after he was killed:—

"Great was our triumph as we gazed on the huge animal dead at our feet, and proud were we of having shot the first orang we had seen, and shot him in his native woods, in a Borneo forest, hitherto untrodden by European feet. The animal was adult, having four incisors, two canines, and ten molars in each jaw; but by his general appearance he was not old. We were struck by the length of his arms, the enormous neck, and the expanse of face, which altogether gave the impression of great height, whereas it was only great power. The hair was long, reddish, and thin; the face remarkably broad and fleshy, and on each side, in the place of a man's whiskers, were the callosities or rather fleshy protuberances, which I was so desirous to see, and which were nearly two inches in thickness. The ears were small and well-shaped, the nose quite flat, mouth prominent, lips thick, teeth large and discoloured, eyes small and roundish, face and hands black, the latter being very powerful. The following are the dimensions:

	ft.	in.
Height from head to heel	4	1
Length of foot	1	0
Ditto hand	0	10½
Length of arm from shoulder-blade to finger-end	3	5¾
Shoulder-blade to elbow	1	6

ON THE MIAS.

		ft.	in.
Elbow to wrist		1	1¼
Hip to heel		1	9
Head to os coccygis		2	5½
Across the shoulders		1	5½
Circumference of neck		2	4
Ditto below the ribs		3	3¼
Ditto under the arms		3	0
From forehead to chin		0	9¾
Across the face, below the eyes, including callosities		1	1
From ear to ear across the top of head		0	9¼
From ear to ear behind the head		0	9¾

The natives asserted the animal to be a small one; but I am sceptical of their ever attaining the growth of a tall man, though I bear in mind that full-grown animals will probably differ as much in height as man."

Some days after this, and about thirty miles distant, I was fortunate enough to kill two adult females (one with her young), and a male nearly adult, all the Mias kassar. The young male was not measured, owing to my having waded up to my neck in pursuit of him, and thereby destroyed my paper and lost my measure; but he certainly did not exceed 3 feet, whilst the two females were about 3 ft. 1 in. and 3 ft. 2 in. in height. The male was just cutting his two posterior molars: the colour of all resembled that of the Mias pappan, but the difference between the two animals was apparent even to our seamen. The kassar has no callosities either on the male or female, whereas the young pappans despatched by the Martin Luther (one of them not a year old, with two first molars) shew them prominently. The great difference between the kassar and the pappan in size would prove at once the distinction of the two species; the kassar being a small slight animal, by no means formidable in his appearance, with hands and feet proportioned to the body, and they do not approach the gigantic extremities of the pappan either in size or power; and, in short, a moderately powerful man would readily overpower one, when he would not stand the shadow of a chance with the pappan. Besides these decisive differences may be mentioned the appearance of the face, which in the Mias kassar is more prominent in the lower part, and the eyes exteriorly larger, in proportion to the size of the animal, than in the pappan. The colour of the skin in the adult pappans is black, whilst the kassar, in his face and hands, has the dirty colour common to the young of both species. If further evidence was wanted, the skulls will fully prove the distinction of species; for the skulls of two adult animals compared will shew a difference *in size alone* which must preclude all supposition of their being one species. Mr. Owen's remarks are, however, so conclusive, that I need not dwell on this point; and with a suite of skulls, male and female, from the adult to the infant, of the Mias kassar, which I shall have the pleasure to forward, there can remain, I should think, little further room for discussion. I may mention, however, that two young animals I had in my possession alive, one a kassar, the other a pappan, fully bore out these remarks by their proportionate size. The pappan, with two molars, shewed the callosities distinctly, and was as tall and far stouter than the kassar with three molars, whilst the kassar had no vestige of the callosities. Their mode of progression likewise was different, as the kassar doubled his fists and dragged his hind quarters after him, whilst the pappan supported himself on the open hands sideways placed on the ground, and moved one leg before the other in the erect sitting attitude; but this was only observed in the two young ones, and cannot be considered as certainly applicable to all.

On the habits of the orangs, as far as I have been able

to observe them, I may remark, that they are as dull and as slothful as can well be conceived, and on no occasion when pursuing them did they move so fast as to preclude my keeping pace with them easily through a moderately clear forest; and even when obstructions below (such as wading up to the neck) allowed them to get way some distance, they were sure to stop and allow us to come up. I never observed the slightest attempt at defence; and the wood, which sometimes rattled about our ears, was broken by their weight, and not thrown, as some persons represent. If pushed to extremity, however, the pappan could not be otherwise than formidable; and one unfortunate man, who with a party was trying to catch a large one alive, lost two of his fingers, besides being severely bitten on the face, whilst the animal finally beat off his pursuers and escaped. When they wish to catch an adult, they cut down a circle of trees round the one on which he is seated, and then fell that also, and close before he can recover himself, and endeavour to bind him.

In a small work entitled " The Menageries," published in 1838, there is a good account of the Borneon orang, with a brief extract from Mr. Owen's valuable paper on the Simia morio; but, after dwelling on the lazy and apathetic disposition of the animal, it states in the same page that they can make their way amid the branches of the trees with surprising agility; whereas they are the slowest and least active of all the monkey tribe, and their motions are surprisingly awkward and uncouth. The natives on the northwest coast entertain no dread, and always represent the orangs as harmless and inoffensive animals; and from what I saw, they would never attack a man unless brought to the ground. The rude hut which they are stated to build in the trees would be more properly called a seat or nest, for it has no roof or cover of any sort. The facility with which they form this seat is curious, and I had an opportunity of seeing a wounded female weave the branches together, and seat herself within a minute; she afterwards received our fire without moving, and expired in her lofty abode, whence it cost us much trouble to dislodge her. I have seen some individuals with nails on the posterior thumbs, but generally speaking they are devoid of them: of the five animals sent home, two have the nails, and three are devoid of them; one has the nail well formed, and in the other it is merely rudimentary. The length of my letter precludes my dwelling on many particulars which, as I have not seen the recent publications on the subject, might be mere repetitions; and I will only mention, as briefly as I can, the skulls of these animals in my possession. From my late sad experience I am induced to this, that some brief record may be preserved from shipwreck. These skulls may be divided into three distinct sorts. The first presents two ridges, one rising from each frontal bone, which joining on the top of the head, form an elevated crest, which runs backward to the cerebral portion of the skull.

The second variety is the Simia morio; and nothing need be added to Mr. Owen's account, save that it presents no ridge whatever beyond the frontal part of the head. No. 9 in the collection is the skull of an adult male: No. 2 the male, nearly adult, killed by myself: Nos. 11 and 3 adult females, killed by myself: No. 12 a young male, with three molars, killed by myself: No. 21 a young male, died aboard, with three molars: No. 19, young male, died aboard, with two molars. There are many other skulls of the Simia morio which exactly coincide with this suite, and this suite so remarkably coincides through the different stages of age, one with another, that no doubt can exist of the Simia morio being a distinct species. The different character of the skull, its small size and small teeth, put the matter beyond doubt, and completely establish Mr. Owen's acute and triumphant argument, drawn from a single specimen.

The third distinction of the skulls is, that the ridges rising from the frontal bones do not meet, but converge towards the top of the head, and again diverge towards the posterior portion of the skull. These ridges are less elevated than in the first-mentioned skulls, but the size of the adult skulls is equal, and both present specimens of aged animals. For a long time I was inclined to think the skulls with the double ridge were the females of the animals with the single and more prominent ridge; but No. 1 (already described as killed by myself) will shew that the double ridge belongs to an adult and not young male animal, and that it belongs to the Simia Wurmbii with the huge callosities. The distinction therefore cannot be a distinction of sex, unless we suppose the skulls with the greater development of the single ridge to belong to the female, which is improbable in the highest degree. The skulls with the double and less elevated ridges belong, as proved by No. 1, to the Simia Wurmbii; and I am of opinion the single and higher ridge must be referred to another and distinct species, unless we can account for this difference on the score of age. This, I conceive, will be found impossible, as Nos. 7 and 20 are specimens similar to No. 1, with the double and less elevated ridges decidedly old, and Nos. 4 and 5 are specimens of the single high ridge, likewise decidedly old.

These three characters in the skulls coincide with the native statements of there being three distinct species in

Borneo, and this third Borneon species may probably be found to be the Simia Abelii, or Sumatran orang. This probability is strengthened by the adult female on her way home: her colour is dark brown, with black face and hands; and in colour of hair, contour, and expression, she differs from the male orangs with the callosities to a degree that makes me doubt her being the female of the same species. I offer you these remarks for fear of accident: but should the specimens, living and dead, arrive in safety, they will give a fresh impetus to the inquiry, and on my next return to Borneo I shall, in all probability, be able to set the question at rest, whether there be two or three species in that country. Believe me, my dear sir, with best wishes, to remain,

Yours very truly,

J. BROOKE.

BORNEO, like Celebes, teems with Natural History unknown to European science; and Mr. Brooke has sent some remarkable specimens to England, though his own large collection was, unfortunately, wrecked on its voyage homewards. Every arrival, however, is now adding to the stores we already possess. The British Museum has been much enriched, even within the last year, with rare specimens of zoology and botany; and at the Entomological Society there have been exhibited and described many curious insects hitherto strange and unclassified. During this rapidly progressing development, the list that we might furnish would hardly merit the space that must be devoted to a mere catalogue, without that comprehensiveness and those scientific descriptions which are requisite for philosophical arrangement. As we have remarked on philology, so we may repeat here, that either public or private occasion will find us prepared to communicate to the extent of our information in this respect.

No. II.

Philology.

IT was intended in this work to convey to the studious in philology,—upon which science, rationally investigated, so much depends of our ability to ascertain the origin and trace the earliest relations of mankind, —as copious a vocabulary of the Dyak language, with definitions of meaning and cognate references, as might be considered a useful contribution to that important branch of learning. But various considerations have crippled the design; and not the least of them has been, not the difficulty, but the impossibility of reducing the whole collection to a system, or of laying down any certain rule of orthography in this oriental confusion. Nearly all the vowels, for example, have been found of equal value; and as they have but one general Malay name, so it happens that (for instance) the consonants *b d* might be pronounced with the intervening sound, *bad, bed, bid, bod, bud*, and sundry variations besides, unknown to the English tongue. This will in a great degree account for the universally vexatious, because puzzling, spelling, inflections, and pronunciation of Eastern names, which is so injurious to the literature and knowledge of those countries amongst Europeans. And when it is superadded to this, that the Dyak dialects, as far as they are concerned in this inquiry, are almost exclusively corrupt Malay, and the Malay itself a mosaic, in which Persian and Sanscrit are prominently intermixed, and Dutch and Portuguese not uncommon elements, it may fairly be conceded that a very imperfect glossary was as much as could be attached to a publication of the kind. At a future time, should opportunity offer, very considerable additions and improvements may be made in the following notes on Malayan and Dyak vocabularies, which have been taken from natives of the tribes, except the Kayan, which was obtained from a Meri man who had lived amongst them, and has been checked by an old vocabulary furnished by a Bintula man well conversant with the Kayan dialect.

The vowel-sounds adopted are :

a	like	*a* in *father*.
e	,,	*a* in *fan*.
i	,,	Italian *i*, or *ee* in *thee*.
ĭ	,,	*i* in *pin*.
o	,,	*o* in *spoke*.
u	,,	*oo* in *cool*.
ŭ	,,	*u* in *run*.

y occasionally like *ĭ*.

ow (*ou*) like *ow* in *cow*.

The final *k* in Malayan is frequently mute : thus Dyak is pronounced Dya*h*, with the slightest possible aspiration.

The acute accent is used to shew on what syllable the accent falls, and when necessary for the pronunciation the syllables are divided thus, *apĭ,ŭn,dòw*.

gn is a liquid sound.

PHILOLOGY.

ENGLISH.	MALAY.	SUNTAH.[a]	SOW.	SIBNOW.[b]
one	satu	níh	níh	sa
two	dua	du͵úh	du͵óh	dua
three	tiga	taru	taru	tiga
four	ampat	ampat	pat	ampat
five	lima	riméh	limo	lima
six	anam	naum	naum	anam
seven	tuju	joh	joh	tuju
eight	slappan[h]	mĭ͵ih	mĭ͵ih	slappan
nine	sambilan	pri͵ih	pri͵ih	sambilan
ten	sapuluh	simong	simong	sapuluh
husband	laki	bun͵óh	bun'on	lelaki
wife	bini	sa͵wun	sa͵wun	bini
father	bapa	sama	sama	apĭ
mother	ma	sindo	sindo	indĭ
man	orang	dari	dali	orang
woman	perampuan	dyong	dyong	indo
child	anak	anak ŭnia	anak kupot	anak
infant	kanak kanak	anak pera	anak kila	kanak kanak
sun	mata'an	bat'ŭndu	battŭn undu	mata'an
moon	bulan	buran	bulan	bulan
head	kapala	obak	bāk	pala
hair	rambut	ubok	bōk	bōk
ear	telinga	kajĭt	kajĭt	pŭndĭn
eyes	mata	bŭttúk	bŭt͵ton	mata
nose	idong	undong	indong	idong
mouth	mulut	bŭbbah	bŭbbah	mulut
teeth	gigi	jip͵úh	jipŭn	gigi
tongue	lida	jurah	jurah	dila
hand	tangan	tang͵an	tongan	lŭng͵an
leg	kaki-betis	kŭj͵ah	pohon	kaki

PHILOLOGY.

SAKARRAN.	MERI.[c]	MILLANOW.[d]	MALO.[e]	KAYAN.[f]
sa	séh	jà	sera	gí
dua	duvéh[g]	dua	dua	dua
tiga	tŭllow	tŭllow	talo	tŭllo
ampat	pat	pat	ampat	pat
lima	lima	lima	lima	lima
anam	nŭm	naum	anam	anŭm
tuju	tujoh	tŭjŭ	tuju	tujak
dualapan	madeh	ĭ‚an	slappan	say a
salapan	supĭ	ulan	salapan	tapitan
sapuloh	pulo	pluan	sapuluh	pulo
laki	lakĭ	sawa	laki	lake
bini	turĭ	sawa	—	dó
apĭ	tama	ama	ama	amĭ
indĭ	tina	in‚na	indo	inĭ
orang	idéh	to‚o‚lĭ	babaka	daha
indo	turĭ	marōw	ba‚be‚gni	dó
anak	anak	anak	anak	anak
kanak kanak	anak di‚ĭk	umi	anak keke	anak ok
mata'an	matta dŭllo	mata low	matasu	mata dow
bulan	tŭkka	bulan	bulan	bulan
pala	uh‚ó	ulow	ulu	uhong
bōk	fok	bōk	bōk	bōk
pŭndĭn	telinga	ling‚a	telinga	telinga
mata	mata	mat‚tá	mata	matan
idong	sing‚ote	udong	ing‚ar	urong
mulut	munong	bāh	baba	
gnali	nipŭn	nipŭn	isi	nipŭn
dila	jillah	jŭllah	lela	jĭllah
tangan	tu joh	a‚gŭm	tangan	usu
kaki-betis	paka	—	bangkang	

VOL. I.   A A

ENGLISH.	MALAY.	SUNTAH.	SOW.	SIBNOW.
foot	kaki	purah	lupa pohon	tapa
dog	anging	kŭs‚ong	kosong	asu
deer	rusa	pĭ‚ŭh	rusa	hussa
wild hog	babi utan	pung‚an	pong‚an	laba kampo
water	ayer	pĭ‚in	pi‚in	a‚i
sea	laut	raut	laut	tasik
house	rumah	ramĭn	lomin	huma
head-house	—	pang‚áh	baluk	—
mountain	gunong	darud	dolud	bukĭt[1]
dead	mati	kabus	kobos	mati
sick	sakĭt	barŭndŭm	di‚go‚ga	sakĭt
go	pergi[j]	adi	adi	pergi
go to Kuching	pergi akun K.	adi ka K.	adi ka K.	pergi akun
come here	mari sini	kamati dow	kati kati	mari sini
sick head	sakĭt kapala	namŭn bak	mŭndŭm bāk	sakĭt pala
belly	prut	tĭ‚ĭn	ti‚in	prut
cholic	sakĭt prut (sick belly)	namŭn tĭ‚ĭn	mŭndŭm ti‚in	sakĭt prut
run (be off)	lari	bu	bu	lari
white	putah	buda	mopu	putah
black	etam	sing‚ote	sing‚ote	chĭllum
good	baik[m]	mŭndi	pago	baik
fire	api	a‚pu‚i	opui	api
cocoa-nut	kalapa-nior	butan	butan	nio
rice	bras	bras	blas	bras
God	Allah Taala	Tŭppa	Jowata, Tŭppa	Battara[n]
country	benua	benua	benua	menua
quickly	lakas	rikas	likas	lakas
slowly	lambut	sĭ‚ih	tu‚ih	low‚un
enemy	mirsuh—satru	tŭm‚me	tŭm‚me	munsu
bathe	mandi	mamu	mamo	mandi

SAKARRAN.	MERI.	MILLANOW.	MALO.	KAYAN.
kaki	dattafa	tabŭlla	kaki	—
okoé	ow	asow	asu	asu
rusa	tukkĭ	pĭow	pi͵ang	—
babi jani	baha	baboé tang	babi tuan	—
ai	féh	anom	danum	danum
tasik	lāūd	kala	laut	—
rumah	amĭn	lŭbbu	sow	—
—	—	—	—	—
bukĭt	lŭd	gunong	ukĭt	—
parĭ	matĭ	matĭ	mate	mate
tabin	sa͵hĭ͵it	bĭj͵ji	mekar	—
namu'ĭ	matahow [k]	mŭlla	lamba	—
namuĭ ka K.	mĭ ka K.	mŭlla ka K.	lamba ka K.	—
rito kĭ	uleta	kidĭ mow	la koko	—
pud͵ĭs pala	sahĭit uho	pud͵ŭs ulow	uluko pud͵ĭs [l]	—
prut	tŭj͵jŭn	nĭ	batang	—
pudĭs prut	sahĭit tŭj͵jŭn	pud͵ŭs nĭ	pud͵ĭs batang ko	—
lari	dure	mulli mow	—	—
burak	futĭh	putīh	ute ute	—
chĭllum	mitŭm	bilŭm	lanarum	—
baik	giá	ja͵an	maŭm	—
api	igun	apoé	api	—
gniak	butan	bĭn͵ni͵oh	in͵gniak	—
brow	breh	bras	bras	—
Battara	Allah Taala	Allah Taala	Matasu [o]	—
menua	duŭn	tud	benua	lĭbbo
jŭmpat	merĭ	galŭg͵ga	bari͵al	—
oba	malŭn	kata	malown	—
munsu	bavéh	balum	pangĭow [p]	—
mandi	matok	tummo	mandi	—

xviii PHILOLOGY.

ENGLISH.	MALAY.	SUNTAH.	SOW.	SIBNOW.
request	minta-pinta	mĭtté [q]	mĭtté	minta-pinta
give	bri-kasih	ni‚en	ni‚en	bri-kasih
jungle	utan	darumtarun	tarŭn	kampong
a path	jalan-horong	aran	oran	jalan-horon
paddy	paddy	paddy	poddy	paddy
plantain	pisang	brak	bolak	pisang
sky	lang‚it	rang‚ĭt	long‚ĭt	lang‚it
star	bintang	betang	betang	apĭ‚ŭn‚dow
river	sung‚ei	sung‚ei	sung‚ei	sung‚ei
thunder	guruh	dudu	dudu	gunto
brother	sudara	madih	madih	miadih
bee	lebah	bŭn‚u	bon‚i	ma‚ni‚i
salt	garam	garo	galu	garam
kill	bunoh	si‚úh [s]	nio‚óh	bunoh
old	tuah	niambah	numbah	tuĭ
green	ijow	barum	([t])	gadong
red	mera	bire	bile	mang‚sow
yellow	kunong	sia	sia	kunong
bamboo	bulu	buru	buru	bulo
durian	durien	da‚en	di‚en	hien
iron	besi	besi	bos‚i	besi
gold	amas	ba‚row‚an	ba‚row‚an	mas
brass	loyang	royang [v]	rasong	sillong
egg	telui	turo	tul‚o	tillo
wind	ang‚in	sabak	sabak	ang‚in
dew	umbun	abun	abun	ambun
stone	batu	batu	batu	batu
fowl	ayam	si‚ok	ok	manuk
blacksmith	tukang besi	pandi [x]	moba	tukang besi
bird	burong	manuk	burong	buhong
walk	jalan	pŭn‚úh	pŭn‚óh	jalĭ

Appendix II.] PHILOLOGY. xix

SAKARRAN.	MERI.	MILLANOW.	MALO.	KAYAN.
minta-pinta	nŭnnōūm	niabi	—	—
bri-kasih	mumo	jok	—	—
kampong	talon	tang	tu,an	—
jalï	galan	aro	—	—
paddy	paddy	paddï	ase	—
pisang	futtï	balak	unti	pute
lang,it	lang,ït	rang,it	suan	—
bintang	futtak	bintang	bintang	—
sung,ei	liko	sung,ei	sung,ei	—
guruh	grong	lito	dalak	—
maideh	—	janak	—	—
ma,ni,i	motït	ani,ï	wa,gni	—
garam	u,ï	si,áhʳ	sia	—
bunoh	mun,óh	bino	—	—
tuï	mara,hon	lak,ï	—	—
ijow	ijow	ijow	—	—
mang,sow	ma,ang	sāk	dadara ᵘ	—
kunong	kuning	kunong	—	—
bulu	bulu	bulu	bulu	—
rien	tabedïk	durien	durien	—
besi	besi	besï	basi	—
mow	mas	mas	amas	—
sillong	sarïm	lasong	langsun	—
tul,o	tŭj,joh	tello	telui	—
ribut ʷ	baru,i	pang,ï	soang,in	—
jummo	am,bun	mun	ambun	—
batu	batow	sa,now	batu	—
manuk	a,al	si,ow	manuk	i,ŭp
orang tow kambo	fŭndï besi	tukang besï	—	—
burong	manuk	manuk	burong	burong
bejalï	malahow	makōw	—	—

Comparisons of these terms with the languages of Otaheité, New Zealand, and Acheen, afford some very curious data for speculation; but for the reasons assigned, the subjoined notes (from a recent communication of Mr. Brooke) are all that can with propriety be added to our partial illustration. The letters (ᵃᵇᶜ) refer to their correspondents in the preceding tables.

ᵃ Sŭntah is a type of all the Sarāwak Dyaks on the left-hand river of Sarāwak; Sow, of those on the right hand.

ᵇ Sibnow and Sakarran are the same, with very slight variations, as the dialects of Sarebus, Balow, Undop, Lamanak, and the numerous tribes of the Batang Lupar—all those which I denominate Sea Dyaks or Dyak Laut.

ᶜ Meri is a river near Tanjong Barram.

ᵈ The Millānow are an inoffensive and agricultural people, located chiefly on the rivers of Muka, Oyer, Igan, &c., near Tanjong Sirĭk.

ᵉ Malo is a large Dyak tribe located on a small river of the same name, which discharges itself into the Pontiana river. It takes a small fast-pulling boat six days to arrive at Santang from Pontiana, and three days from Santang to the mouth of the Malo. (Native information.)

ᶠ Kayan is a general term for a very numerous and powerful race in the interior of the island. They have probably specific names besides, and different dialects.

ᵍ Duveh. Here we find the letter *v*, which is unknown in Malay, in consequence of their adoption of the Arabic letters.

ʰ Commonly dilapan.

ⁱ Bukĭt signifies, in Malay, "a hill." In this dialect the terms are reversed. Gunong is "a hill."

ʲ *Vulgo* pīggi.

ᵏ Matahow is, probably, "let us walk :" mĭ being strictly "to go." So, many of these tribes use the verb "to walk" or "to paddle" instead of "to go."

¹ Uluko. The ko means "my." Uluko pudis, "my head is sick, or hot."

ᵐ In Moluccas, &c. the *k* is mute.

ⁿ Thus we have "Tŭppa," "Jowata," and "Battara," as Dyak gods. Besides these, the Hill Dyaks acknowledge Sakarra. Tŭppa is an invisible god; but he warns the Dyaks through the birds of omen; and the Dyaks offer meat-offerings, and offerings of rice, fruit, &c. at his shrine, which is usually near the village, or under the shade of a yellow-stemed species of bamboo, which seems to be considered sacred. Of the gods here mentioned, Jowata and Battara are certainly Hindoo. Sakarra and his tradition is very Hindoo, though I have not time to look for him amid their host of divinities. Tŭppa alone remains a god of the Dyaks, and he likewise may probably be traced to the same source. These names, together with the burning of their dead, and other customs, leave no doubt on my mind that the Hindoo religion penetrated to this remote region, and most probably was implanted on some original Dyak superstitions.

º The Malo man was clear and decided that matásu, "sun," was their word for God.

ᵖ Pangȷow—derived from kayūh, "to row," "to paddle"—mengayuh, "to go on a piratical expedition." Vide Marsden, Dict. p. 251, under head Kay͏̈ūh.

ᑫ Mitté becomes mït in talking. Mït pïm, "I request some water."

ʳ Siáh. The last syllable is gently jerked out of the throat.

ˢ The *uh* is guttural.

ᵗ The man would not or could not give a term but black. When asked the colour of a green leaf he said "singote."

ᵘ Dadara—from "dara," blood.

ᵛ The sense of "royang" is restricted to brass wire.

ʷ Ributt, in Malay, is "a storm."

ˣ Pandï signifies "clever," which the Dyak applies, *par excellence*, to the blacksmith.

I conceive it beyond question, that the whole of these dialects form links in the chain of that primitive language entitled by Marsden the Polynesian. Marsden in the introduction to the Grammar, p. 18, remarks: "The doubts which have arisen respect only the third, or that original and essential part which, to the Malayan, stands in the same relation as the Saxon to the English, and which I have asserted to be one of the numerous dialects of the widely extended language found to prevail, with strong features of similarity, throughout the Archipelago on the hither side of New Guinea, and, with a less marked resemblance, amongst the islands of the Pacific Ocean or South Sea. This language, which, in its utmost range, embraces Madagascar also, to the westward, may be conveniently termed the Polynesian, and distinguished, as already suggested, into the Hither (frequently termed the East insular language) and the Further Polynesian." It is an extraordinary confirmation of these just views to find the dialects of the wildest and rudest tribes in Borneo—tribes far removed, and holding no communication one with another—forming links of the chain which extends so far over the insular portion of the globe, and is as yet untraced to either continent. Good vocabularies of the language of some of the South Sea islands, New Zealand, and Madagascar, might even at the present day throw farther light on our knowledge of these dialects, which at the time that Marsden wrote was far inferior to what has subsequently been attained. The Orang Laut, or the Orang de bower ang,in—for they disown the term of Malay—inhabiting the various rivers on the N.W. coast, all speak dialects of their own. Bruni, the capital, is stated to have been peopled by the Orang Laut from Johore; Sarāwak from Java; Sadong, probably the same; Samarahan *from Pegu!* Linga from the island and kingdom of that name, corruptly called Lĭngĭn; Sarebus from Menangkabau in Sumatra: and all these may be called patois of the Malay language, mixed and corrupted by the Dyak dialects of the neighbourhood.

We add an alphabetical list of some other words which have occurred in the preceding pages.

Arafuras, or *Haraforas*, natives of Papua.
Balanian, wild tribes in Borneo.
Bandar, or *Bandhāra*, treasurer, high steward, high officer of state.
Basaya, tribes in the interior of Borneo Proper, locating near and resembling the Murut.
Battara, one of the Dyak names of God (the Hindu *Avatara*).
Borneo, the island of, written ' Brūnī' by the inhabitants.
Borneo Proper, the northern and north-western part of the island ; an independent Malay state.
Borneons, the Malay inhabitants of Borneo Proper.
Bugis, natives of Celebes.
Bulan, the Moon, a poetical title of honour to a pirate-chief.
Brūnī, the native name for Borneo.
Campong, a native village, or town.
Datu, a cape or point of land to the north-west of the river Banjamassim.
Datus, strictly, native chiefs, heads of tribes.
Dusun, agricultural villagers on the northern extremity of Borneo.
Dyaks, or Dyak, aborigines of Borneo, and generally pronounced Dyah.
Dyak Darrat, Land Dyaks.
Dyak Laut, Sea Dyaks.
Gantong, a Malay measure for rice.
Gunong, a mountain.
Hadji, a Mahomedan who has made a pilgrimage to Mecca.
Haraforas, or *Arafuras*, natives of Papua.
Idaans [Kadiens], Borneon tribes, and the name generally given to most of the varieties of the Indian Archipelago.
Illanuns, or *Lanuns*, pirates inhabiting the small cluster of islands between Borneo and Magindano.
Kadiens, Borneon tribes, Mahomedans, the Idaan of preceding voyagers and writers. See *Idaans*.
Kanowit, wild tribes in Borneo.

Kaya, a title of authority, Orang Kaya de Gadong, chief man of Gadong.
Kayans, the most powerful and warlike people of Borneo, living inland.
Kalamantan, an original name of Borneo.
Kuching, the former name of the town of Sarāwak.
Labuan, the island off Borneo river, ceded by the Sultan to the British crown.
Lelas, guns.
Magindano, an island off the north-east of Borneo, the natives of which are pirates.
Makassar, the straits of, usually written Macassar, but more accurately Mangkassar.
Malays, settled on the Malayan peninsula, coasts of Borneo, &c. &c.; a race of seafaring character, often piratical, and conquerors of various native tribes in the Indian Archipelago.
Murrundum, an island off Borneo.
Morotaba river, one of the mouths of the Sarāwak.
Millanows, a tribe resembling the Kayans, living near the river Meri, river Bentulu, tolerably civilised, and fairer than the Malays.
Minkokas, a wild tribe near the Bay of Boni.
Montrado, a very large and populous Chinese settlement near Point Datu.
Murut, inhabitants of the interior of Borneo Proper.
Matari, or *Mata-hari* (the eye of day), the Sun, a poetical title of honour to a pirate-chief.
Malukus, pirates from a bay in Gillolo, whose country is in the possession of the Dutch.
Mias Rombi and *M. Pappan*, two species of orang-outang, determined by Mr. Brooke.
Natunas, islands off Borneo.
Ondong-ondong, the written law of Borneo.
Orang, a man.
Orang-outang, a wild man.
Pangeran, or *Pangiran*, the title of a high Malay authority.
Patingi, or *Patingue*, a high local officer.
Patobong, the name of the ranjows and sudas, defences in war.

Pontiana, one of the finest rivers in Borneo; also the name of natives on its banks.

Patakan Dyaks, said by the Malays to be cannibals.

Ranjows, bamboo-spikes stuck in the ground to wound the feet of attacking enemies, or concealed in pits to wound or destroy them.

Rhio, a Malay settlement, under Dutch control.

Sadung, a river adjoining the Sarāwak.

Sakarran, a river like the Sarebus (which see), with a similar native population on its banks.

Sarebus, a river flowing into the deep bay between Tanjong Sipang and Tanjong Sirak.

Sarebus, powerful Dyak tribes and pirates, located on the above, and other rivers flowing into the bay. They have thrown off the Malay yoke, and plunder as far as Celebes.

Sibnowans, or *Sibnyows*, Mr. Brooke's favourite tribe of Dyaks, of superior character.

Singè, Dyak tribes.

Songi Besar, large river.

Sooloo, on the north-east of Borneo, a powerful piratical nest, the natives of which massacred the garrison of Balambangan in 1775.

Sampan, a small prahu.

Sumpitan, or *Simpote*, a tube seven or eight feet in length, through which the Borneons blow small sharp-pointed poisoned arrows.

Satīgī, a wooden spear, or dart.

Sudahs, defences to wound the feet of attacking enemies.

Seriff, or *Sheriff*, a high Malay title.

Tanjong, a point of land.

Taraj, or *Tarajahs*, natives of Celebes.

Tatows, wild tribes in the interior of Borneo.

Tiran, natives on the north of Borneo, reported (on doubtful authority) to be pirates and cannibals.

Tuppa, a Dyak god.

Tumangong, a local Malay officer.

Tuan, Sir, an exclamation of assent to an approved speaker, instead of 'hear, hear,' or 'yes.'

Tuan Besar, Sir, great, great chief, higher applause and deference.

Tumbilans, a beautiful group of about 150 small islands between Borneo and Singapore.

Wakil, a deputy.

Zedong, like the Tiran, which see.

No. III.

This is the Epistle of Laputongei, Rajah of Waju, and Consort, to Mr. James Brooke, and to the company of Merchants at Singapore.

THE Prince Laduka bows, embraces, and kisses his (adopted?) father Mr. Brooke, and presents the compliments of the Queen Arutempih.

This is our statement. We have all conferred as to making Reuring Tuah the Arongmatuah, and did so after your departure. The people of Waju have also conferred with their Rajahs, and have sent to Boni and Sopeng twice, but have not yet received an answer. Sopeng would have given an answer, but was afraid to do it before Boni. This is the reason why we have as yet received no answer.

We now let fly this writing to Singapore, under this our seal, both we and our people earnestly hoping to meet Mr. Brooke, as soon as may be, in the Bugis country, now in this monsoon. We make known to the Singapore merchants, that all our traders are in the habit of coming to us, declaring that they can in nowise endure the restraints of the Dutch, since once we could bring English goods to this and other countries; whereas now they utterly forbid us. How can we get a livelihood in this way? We now ask, we and our traders, what think ye? Is this right? To us it seems out of the question, if things go on so, that Singapore can ever be much of a place.

As a mere *sign* of our regard (for there is no *substance*

to it), Laputongei sends to Mr. Brooke two pieces of Bugis cloth, and to Mr. Boustead a couple of bags of coffee.

Given in the country of Waju, on the 15th day of the month Jumadal Akhir, on Tuesday, 1257.

END OF VOL. I.

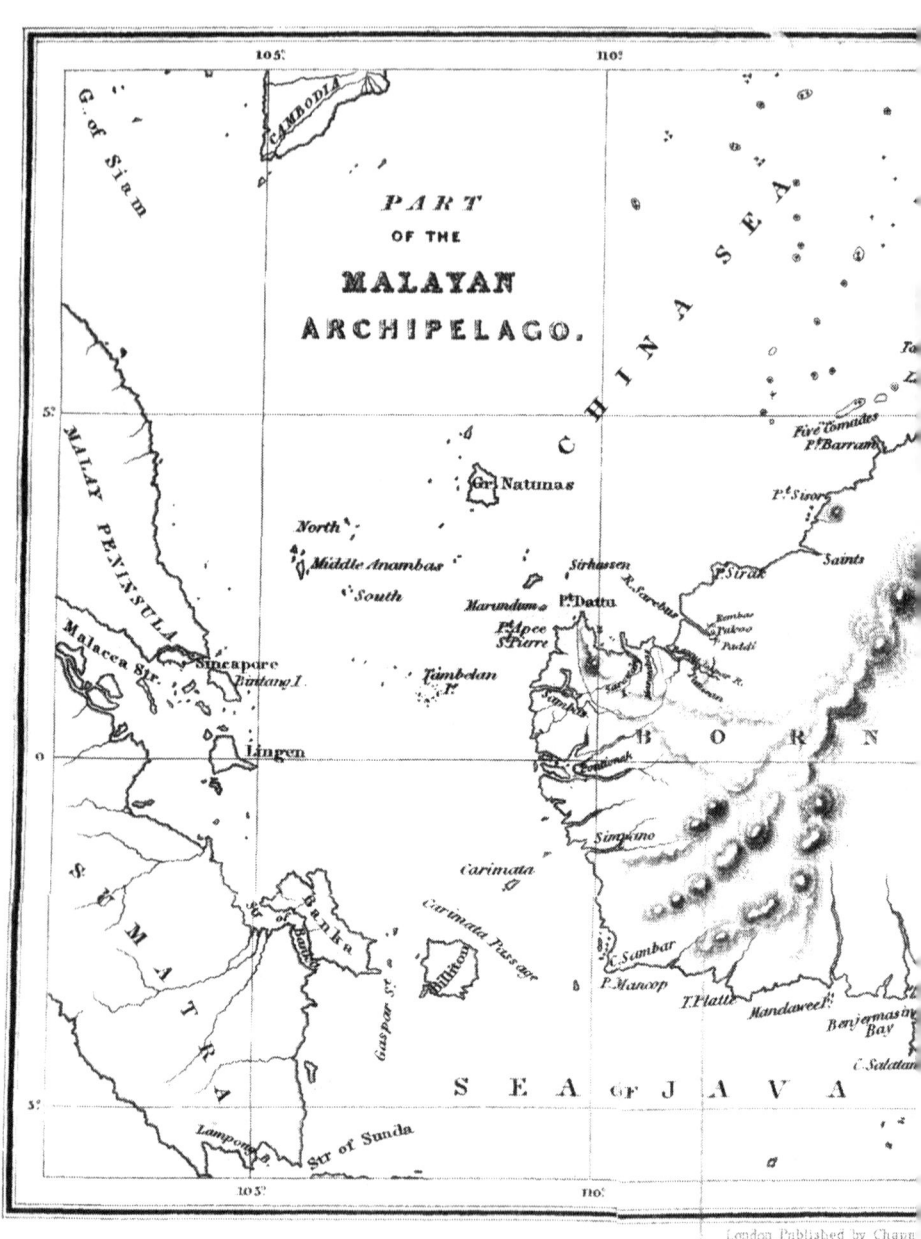

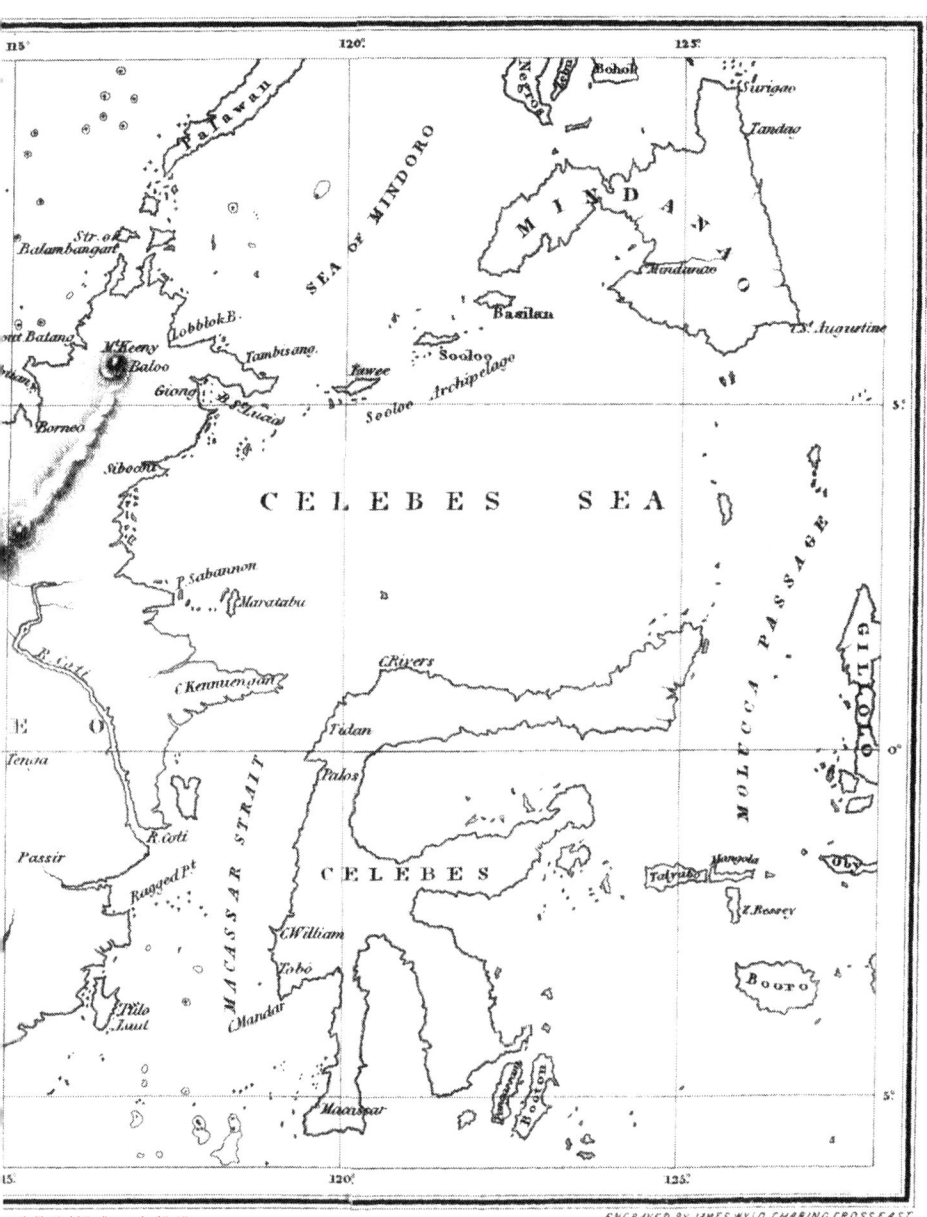

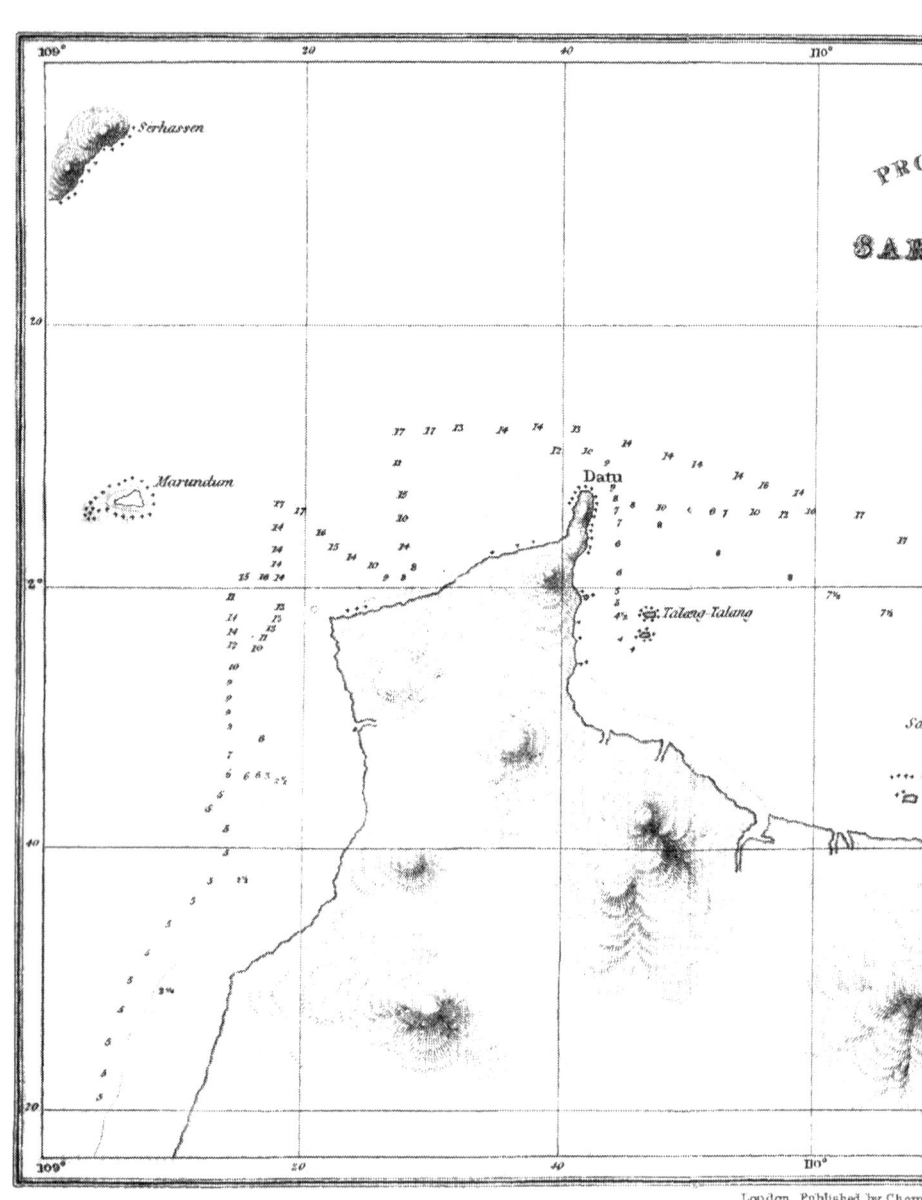

www.ingramcontent.com/pod-product-compliance
Lightning Source LLC
Chambersburg PA
CBHW061928220426
43662CB00012B/1836